Ready for Dessert

Ready for Dessert

MY BEST RECIPES

David Lebovitz

PHOTOGRAPHY BY Maren Caruso

TEN SPEED PRESS
Berkeley

Certain recipes in this work, some in different form, were originally published
in *Room for Dessert* (HarperCollins Publishers, NY, 1999)
and in *Ripe for Dessert* (HarperCollins Publishers, NY, 2003)

Ten Speed Press and the Ten Speed Press colophon
are registered trademarks of Random House, Inc.

Library of Congress Cataloging-in-Publication Data

Lebovitz, David.
 Ready for dessert : my best recipes / David Lebovitz ; photography
by Maren Caruso.
    p. cm.
 Includes index.
 Summary: "A compendium of recipes for desserts, including cakes,
pies, tarts, fruit desserts, custards, soufflés, puddings, frozen treats,
cookies, candies, and accompaniments, from noted pastry chef,
cookbook author, and food blogger David Lebovitz — Provided by
publisher.
 1. Desserts. I. Title.
 TX773.L383 2010
 641.8'6—dc22
                                            2009049281

ISBN 978-1-58008-138-2

Printed in China

Design by Nancy Austin
Food styling by Christine Wolheim

10 9 8 7 6 5 4 3 2 1

First Edition

Contents

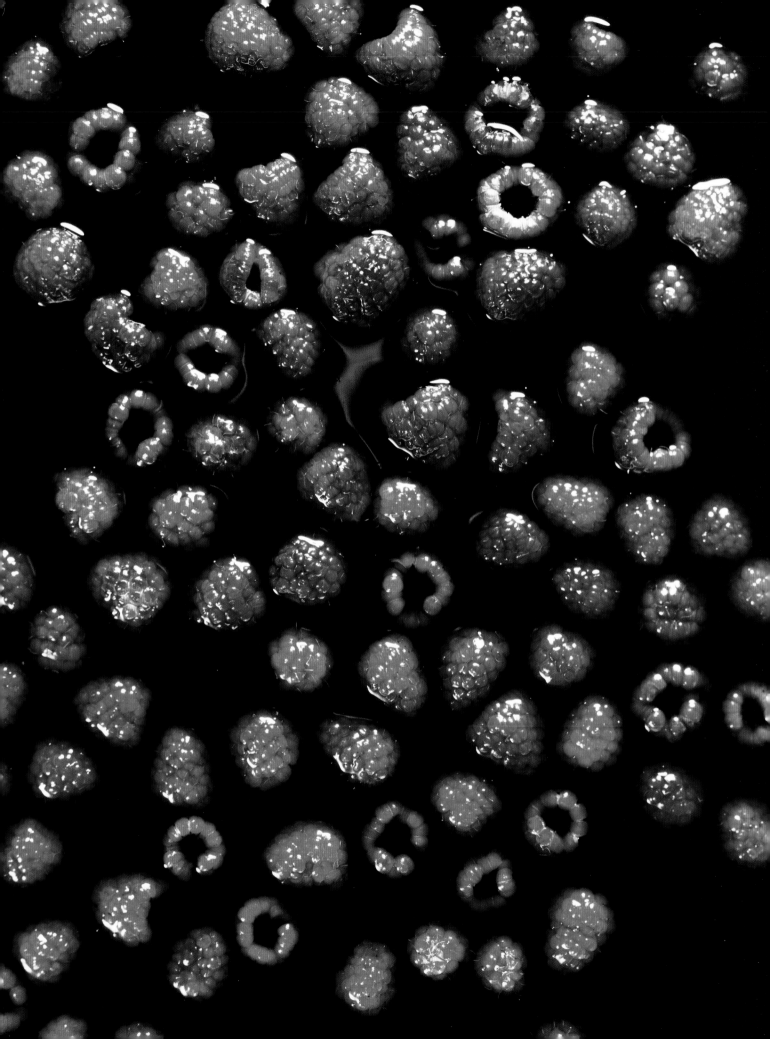

Introduction

Each year, hundreds of cookbooks are released, which means that inevitably, many must go to make room for the new. But I was always surprised, and delighted, to hear from so many people that mine were the ones in their collection that they used the most.

When I began writing cookbooks over a decade ago, someone told me, "If a book has one great recipe in it, then it's a good book." So while I considered calling this book *David's Greatest Hits,* that idea was (wisely) nixed by the powers that be. But, from all the positive feedback my cookbooks have received, I don't know if that title would've been all that far off. Over the years, I've heard again and again from enthusiastic home bakers that many of the recipes from my first two books were their all-time favorites.

Room for Dessert was released in 1999. I hadn't written a book before, but was thrilled when the *New York Times* singled it out for praise in a very crowded field of cookbooks. It was also lauded by colleagues such as food writer Arthur Schwartz, who complimented the book as "deceptively slim," meaning it packed an expansive variety of desserts in a very approachable, and not at all daunting, format.

My second book, *Ripe for Dessert*, continued that philosophy with an emphasis on baking with fruit. I'm very keen on incorporating fruits and berries into my desserts and know that many people share my affection for fruit desserts. The book came out in 2003 just as Americans were rediscovering the rewards of using regional ingredients. At the same time, there was a rising national awareness about healthy eating. Although it was certainly not a diet book, fruits played a central role in all of the desserts, rather than just an ornamental one, and the recipes let home bakers put to delicious use the new abundance of fruit available in farmers' markets and at their local grocers. Shopping baskets overflowed with long-forgotten varieties of heirloom apples, unusual and exotic tropical fruits, deep-red cherries, and soft, tangy raspberries, all of which simply begged to be used during their all-too-brief seasons. I also included recipes starring some of the more elusive fruits—such as quince, figs, and persimmons—which were slowly becoming more familiar as they made their way from upscale farmers' markets into mainstream grocery stores.

And it wasn't just home bakers who were using my books. I got a great thrill out of spying a flour-dusted copy of one of my books on a shelf in a restaurant or bakery kitchen. It was tremendously gratifying to know that the recipes met the demanding standards of professionals.

After a long run, both *Room for Dessert* and *Ripe for Dessert* went out of print. In the meantime, through my website and blog, www.davidlebovitz.com, I was able to introduce my recipes to a whole new audience and to those who were disappointed that my books were no longer available. Needless to say, when

I was offered the chance to update the recipes and present them in this all-new edition, I jumped at the opportunity to do so.

Like so many other things, techniques, tastes, and even the availability of ingredients change over time. At first, I thought I'd just revisit a few recipes and make some minor changes. But as I flipped through the pages, invariably I'd land on a recipe and say, "Hmm, I wonder what that would be like if I reduced the sugar, and melted the butter instead of creamed it?" Or, "What about sharing those cookies I made last Christmas that everyone loved?" Off to the kitchen I would go to try out these new ideas.

So just about every recipe has been revised in some way—ingredients were added or swapped out with another or techniques have been changed. Plus, I couldn't resist including a dozen new recipes, ones that have become favorites of mine, which I hope will become favorites of yours as well.

• • •

As a baker, my strongest influence was Lindsey Shere, the founding pastry chef at Chez Panisse, whose ideas prompted some of my favorite desserts in this book, including Blanco y Negro (page 176) and Champagne Gelée with Kumquats, Grapefruits, and Blood Oranges (page 114), as well as her now-classic recipe for Chocolate Pavé (page 25), which she kindly allowed me to share. Some of these recipes were from our repertoire at Chez Panisse, and like many good recipes, they're the result of a variety of influences, an appreciation for delicious desserts, and years of kitchen experience.

I was fortunate to work with the same people for nearly thirteen years, and I learned almost everything I know from working with them, most notably Mary Jo Thoresen, Lisa Saltzman, Shari Saunders, Diane Wegner, and Linda Zagula. Every day was a collaboration—there was no finer dessert "think tank" than the pastry team at Chez Panisse.

At Chez Panisse, some of the world's best cooks were welcomed into the kitchen to collaborate with us, including Bruce Cost, Marion Cunningham, Niloufer Ichapouria King, Richard Olney, Jacques Pépin, and Shirley Sarvis, as well as our own chefs, David Tanis, Catherine Brandel, Paul Bertolli, Jean-Pierre Moule, Peggy Smith, Gilbert Pilgram, and, of course, Alice Waters, who wrote the introduction to my original book.

• • •

Pastry whiz Nick Malgieri likes to say, "Bake something. You'll feel better!" And nothing could be truer. People constantly ask me, "Why do you bake?" It took me over a decade (I'm a slow learner) to come to the conclusion that baking is about sharing. The best bakers I know aren't merely armed with a bunch of recipes, but baking is truly their passion, as it is my passion. We just love to do it, not just for ourselves, but for others—I've yet to come across a dessert recipe that makes only one serving. Cakes, pies, and batches of cookies are meant to be shared.

When people tell me "I can't bake," I'm truly puzzled because baking is the least fussy of the culinary arts. Sure, you need to measure carefully, but 1 cup of sugar is 1 cup of sugar. Eight tablespoons of butter isn't really open to interpretation. To me, baking has much of the guesswork taken out of it. (I often think the world would be a safer place if people would drive with the same exactitude and precision that they think is necessary when baking.)

As much as I'd like to be baking right beside you, I can't be. You'll often need to make some of your own judgment calls, but there's no need to panic. The French have a wonderful term, *au pif* ("by the nose"), that is used to describe cooking or baking in that fashion. If the cookie recipe says, "Bake for 11 minutes" and in your oven they look done at the 10-minute mark, take them out. (I've never met two ovens that bake the same, no matter how fancy they are.) Your pears may not be as sweet as the ones I call for. Or you might have decided to use one of the newer high-percentage chocolates or European-style butters available these days, both of which can alter textures as well as baking times. So once in a while, don't be afraid to do a little bit of baking "by the nose."

—————— ⚬⚬⚬ ——————

Although lots of things have changed over the years, my tastes remain the same. I still crave chocolate cakes that have the "screaming chocolate intensity" that I wrote about ten years ago. I still don't think that desserts need to be fussy or overly elaborate. And I'm even more convinced nowadays that it's easier to make something tasty if you start with good ingredients and do as little to them as possible. So if you're going to take the time to make a dessert, select your ingredients with care. I'm confident that no one ever tasted something delicious and sighed, "Gee, I wish I had used cheaper ingredients."

So here's a collection of many of my all-time favorite recipes, the ones I turn to over and over again. It's not often that one gets a chance to revisit his or her work, update it, and make it even better. Thankfully, I got the chance, and I couldn't be happier to have the opportunity to share these recipes with you, once again.

Ingredients

If you're going to take the time to bake a cake or churn up a batch of homemade ice cream, the results should truly shine. My desserts don't have a lot of fussy decoration. Instead, they impress with pure flavors, so it's imperative that you begin with good-quality products. But you need not go broke buying the most expensive or exotic ingredients. Good-tasting chocolate costs only slightly more than the mediocre stuff. And ripe fruit in season is a lot cheaper and infinitely better tasting than its out-of-season counterpart. There's absolutely no reason to use rock-hard blackberries from the other side of the world or apples that have spent eight months in storage when there's so much to choose from that's fresh and local.

There's been a spate of "premium" or "European-style" products on the market, everything from baking flours and sugars to high-fat butter. Aside from a few recipes that benefit from high-percentage chocolate, I don't use specialty ingredients when creating recipes since the results can vary widely and I strive for everyone to have the same results that I do. If you do want to use them, just keep in mind that they'll sometimes behave differently and you may have to rely on your baking instincts when working with them.

"Organic," "locally produced," and "sustainable" are important factors to consider when shopping. I don't like to get preachy, but I do my best to try to buy products that I feel make the most sense for my circumstances. When you shop, you'll need to make some decisions, too. Should you buy organic and locally grown or conventional strawberries? Is that organic milk in the glass bottle really worth the additional cost? Will farm-fresh eggs make a more flavorful ice cream? In spite of how much we all like to economize, I think it's okay to splurge for your family and guests. Not only is it a nice gesture, but it's fun to discover new products. And it feels good to support the local growers and producers who are part of your community.

I'm often asked about ingredient substitutions. For the most part, in recipes, I've reduced my use of sweeteners and fats to modest amounts without sacrificing flavor or texture, and I strongly encourage you to make the recipe as written for best results. Substituting nonfat milk for whole milk for custards and ice cream bases is inadvisable, and I avoid using artificial sweeteners. For those on restricted diets or with food allergies, you're likely familiar with how to choose and modify recipes, and which ingredients will work for your particular needs.

ALCOHOL

Any alcohol used in baking should always be of good quality, especially since it will likely be consumed outside the kitchen, too (at least in my house it is). I always have on hand: dark rum, Cognac, bourbon, Chartreuse, kirsch, pear eau-de-vie, and an orange-flavored liqueur such as Grand Marnier, Cointreau, or Triple Sec. You don't need to buy the most expensive brands, but do buy ones that are drinkable.

ALMOND PASTE

This rich mixture consists of nearly equal parts ground blanched almonds and sugar kneaded into a paste. You can find it in the baking aisle of most supermarkets and specialty food stores. Or you can order a very good-quality almond paste from Love 'n Bake (see Resources, page 270). Note that almond paste is not the same as marzipan, which contains more sugar and is mostly used for modeling and shaping.

BAKING POWDER

This is a leavening agent. I use only baking powder that is aluminum free because it has no bitter, metallic aftertaste. Rumford is the most common brand, available at natural food markets and well-stocked grocery stores. Replace baking powder that is over 6 months old, or test its efficacy by mixing some with a small amount of hot water—it should bubble vigorously.

BAKING SODA

This leavening agent usually appears in recipes that also contain an acid ingredient to activate it. Often it's a partner to natural cocoa powder, which is more acidic than Dutch-process cocoa powder (see page 8). Unlike baking powder, baking soda doesn't lose its oomph over time.

BUTTER

I prefer the wonderful, natural flavor of butter to that of margarine or vegetable shortening, products I don't use. For most cakes, it is important to use room-temperature butter and cream it with the sugar (beat the mixture until light and fluffy) to incorporate air into the batter. When making cookies, however, you need to cream the butter only long enough to thoroughly combine it with the sugar, about 1 minute. Don't overbeat the butter or the cookies will spread too much during baking.

The recipes in this book mostly call for unsalted butter, although in recent years I've become fond of using salted butter. When small amounts of salted butter are called for—a tablespoon, for instance—the quantity of salt added isn't going to make a difference in a dessert, so I often call for either. But since most people are accustomed to using unsalted butter for baking, a majority of the recipes call for that. Salted butter contains about $1/4$ teaspoon of salt per stick; if you prefer to use salted butter, adjust the salt in the recipe accordingly.

CHOCOLATE

I love chocolate and you'll notice there are quite a few chocolate recipes in this book, something I feel no need to apologize for. Americans have always been chocolate lovers, and a recent surge in bean-to-bar chocolate makers has made the chocolate aisle a much more interesting place. Until the last decade or so, if you wanted good chocolate, you had to choose one that was European. And while a lot of European chocolates are excellent, you now have the choice of some really good American-made chocolates as well. (See Resources, page 270, for ordering information for some of my favorites.)

I normally don't recommend specific brands unless it's very important to the recipe. Instead, I encourage you to discover on your own which brands you prefer. The best way to find a good chocolate, and one that you like, is to taste as many as you can, a task that most people won't find all that difficult. I'm often asked what's a "good" chocolate. My response: "If *you* like the taste and think it's good, then it's good chocolate." If price is a concern, buy chocolate in bulk or large tablets, which are much more economical than individual bars.

Unsweetened, bittersweet, and semisweet chocolates will keep for several years if well-wrapped and stored in a cool, dry place. Milk chocolate is more delicate—wrapped well, it will keep in a cool, dry place for up to 1 year. White chocolate is perishable and should be purchased in small quantities as needed.

Unsweetened Chocolate

If a recipe calls for unsweetened chocolate, that means chocolate without any added sugar. Sometimes it's labeled "99 percent" or "100 percent" unsweetened chocolate, references to the percentage of cacao solids. If you come across "bitter chocolate," verify that it's unsweetened chocolate by looking at the ingredients list (it shouldn't contain any sugar) or look carefully for the percentage of cacao solids.

Bittersweet or Semisweet Chocolate

If a recipe calls for bittersweet or semisweet chocolate, you can use either as they're interchangeable. Both, by law, are required to have a minimum of 35 percent cacao solids, but many premium brands have much higher percentages, sometimes over 70 percent.

The recipes in this book that call for bittersweet or semisweet chocolate were tested with chocolate that's between 50 percent and 65 percent cacao solids. I like a lot of the high-percentage chocolates (ones with more than 70 percent cacao solids) for eating. I don't bake with them, however. One can run into problems due to their lack of fluidity, a result of reduced amounts of sugar and cocoa butter. And their greater acidity can cause mixtures to curdle.

Milk Chocolate

Not too long ago, our only option for milk chocolate was those vapid brown bars sold in the candy aisle of the supermarket. But milk chocolate has come a long way and we now have good-tasting choices. Contrary to my advice for buying dark chocolate, I recommend getting milk chocolate with the highest percentage of cacao solids as possible. Standard milk chocolate bars usually contain about 10 percent whereas some of the new "dark" milk-chocolate bars have 35 to 40 percent and taste a lot better. I use those.

White Chocolate

Buy only real white chocolate, one that contains cocoa butter, sugar, and milk powder. In products labeled "white coating," the flavorful cocoa butter has been replaced with vegetable fat. It's awful and I don't use it—and neither should you.

CHOPPING CHOCOLATE

When a recipe calls for "chopped chocolate," the pieces should be in coarsely chopped $^1/_2$-inch (1.5 cm) chunks. If it specifies "finely chopped chocolate," the pieces should be in very small bits, about the size of tiny peas, so they'll melt very quickly. I use a serrated bread knife for chopping chocolate. If chopping from a block, start at a corner and shave downwards with the knife, rotating the block and beginning at another corner when you've reached a point that's too wide and the chocolate block gets difficult to chop.

MAKING CHOCOLATE CURLS

To make chocolate curls, use a sharp vegetable peeler to shave thin curls of chocolate in long strokes from the sides of a tablet of dark or milk chocolate. Milk chocolate works best for shaving, though a mix of milk and chocolate curls makes for a more dramatic presentation.

MELTING CHOCOLATE

Chocolate melts at a relatively low temperature and can easily burn if overheated, so always melt it in a heatproof bowl set over a saucepan of barely simmering water, or what's known as a double boiler. Make sure the hot water does not touch the bottom of the bowl. Stir the chocolate gently as it melts, and take it off the heat just when, or slightly before, it's completely melted. If you're very familiar with all those buttons on your microwave oven, you can melt chocolate in the microwave at low power, opening the door and stirring it as it warms, to make it more fluid.

When melting chocolate by itself (without any other ingredients), it is extremely important that no moisture gets into the chocolate, or it can seize and turn into a grainy mess. Check your utensils and bowls and wipe them completely dry before using them. For the same reason, do not let steam from a neighboring pot or from the bottom of the double boiler get into the chocolate. If your chocolate does seize, you can turn it into chocolate sauce by adding some water, cream, and maybe some butter. Then you'll need to start again with some fresh chocolate—and be more careful.

Chocolate Chips

A majority of the chocolate chips are made of what's called "baking resistant" chocolate, which means that they have less cocoa butter so that they hold their shape during baking. This makes them suitable for cookies but not great for melting. Some upscale brands are made from regular (melting) chocolate. But with so many brands out there, unless you know for sure that the chips melt smoothly, don't use them in place of bittersweet or semisweet chocolate that will be melted.

Cocoa Powder

To make cocoa powder, cocoa butter is pressed out of unsweetened cacao paste until the paste is reduced to a powder. There are two kinds of cocoa powder: natural and Dutch-process. "Dutching" cocoa powder involves treating the cacao with an alkalizing agent to neutralize acidity, which also darkens the color of the cocoa.

I generally use Dutch-process cocoa since it tastes better to me. But there are some good natural cocoa powders out there, although they're not easy to find (see Resources, page 170). Dutch-process cocoa is usually labeled as such. If you're questioning whether it is, check for an alkalizing agent (potassium bromate or carbonate) in the ingredients list; if it's listed, then it's Dutch-process. Always use the type indicated in the recipe. In some cases, I give you the option to use either. If your cocoa powder is lumpy, sift it before using.

COCONUT

When using dried coconut, I use unsweetened, which can be found in natural and specialty food stores. If a recipe specifies unsweetened coconut and you don't have unsweetened coconut, you can soak sweetened coconut in boiling water, wring it out well in paper towels, and dry it in a low oven. I use dried shredded coconut (sometimes labeled "desiccated") that resembles coarsely grated Parmesan cheese. Dried coconut sold in larger, longer shreds can be pulsed in a food processor until it's in smaller pieces.

TOASTING DRIED COCONUT

Toasting doesn't just give the coconut a nice brown color; it also gives it a much deeper flavor. Spread the dried coconut out on an ungreased baking sheet in an even layer and toast in a 350°F (175°C) oven for 5 to 10 minutes. Stir it several times for even baking, as most ovens have hot spots. The coconut is done when the flakes are uniformly deep golden brown and smell nutty and toasty. Let cool before using.

COCONUT MILK

Canned coconut milk is not the watery liquid from inside the coconut, but a mixture of the flavorful, rich meat blended with the liquid. It's very time-consuming to make, so I use Thai canned coconut milk, available in Asian food stores and well-stocked supermarkets. My favorite brand is Chaokoh (beware of similar-sounding brands). Always shake the can before opening because the milk separates as it sits. Unused coconut milk can be frozen in a plastic container for future use.

EGGS

All the recipes in this book use large eggs. For purposes of measurement, one large egg contains 2 tablespoons of white and 1 tablespoon of yolk. When a recipe calls for room temperature eggs, remove them from the refrigerator 30 minutes before using. If you forget to take them out, put the eggs (in their shells) in a bowl filled with warm water for 5 minutes before using.

EGG SAFETY

Salmonella in raw eggs is a rare occurrence. According to the American Egg Board, the average consumer "might encounter a contaminated egg once every 84 years." Still, salmonella is cause for concern for some people. You can mitigate risk by buying eggs from a trusted source. When cooking custards on the stovetop (for ice cream, pastry cream, and crème anglaise), check their temperature with an instant-read thermometer. Health experts say eggs should be brought up to a temperature of at least 160°F (70°C) in order for them to be considered "safe." Almost all the recipes in this book call for eggs to be cooked. In those that call for uncooked eggs, I offer alternative methods.

ESPRESSO

The bold flavor of espresso is important in my recipes that call for it, so do not substitute coffee. If you don't have an espresso machine, consider making a deal with your local barista, trading a slice of cake for a few shots. Otherwise, I recommend an inexpensive stove-top espresso-maker called a *moka* pot. Non-purists can mix 1 heaping teaspoon of instant espresso powder (or to taste, depending on the brand) with $^{1}/_{4}$ cup (60 ml) of boiling water and use that in place of espresso.

FLOUR

Nearly all of the recipes in this book that use flour use all-purpose flour. Either bleached or unbleached is suitable. There are a couple recipes that call for cake flour and one that calls for buckwheat flour. Buckwheat flour is available in well-stocked supermarkets and natural food stores.

GELATIN

Granules of gelatin need to be softened before they're heated or added to other ingredients. To soften, sprinkle them evenly over the surface of the cold water called for in the recipe, then let stand for 5 minutes. Once "bloomed," stir the swollen granules and the liquid over very low heat until just dissolved, or heat the water or liquid called for in the recipe, then pour over the softened gelatin and stir until dissolved.

Gelatin-based desserts need to chill for several hours or overnight to set, so plan accordingly. If you want a gelatin dessert (such as panna cotta, page 135, or gelée, page 114) to set quickly, put the mixture in a metal bowl set over an ice bath and stir constantly with a rubber spatula to promote even jelling and discourage lumps from forming until the mixture is cool but still fluid. Pour it into the serving dishes or molds and refrigerate until set. Chilling the serving or storage containers before filling them will speed things up, too.

Most packets of gelatin contain 2 $1/4$ teaspoons (7g) of powder. If you purchase gelatin that's loose, use that measurement as your guideline.

MILK, CREAM, AND CRÈME FRAÎCHE

In this book, "milk" always means whole milk. Do not substitute low-fat or nonfat milk unless the recipe indicates you can, as you won't be satisfied with the results.

I strongly recommend finding good heavy cream from a local dairy that has not been ultrapasteurized and has a fresh, sweet taste. Keep it well chilled until ready to use. If you are making whipped cream, it's a good idea to chill the bowl and the beaters before whipping the cream.

Crème fraîche is cream that has been cultured, giving it a slight tang and a thick, silky richness. You can make your own version of crème fraîche: mix 1 cup (250 ml) of heavy cream with 1 tablespoon of buttermilk (or crème fraîche from a previous batch) and store it in a warm place until thickened, about 24 hours. Crème fraîche is also available in well-stocked supermarkets and online (see Resources, page 270). Homemade crème fraîche will keep for about 1 week.

NUTS

Most of the nuts called for in this book are easily obtainable. Nuts do not improve with age, so buy them from places that sell lots of them and whose supply is constantly refreshed. Farmers' markets are wonderful sources of nuts, as growers usually sell them as close to harvest as possible.

The primary enemy of oil-rich nuts is rancidity. Pecans and hazelnuts are especially vulnerable. Check for visible mold or signs of infestation before buying. Bakers with lots of freezer space at home, which excludes me, may wish to store them in the freezer.

CHOPPING NUTS

In a recipe, when nuts are called for—1 cup (100 g) pecans, for example—I mean whole nuts. If coarsely chopped nuts are specified, the pieces should be cut into large, irregular pieces about one-quarter or one-third the size of the whole nut. If you need finely or very finely chopped nuts, make the pieces about the size of peppercorns.

TOASTING NUTS

Toasting enhances the flavor of nuts and makes them crisp. Nuts should be toasted on an ungreased baking sheet in a 350°F (175°C) oven for approximately 10 minutes. When done, they'll smell, well, nutty and have light brown flesh when one is cracked open. Keep an eye on the nuts and stir them occasionally while toasting to prevent burning.

OIL

Some recipes in the book call for vegetable oil. Any neutral-tasting, unflavored oil is suitable. One exception to the unflavored rule is Lion & Globe peanut oil, which has the flavor of roasted peanuts. It's stocked in Asian markets. When available, I like to use it in my Fresh Ginger Cake (page 42).

SPICES

Most of the recipes specify ground spices. But certain spices, like nutmeg and cardamom, should be freshly ground right before using, because once ground, they quickly lose their distinct aroma. Nutmeg can be grated with a rasp-style grater; cardamom seeds are best ground with a mortar and pestle or spice grinder, or can be crushed in a sturdy freezer bag with a rolling pin.

Buy ground spices in small quantities and use them within a year. There are excellent spice merchants in cities and online (see Resources, page 270), and it's always worth searching out top-quality spices for best results.

SUGAR AND OTHER SWEETENERS

Sugar is, of course, a sweetener. It also provides moisture, and in small quantities, it heightens the flavors of fruits, chocolate, and other ingredients. Granulated white sugar is the most widely used type, but there are a few other sugars and liquid sweeteners that I bake with.

Granulated White Sugar

When "sugar" is called for in the recipes, I mean granulated white sugar. Baker's sugar or superfine sugar is finely ground granulated sugar. It can be used anywhere granulated sugar is called for.

Brown Sugar

Both light and dark brown sugars are fluffed up during processing and need to be firmly packed into a measuring cup for proper measurement. Use the type of brown sugar called for in the recipe for the best results.

Coarse-Crystal Sugar

Just as its name suggests, granules of coarse-crystal sugar are large and coarse. When sprinkled over a cookie or pastry before baking, the sugar gives the finished dessert a pleasant crackly crunch. Raw coarse-crystal sugars, some known as turbinado or demerara sugar, are amber in color, while other types are white or translucent. I prefer the raw ones. Hawaiian washed raw sugar made by C&H Sugar Company is available in supermarkets on the West Coast. You can buy coarse-crystal sugar online (see Resources, page 270) or in natural food and baking supply stores.

Powdered Sugar

Sometimes called confectioners' sugar, this is pulverized white sugar with a small amount of starch added to prevent caking. If it's lumpy, sift before using. Because it contains starch, powdered sugar shouldn't be substituted for granulated sugar.

Agave Nectar

Obtained by juicing agave plants, this naturally sweet nectar has become popular because of its low glycemic index and because it's a natural alternative to refined sugars. I like it because the taste doesn't overpower other ingredients. It's available in natural food stores in light and dark varieties, and I've offered it in a few recipes as an alternative to corn syrup. If using it in place of corn syrup, use a light agave nectar that has a mild flavor.

Corn Syrup

Light corn syrup is vital in a few recipes to prevent sugar from recrystallizing or because it provides the correct texture. If it's possible to substitute another liquid sweetener, I've indicated so in the recipe.

Honey

Any locally produced honey is always better than bland supermarket varieties. Some are syrupy sweet and others, such as chestnut and buckwheat, have a pleasant bitter edge. My taste tends toward the latter, but you can use any kind when a recipe calls for honey. If your honey crystallizes, warm the jar in a small saucepan of barely simmering water, or in a microwave, until it liquefies.

Maple Syrup

This natural product comes in various grades. I always get one labeled "dark amber," which has a stronger maple flavor than light amber syrups.

Molasses

When called for in recipes, use mild-flavored unsulphured molasses (sometimes called "light" molasses, which can be confusing as "light" is a term often used to describe reduced-calorie products). Both "full flavor" and blackstrap molasses have rather assertive flavors that can easily dominate, which is why I prefer lighter-flavored molasses. But, if you like a strong molasses flavor, feel free to use "full flavor" or blackstrap.

TAPIOCA

Pearls of tapioca are made by squeezing manioc (aka cassava) root over a hot plate; when the sap hits the plate, it bounces off and creates little pearls. Grind tapioca pearls into a fine powder and you get tapioca flour, an excellent thickener. Tapioca flour is available at Asian markets and from the King Arthur Flour Company (see Resources, page 270). Small pearl tapioca, which is used in Coconut Tapioca Pudding (page 139), is easily found in Asian markets and is not the same as the boxed quick-cooking tapioca stocked in supermarkets.

VANILLA

I don't mind spending top dollar for wonderful vanilla and I treat my bottles of extract and vanilla beans like precious jewels. Store vanilla beans in an airtight container in a cool, dry place—but not in the refrigerator where the moisture invites mold.

Even if I use a vanilla bean in a recipe, I always add a capful of vanilla extract as well, as I find that the extract provides a dynamic vanilla flavor, while the bean provides something more perfumed and aromatic.

If you wish to substitute one for the other, 1 vanilla bean is the equivalent of 2 to 3 teaspoons of extract, depending on the quality of the bean. Due to variations in strength, substitutions using vanilla bean pastes and powder can vary. I find $^1/_2$ teaspoon powder or paste equals the strength of 1 teaspoon vanilla extract.

Vanilla Extract

Be sure to only use pure vanilla extract. There simply is no substitute. Tahitian vanilla has a delicate floral scent and flavor and I like it with desserts that feature tropical fruit. Bourbon vanilla is more assertive and is best used in cakes and cookies as it stands up well to baking. Real Mexican vanilla is excellent, although hard to find. It's my favorite vanilla of all. (Beware of the cheap imitation stuff that's sometimes labeled "real" and sold by the quart to tourists south of the border.) Vanilla extract should be stored in a cool, dark place and kept tightly capped.

Vanilla Beans

The fragrant dried and cured pods of a tropical orchid are ideal for steeping in ice cream and custard mixtures. Avoid cheap vanilla beans, which often smell smoky, as well as beans that are dried out and brittle. A good sniff should help you gauge the quality of the vanilla beans.

To use vanilla beans, split them lengthwise with a paring knife and scrape the tiny flavorful seeds into whatever you're cooking. The pod can be used for infusing flavor as well. You can reuse the pods by rinsing and drying them thoroughly, then storing them embedded in white sugar, or in a jar of rum or bourbon.

Vanilla Bean Paste and Powder

Both of these are made with dried vanilla beans and seeds that are ground to a fine powder. Vanilla bean paste is made by macerating the powder in a sweetened liquid base. See above for substitutions.

Equipment

While it's nice to have an arsenal of fancy equipment, most bakers can get by pretty well with the basics: a set of measuring spoons and cups, a couple of nesting bowls, a saucepan and a skillet, a spatula, a few knives, and a whisk. Of course, baking is much easier and more enjoyable if you have a few extra spatulas on hand; a top-quality, sharp knife is not only easier to use, but safer too; and an electric stand mixer makes beating batters and doughs a breeze.

I've enjoyed a grand American-style designer kitchen equipped with a professional multiburner stove with enough BTUs to cater dinner for a few hundred. I've also baked in a tiny apartment with an oven I wouldn't wish on my worst enemy and a counter so small that two bowls couldn't sit on it side by side. The two kitchens produced identical results. The secret is being able to adapt to your circumstances.

I don't call for any fancy equipment. Everything used in this book can be found in most hardware or cookware stores, or even in the housewares aisle at your local supermarket. And, of course, with the Internet, everything is just a few clicks away.

The biggest tip I can offer about kitchen equipment is to buy the best you can. Fortunately, the best isn't always the most expensive. When in doubt, commercial-quality gear from a restaurant supply store is a good bet. Anything that can stand up to abuse day after day will likely do pretty well in your home kitchen, too.

BAKING DISHES

Recipes in this book that require a baking dish are scaled for 2-quart (2-liter) rectangular or oval baking dishes. Porcelain, ceramic, and earthenware are the most common materials. Enamel-coated cast iron bakers don't break as easily but are heavier and more expensive. A very large baking dish or roasting pan is necessary to make a water bath for gently baking custards and delicate cakes such as Chocolate Orbit Cake (page 26).

BAKING SHEETS

You should have at least two baking sheets. Mine measure about 12 by 18 inches (30 by 46 cm) and have sides that can contain runny cake batters and give me something to grip when moving cookies about during and after baking. If you prefer, you can use rimless baking sheets for cookies. Avoid flimsy baking sheets and ones with a dark finish as they heat too quickly, causing cookies to burn on their bottoms. Insulated baking sheets, dark or otherwise, protect against burnt bottoms, although you may need to increase the baking time if using this type.

CAKE DOME

If you make lots of cakes, a covered cake stand, or cake dome, is a worthwhile purchase. It's a great way to present and store cakes, especially ones that are glazed, frosted, or have sticky surfaces, because the domed cover leaves the icing unscathed. Cake stands can be found at cookware stores and restaurant supply shops. Beautiful vintage stands can be sleuthed out in antique shops and flea markets by those with a sharp eye.

CAKE PANS

Cake pans come in a variety of shapes, sizes, and materials. The recipes in this book use only a few different types, but it's important to use the right shape and size so that your cake bakes up properly.

Round Cake Pans

Many of the cake recipes in this book call for a 9-inch (23-cm) round cake pan with sides 2 to 3 inches (5 to 8 cm) high. Pans that are shallower don't hold enough batter for these cakes.

Springform Pans

A 9-inch (23-cm) springform pan is necessary for delicate cakes that can't be removed from their pans by flipping them out. I use one with a glass bottom, which makes serving a whole lot easier (and prettier). Most springform pans leak, so before filling it with batter, wrap yours securely on the outside and up the sides with a single sheet of aluminum foil, making sure there are no tears or openings.

Bundt Pans

For some recipes, you'll need a 10-cup (2.5 liter) Bundt cake or tube pan about 10 inches (25 cm) in diameter. These days, Bundt pans are made with a variety of decorative patterns and elaborate designs, but I'm a bit of a traditionalist and prefer those that are simple and elegant. Note that the shape and design of the Bundt pan can affect the cake's baking time.

Muffin Tins

For cupcakes, I use a standard muffin tin with cups that are $2\,^1/_2$ inches (7 cm) across the top, and hold $^1/_2$ cup (125 ml) of batter in each. For Green Tea Financiers (page 208), I use a mini muffin tin with 24 tiny cups, each with a $1\,^1/_2$-tablespoon capacity.

COOLING RACKS

A flat wire rack is useful for cooling cakes and sheets of just-baked cookies. You may need more than one if the recipe yields a lot of cookies.

CUTTING BOARDS

I recommend plastic cutting boards for baking tasks because they don't absorb odors and are dishwasher safe. I reserve one specifically for cutting fruits, which garlic and onions aren't allowed anywhere near. (I pity the person who grabs the wrong one in my kitchen and begins mincing garlic without asking first.)

FOOD MILL

They've fallen out of favor, but food mills do a great job of separating the seeds from the pulp of raspberries and blackberries without cracking the seeds, which causes bitterness. If you don't have one, purée berries in a food processor, then press the pulp through a mesh sieve to separate out the seeds.

FOOD PROCESSOR AND BLENDER

I use a food processor fitted with the metal blade to chop lots of fresh ginger for recipes such as my Fresh Ginger Cake (page 42) and to prepare certain types of pastry doughs. I prefer to chop nuts by hand because I find the processor does an uneven job, leaving some nuts almost whole, while turning others to dust.

A blender is great for puréeing cooked fruits for sorbets and preserves. If you are puréeing something hot, remember to fill the jar of a blender no more than halfway full or the hot liquid and steam can shoot out over the top and cause injury. A handheld immersion blender has the advantage of letting you purée directly in a saucepan, bowl, or measuring cup, eliminating the chore of washing the blender jar.

GRATERS AND VEGETABLE PEELERS

In baking, the job of graters is to remove the colorful and highly flavorful part of the citrus skin that contains the essential oils. I use a rasp-style grater, working directly over the pan or bowl to collect the oil that sprays as you grate as well as the zest itself. That's why in many recipes, I call for the "zest of $1/2$ lemon" rather than a specific quantity, which would require zesting over a cutting board and losing all that lovely citrus oil. If you don't have a rasp-style grater, use a regular grater or a zester, then chop the peel very fine.

A sharp-bladed vegetable peeler is the tool for stripping off large, wide pieces of zest. Avoid using too much pressure; it's best to leave as much of the bitter white pith behind as possible. Some people use a peeler to pare the skin off apples and pears, although I always use a paring knife. As with other kitchen tools, get a vegetable peeler that feels good in your hand.

ICE CREAM MACHINE

Thankfully, there are several inexpensive machines on the market with motors that simply snap on and put homemade ice cream within anyone's reach. These machines work well, although the churning containers must be frozen a full 24 hours before use. (In spite of what the instructions might say about pre-freezing time, I find they're being hopelessly optimistic if they call for less.) Folks with plenty of freezer space often store their canister in there all the time so that it's ready whenever they need it.

If you like ice cream (as I do), and make it regularly (as I do), you should treat yourself to a machine with a self-contained internal refrigeration unit. It lets you freeze ice cream with a lot less hassle, though price can be a deterrent.

Cuisinart makes good ice cream machines in various price ranges, including a relatively affordable model that's self-refrigerating. Rival-White Mountain makes models that require ice and rock salt, which are nice if you like to churn your ice cream in the great outdoors. And KitchenAid makes a stand-mixer attachment specifically for freezing ice cream.

If you don't have an ice cream machine, you can make ice cream and sorbets by freezing the mixture in a shallow plastic container. As it begins to freeze, beat it vigorously by hand or with a handheld mixer, then return it to the freezer. Repeat every 30 minutes or so. When it becomes too hard to stir, it's done.

JUICER

I use a Mexican-style metal citrus press for juicing lemon, lime, and orange halves. The press simply squeezes the juice out of the fruit, and a bowl or measuring cup placed under the juicer catches the liquid. If you need a lot of juice, an electric juicer is likely faster.

Citrus fruit for juicing should be room temperature, not cold. Before juicing, roll the whole fruit on the counter, pressing down firmly to rupture the juice sacs within. Then, halve it and press out the juice.

KITCHEN TORCH

Small butane-fueled kitchen torches are now sold in many cookware shops and are great for caramelizing the sugar on top of crème brûlée. Or, you can use a regular propane blowtorch—its size makes it a little unwieldy, but it does a good, quick job.

KNIVES

As a baker, I use stainless steel knives and avoid ones made of carbon steel, which can react unappetizingly with fruit. Take care of your knives and don't run them through the dishwasher, which brutalizes them and can damage the blades. You'll need three different types of knives for these recipes: A long, sharp serrated bread knife with a 12- or 14-inch (30- to 36-cm) blade is a must for cutting cakes neatly. A high-quality 8-, 10-, or 12-inch (20-, 25-, or 30-cm) chef's knife—whichever size feels right in your hand—is important for chopping ingredients. For peeling and slicing fruit, I recommend a 3- to 4-inch (8- to 10-cm) paring knife.

MEASURING SPOONS AND CUPS

If you bake frequently, you should have at least two sets each of measuring spoons and dry measuring cups. Otherwise, you'll have to interrupt what you're doing to do some speedy washing and drying in order to measure something else.

Measuring Spoons

I'm fond of the OXO measuring spoons that don't tip over when filled and set on a countertop. But any kind of measuring spoons will do. Be sure when measuring something acidic, like lemon juice, that you use spoons made of a nonreactive material, such as stainless steel or plastic.

Dry and Liquid Measuring Cups

For accurate measuring, you need both dry and liquid measuring cups. Dry measuring cups come in nested sets with cups that hold $^1/_4$, $^1/_3$, $^1/_2$, and 1 cup (60, 80, 125, and 250 ml). The level edges make it easy to scoop up flour, for example, and sweep away the excess with a straight-edged utensil or the back of a knife—the correct way to measure flour, sugar, and other dry ingredients. Liquid measuring cups have handles and spouts and come in 1-cup (250-ml), 2-cup (500-ml), and 1-quart (1-liter) capacities, with measurements indicated on the sides of the cup.

MIXING BOWLS

In my pantry, I have stacks of these in various sizes because baking often requires the use of many bowls at the same time. A good choice is nested stainless steel or heavy-duty plastic bowls, which are lightweight, durable, and space efficient. Those with rubberized bases make tempering egg yolks for custards, which involves simultaneous pouring and whisking, much easier. (You can also dampen a kitchen towel, twist it like a rope, form it into a ring on the counter, and set the bowl in the center to hold it steady.)

For the purposes of the recipes in this book, a small bowl is one that holds up to 2 quarts (2 liters), a medium bowl holds up to 4 quarts (4 liters), and a large bowl holds more than 4 quarts (4 liters).

PARCHMENT PAPER AND SILICONE MATS

Lining a pan with parchment paper ensures that cookies or cakes don't stick. Rolls of parchment are sold in supermarkets and cookware stores. Some cookware and restaurant supply stores sell parchment paper in half-sheet sizes (professionals refer to home-size baking sheets as "half-sheet" pans). Another option for lining baking sheets is silicone baking mats, flexible sheets of a nonstick material strong enough to withstand even the high heat of caramel. They are reusable and available at most cookware stores or online.

In most recipes, I advise that it's fine to use either. But for a few, like Sesame-Orange Almond Tuiles (page 212), using thin parchment paper makes it easier to lift the fragile cookies from the baking sheet.

PASTRY BRUSHES

I use pastry brushes for applying glazes, buttering pans, and brushing cakes to saturate them with syrups. When I roll out dough, I use a wide, dry brush to remove excess flour, which could otherwise toughen the pastry. Buy inexpensive soft-bristled brushes at cookware or hardware stores, ones that you have no qualms dicarding when they start losing their bristles. This will save you the embarrassment of a guest finding a hairlike filament sticking out of his or her wedge of pie.

PASTRY SCRAPERS

I wouldn't bake without one of these within reach. Rectangular metal scrapers, also called "bench scrapers," are indispensable for lifting dough while rolling it, moving chopped chocolate and nuts, and scraping work surfaces clean. Flexible plastic scrapers are handy for getting all the dough cleanly out of mixing bowls. It's rare to find a professional pastry chef who doesn't keep a pastry scraper nearby at all times.

PIE PLATES AND PIE WEIGHTS

I use both 9- and 10-inch (23-cm and 25-cm) pie plates. My favorites are made of heavy glass, which allows you to see how your bottom crust is browning during baking. In my recipes, you can substitute a 9-inch (23-cm) pie plate if you don't have a 10-inch (25-cm) one, and feel free to use one made of whatever material you choose. Metal conducts heat more efficiently than glass, so check pies baked in metal tins before the end of the recommended baking time.

For weighting pie and tart crusts that need to be prebaked (baked before the filling is added), you can use dried beans, pennies, or pie weights, which are sold in cookware stores. Weighting the crust prevents the dough from shrinking.

RAMEKINS AND CUSTARD CUPS

You can use elegant porcelain 4-ounce (60-ml) ramekins or basic 6-ounce (180-ml) Pyrex custard cups that are available in supermarkets and hardware stores. Really, any ovenproof custard cups are fine to use. You may have good luck searching garage sales and antique stores for vintage sets.

ROLLING PIN

There are lots of rolling pins out there made from modern materials, but I'm hopelessly attached to ones made from good old-fashioned wood. I've switched from one with handles and ball bearings to the simple kind, just a spindle of wood, otherwise known as a French rolling pin. Use whichever kind of rolling pin you prefer.

SAUCEPANS AND SKILLETS

Cheap pots and pans are badly balanced, warp easily, and don't last. They also have hot spots which will cause your food to cook unevenly. Worst of all, they're a pain to clean. This is one category of kitchen equipment that I refuse to compromise on.

My favorite cookware is made by All-Clad. It's well designed, solid, cooks evenly, and has handles that stay cool on the stovetop. If you can, go to a cookware store, heft as many pans as you can, and get what feels right for you. Good cookware is an excellent investment that few cooks regret making, and starter sets are an inexpensive way to start a collection.

For the purposes of the recipes in this book, a small saucepan is one that holds up to 2 quarts (2 liters), a medium saucepan holds up to 4 quarts (4 liters), and a large saucepan (or Dutch oven) holds more than 4 quarts (4 liters). A large skillet measures at least 10 inches (25 cm) in diameter.

I use nonstick skillets for frying crêpes. When the nonstick finish begins to show any signs of aging, I replace the pan. Recent to the market and worth investigating are "green" nonstick cookware that claim to be made by eco-friendly methods.

SCALE

Since many pastry recipes call for ingredients that are impractical to measure by volume, like chocolate, you'll want to have an accurate scale. I recommend a digital one. Unless you're a scientist, it need not be the pinnacle of precision. A reasonably priced one is adequate for home bakers.

SPATULAS, SPOONS, AND LADLES

I favor heatproof silicone spatulas. Since discovering them, all other rubber spatulas have been relegated to the drawer of RIP kitchen utensils. I use a heatproof spatula for everything from mixing ice cream custards to stirring caramel. I'm partial to Le Creuset spatula "spoons," which have a slight curve to their blades and are good for scooping and folding ingredients; they just feel right in my hand. I keep at least five or six heatproof spatulas in my kitchen.

Both straight and offset (angled) metal icing spatulas are good for decorating, spreading icings, and leveling the surface of batters. I have both types in two sizes: small, with a 4-inch (10-cm) blade, and large, with an 8- to 10-inch (20- to 25-cm) blade. I don't use them often, but when I need one, I'm always glad that I have it on hand. Wide metal or plastic spatulas are useful for removing cookies from baking sheets.

For stirring, both stainless and wooden spoons are suitable utensils. A 1- or 2-ounce (30- to 60-ml) ladle is handy for tempering eggs for custards, pouring crêpe batter, and, of course, ladling sauces.

STAND MIXER

A good, sturdy stand mixer is likely to be your biggest expense as a baker. I use a KitchenAid 5-quart mixer because that's the machine I feel most comfortable with, having used it as a pastry chef in restaurants.

Make sure that the stand mixer you use is powerful and stable so it doesn't walk off the counter while it's beating a batter and you've turned your back.

I also recommend buying an extra stand-mixer bowl and extra paddle and whisk attachments. Having doubles will save you the trouble of scrambling to wash and dry them when you need clean equipment midway through a recipe. If you don't have room for a stand mixer, a powerful handheld mixer is the next best thing.

STORAGE CONTAINERS

Having frequently used ingredients in easy-to-access containers is a pleasure for any baker. There's nothing more frustrating than trying to scoop flour out of a crinkly paper sack. Plastic tubs with airtight lids will keep things fresh and organized. I keep flour, sugar, and nuts in rectangular plastic containers, available at restaurant supply stores and cookware shops, although to be honest, I've scored a lot of my best ones at garage sales and thrift stores.

Always store cookies in an airtight container at room temperature. Tin or plastic works best. I don't recommend those ceramic cookie jars because they're just too tempting to steal from.

STRAINERS

I use a stainless steel fine-mesh strainer for straining custards and infusions. A strainer can also double as a sieve for sifting, mixing, and aerating dry ingredients, and for dusting baked goods with powdered sugar.

TART PANS

Sometimes called quiche pans, tart pans are two-piece metal pans with removable bottoms that fit into shallow rings with scalloped sides. The tart recipes in this book call for 9-inch (23-cm) round tart pans. You can also use a straight-sided tart ring—a bottomless form that needs to be placed on a flat baking sheet lined with parchment paper or a silicone mat.

THERMOMETERS

Check the accuracy of your oven periodically with an oven thermometer. An instant-read thermometer is useful for checking the temperature of custards, and a candy or jelly thermometer, preferably one with a metal back (ones made entirely of glass break too easily), is handy for ensuring that candies and preserved fruits are cooked to the correct temperature. After using a candy thermometer, clean it and store it right away in a sturdy cardboard tube from a roll of paper towels to prevent breakage.

TIMERS

Since timing is critical for most baked goods, especially cookies, always use a timer. Most stoves have one built in, but it may not be as accurate as a digital or wind-up model.

WHISKS

You should have a wide balloon whisk for whipping anything in a bowl (such as egg whites) and a long, straight whisk for whisking in saucepans. Buy only good-quality whisks that can stand up to being whacked against a bowl or the sides of a pan. Use a metal whisk for whipping egg whites, as a silicone one can harbor oil that will prevent the whites from whipping up properly.

Cakes

When most people think of baking, they think of cake. I love cake in any and all forms, although I'm not one to make fussy, elaborate concoctions—instead, my cakes are straightforward and intensely flavored. A lemon-flavored cake should be tangy-sweet, with the zesty flavor of lemons bursting forth. My Fresh Ginger Cake (page 42) has all the moistness of a classic spice cake with a generous handful of freshly chopped ginger. If I'm going to make (and eat) chocolate cake, I want one like Chocolate Pavé (page 25) that tastes of deep, dark chocolate. I don't want billows of airy buttercream to detract from its intensity.

Speaking of chocolate, I'm crazy for the stuff. You've likely noticed that over the past few years, lots of wonderful types of chocolates have hit store shelves. Not only do I love nibbling on them, but many are available in baking bars, so I use them in desserts. I urge you to sample different brands to find your favorites. But be careful: if your kitchen is anything like mine, chocolate has an odd way of disappearing from the pantry before it can be melted and mixed into a batter.

In this chapter, you'll find a tremendous diversity of cakes, from layer cakes to loaf cakes to cupcakes, but most are made in a 9-inch (23-cm) round cake pan. In general, it's the most commonly used cake pan size, which is why I own four. One day, after cleaning up the aftermath of batter overflow in my oven, I measured the capacity of my 9-inch (23-cm) cake pans that were made by various manufacturers.

I was surprised to find that a slight difference in the height of the pans' sides meant a pretty sizable difference in capacity: filled to the rim, the shallowest pan held only 8 cups (1.9 liters), while the deepest one held 11 cups (2.5 liters). (Of course, when making a cake, you'd never fill a cake pan to the top because the batter requires room for expansion during baking.) For the recipes in this chapter that call for a 9-inch (23-cm) round cake pan, be sure to use one with sides that are at least 2 inches (5 cm) high.

Some of the more delicate cakes, such as the Racines Cake (page 30) and Gâteau Victoire (page 32), are baked in a springform pan set in a bath of warm water for gentle, even cooking. (Many springform pans are made in Europe, so often a pan labeled 9 inches is actually closer to $9\frac{1}{2}$ inches in diameter.) The sides of the springform pan that I use are $2\frac{1}{2}$ inches (6 cm) high.

Don't panic if you don't have a cake pan of the exact size called for in a recipe. Just be prepared to make minor adjustments to the baking time and realize that sometimes a pan of a slightly smaller or larger size can cause the cake to bake up a little differently.

At the end of most of the cake recipes, I offer suggestions for accompaniments, but I encourage you to do your own mixing and matching of cakes with sauces or dollops of something delicious. Some, like the upside-down cakes—plum-blueberry (page 40) and nectarine-raspberry gingerbread (page 41)—are fine just as they are, but they would certainly benefit from a scoop of Vanilla Ice Cream (page 143) or a mound of whipped cream (page 239). Others, like the Lemon Semifreddo (page 65) can be embellished with a fruity accompaniment, such as a spoonful of Blackberry Sauce (page 248). The Basics, Sauces, and Preserves chapter, beginning on page 227, offers a variety of sauces, from elegant Raspberry Sauce (page 246) to a suave, but uncomplicated Tangerine Butterscotch Sauce (page 242), so you can create your own combinations.

Chocolate Pavé

MAKES ONE 9-INCH (23-CM) SQUARE CAKE; 9 SERVINGS

This Chocolate Pavé is an adaptation of a recipe by Lindsey Shere, co-owner and executive pastry chef at Chez Panisse when the restaurant opened, who taught me much of what I know about baking and desserts. Of all the things I learned, the most important lesson was how to appreciate a killer-good chocolate cake just as it is, without dressing it up with fancy swoops and swirls of frosting or layering it with creams or fillings. When I once expressed dismay that I hadn't learned how to make all those fancy, frilly desserts during my tenure with her, she replied, "Why would you want to? They usually don't taste good."

Pavé means "paving stone" in French. This cake is traditionally baked in a square pan so it can be cut into rectangles, creating edible slabs that are delectably rich. After one soft, moist, luscious bite, they'll remind you of paving stones only in appearance.

Cocoa powder, for preparing the pan

1 cup (8 ounces/225 g) salted or unsalted butter, cut into pieces

4 ounces (115 g) bittersweet or semisweet chocolate, chopped

4 ounces (115 g) unsweetened chocolate, chopped

6 large eggs, separated, at room temperature

$^1/_2$ cup (100 g) plus $^1/_2$ cup (100 g) granulated sugar

Pinch of salt

Powdered sugar, for dusting the cake

Melted bittersweet or semisweet chocolate, for decorating the cake

Preheat the oven to 350°F (175°C). Butter the bottom and sides of a 9-inch (23-cm) square cake pan, dust it with a bit of cocoa powder, then tap out any excess. Line the bottom of the pan with parchment paper.

In a large heatproof bowl, combine the butter and both chocolates. Set the bowl over a pan of simmering water, stirring occasionally until the mixture is melted and smooth. Remove the bowl from the heat.

In a stand mixer fitted with the whip attachment, whisk together the egg yolks and $^1/_2$ cup (100 g) granulated sugar on high speed until the mixture leaves a defined ribbon on the surface when you lift the beater, about 5 minutes. Fold in the melted chocolate mixture until fully incorporated.

In a clean, dry bowl and with a clean whip attachment, whisk the egg whites and salt on low speed until they form soft, wet peaks. Gradually beat in the remaining $^1/_2$ cup (100 g) granulated sugar and continue whisking at high speed until the whites hold stiff peaks. Fold the egg whites into the chocolate mixture just until there are no visible streaks of egg whites. Don't overfold.

Scrape the batter into the prepared cake pan and gently smooth the top. Bake until just barely set in the center (it should still feel jiggly), about 35 minutes. The cake will rise as it bakes and form a slightly crackly top. Let cool about 15 minutes.

Run a knife around the sides of the cake to help loosen it from the pan. Invert the cake onto a plate, peel off the parchment paper, and re-invert it onto a large platter or cutting board. Let cool completely.

Dust the top of the cake with powdered sugar and cut the cake into squares. Dip a fork in melted chocolate and wave it back and forth over the cake, creating an abstract design on top.

SERVING: Serve each slab in a pool of crème anglaise (page 237). If you like, a handful of raspberries or a few Candied Cherries (page 250) are delicious alongside.

STORAGE: This cake is best served the day it's made.

> **TIP:** Leftover bits of Chocolate Pavé are wonderful crumbled into just-churned ice cream, especially Caramel Ice Cream (page 144).

Chocolate Orbit Cake

MAKES ONE 9-INCH (23-CM) CAKE; 12 TO 14 SERVINGS

I developed this recipe because I'd been asked by a restaurant to come up with an idiotproof chocolate dessert. Since the cake I created was impossible to mess up, I called it Chocolate Idiot Cake (behind everyone's back, of course). A few years later, I made it in another restaurant and someone commented that the surface of the cake looked lunar, so it was christened with a kinder, gentler name: Chocolate Orbit Cake.

Not that any of you out there is an idiot, but this is the perfect cake for any baker who may not be a rocket scientist in the kitchen. No matter what you call it, it'll surely launch anyone who takes a bite into chocolate heaven.

1 cup (8 ounces/225 g) unsalted butter, cut into pieces

12 ounces (340 g) bittersweet or semisweet chocolate, chopped

6 large eggs, at room temperature

1 cup (200 g) sugar

Preheat the oven to 350°F (175°C). Butter the bottom and sides of a 9-inch (23-cm) springform pan or round cake pan. If using a springform pan, wrap a large sheet of aluminum foil around the outside of the pan, making sure it's absolutely watertight. If using a cake pan, line the bottom with a circle of parchment paper. Set the springform or cake pan in a large roasting pan.

In a large heatproof bowl, combine the butter and chocolate. Set the bowl over a pan of simmering water and stir occasionally until the mixture is melted and smooth. Remove the bowl from the heat.

In a medium bowl, whisk together the eggs and sugar, then whisk in the melted chocolate mixture until completely incorporated.

Scrape the batter into the prepared springform or cake pan and cover the pan tightly with foil. Pour very warm water into the roasting pan to reach halfway up the outside of the cake pan. Bake until the cake appears to be set and your finger comes away clean when you gently touch the center (it will still feel quite soft), about 1 hour and 15 minutes. Remove the cake from the water bath and let cool completely.

To unmold, run a knife around the sides of the cake to help loosen it from the pan. If you've used a springform pan, simply release the sides. If you've used a regular cake pan, invert the cake onto a plate, peel off the parchment paper, then re-invert onto a serving platter.

SERVING: This cake is an overload of chocolate, so serve it in small wedges, accompanied with whipped cream (page 239), crème anglaise (page 237), or a scoop of Caramel Ice Cream (page 144). Chocolate curls and shavings are elegant garnishes (see page 8).

STORAGE: This cake can be refrigerated for up to 5 days.

Marjolaine

MAKES ONE 12-INCH (30-CM) RECTANGULAR CAKE; 12 SERVINGS

I'm not a fan of fancy, complicated desserts, but I am a fan of anything delicious—especially when it involves cara-melized nuts, chocolate ganache, and Cognac-flavored crème fraîche, as this cake does. True, this recipe requires a few steps to gather the components, but slicing layers of nutty meringue and spreading layers of crackly praline cream never feels like work to me. Like all good things, *marjolaine* is worth the effort.

To make things easy, instead of laborious buttercream, I make a simple crème fraîche–based icing, which adds a distinctive tangy flavor and isn't so rich. You can make the praline and the meringue days in advance, and the *marjolaine* should be assembled at least a day before it is served to give the flavors a chance to marry, so you can stage out the preparation. It's really not difficult to assemble once you've gotten the components organized. And I guarantee, when you proudly glide a slick layer of chocolate ganache over the top and then take that first bite, you'll be congratulating yourself on a job well done.

NUT MERINGUE

$^3/_4$ cup (75 g) hazelnuts, toasted

$^3/_4$ cup (75 g) almonds, toasted

$1^1/_3$ cups (265 g) sugar

1 tablespoon cornstarch

8 large egg whites, at room temperature

Pinch of salt

PRALINE

$^1/_2$ cup (100 g) sugar

$^1/_2$ cup (65 g) almonds, toasted and coarsely chopped

CHOCOLATE GANACHE

$^3/_4$ cup (180 g) crème fraîche

10 ounces (280 g) bittersweet or semisweet chocolate, chopped

PRALINE AND VANILLA CREAMS

$^3/_4$ cup (180 g) crème fraîche

$^1/_4$ cup (60 ml) heavy cream

2 tablespoons (30 g) sugar

$^1/_2$ teaspoon vanilla extract

1 tablespoon Cognac or brandy

Before preparing this recipe, see Caramelization Guidelines, page 265.

TIP: Some of the components can be made ahead: The meringue can be made up to 3 days in advance and wrapped in plastic. The praline can be made 1 week in advance, chopped, and kept in an airtight container.

To make the nut meringue, preheat the oven to 350°F (175°C). Coat the bottom and sides of a 12 by 18-inch (30 by 46-cm) baking sheet with nonstick cooking spray and line the bottom with parchment paper. Generously grease the parchment paper, then dust the pan with flour and tap out any excess.

Rub the toasted hazelnuts between your hands or in a kitchen towel to loosen and remove the skins. In a food processor fitted with the metal blade or in a blender, pulverize the almonds and hazelnuts with the $1^1/_3$ cups (265 g) sugar and the cornstarch until finely ground, then transfer the mixture to a bowl.

In a stand mixer fitted with the whip attachment, whisk the egg whites on low speed until frothy. Add the salt, increase the speed to high, and beat until the egg whites form stiff peaks.

Gradually sprinkle the ground-nut mixture over the egg whites, folding it in as you go. Scrape the batter onto the prepared baking sheet and smooth with a spatula. Bake until light golden brown, 20 to 25 minutes. Let cool completely.

To make the praline, lightly coat a baking sheet with cooking spray or line it with a silicone baking mat. Spread the $^{1}/_{2}$ cup (100 g) sugar in an even layer in a medium heavy-bottomed skillet and cook over medium heat until the sugar begins to melt around the edges. Using a heatproof utensil, slowly drag the liquefied sugar to the center and stir gently until all of the sugar is melted. Continue to cook, stirring infrequently, until the caramel is deep amber in color and begins to foam a bit. Remove from the heat, immediately stir in the chopped almonds, then pour the mixture onto the prepared baking sheet and spread it in an even layer. Let cool completely. The praline will harden with cooling.

Once cool, break up the praline with your hands. In a food processor fitted with a metal blade or with a chef's knife, chop the praline into very small pieces. Transfer to a medium bowl.

To make the ganache, heat the $^{3}/_{4}$ cup (180 g) crème fraîche in a small saucepan over medium heat until it just begins to boil. Remove from the heat and add the chocolate. Let stand for a minute, then stir until the mixture is completely smooth. Set aside to cool.

To make the praline and vanilla creams, in a stand mixer fitted with the whip attachment (or in a bowl by hand), whisk together the $^{3}/_{4}$ cup (180 g) crème fraîche, the cream, 2 tablespoons (30 g) sugar, and vanilla on medium speed until the mixture is stiff but still glossy. Don't overbeat.

For the praline cream, stir $^{2}/_{3}$ cup (160 ml) of the whipped crème fraîche mixture into the chopped praline. (The mixture will seem somewhat stiff, but the ingredients will meld and by the time you're ready to use it, the praline cream will be spreadable.) Set aside.

For the vanilla cream, add the Cognac or brandy to the remaining whipped crème fraîche mixture and whisk lightly until firm. Set aside.

To assemble the *marjolaine*, run a knife around the edges of the meringue to loosen it from the pan, place another baking sheet over it, and invert the meringue. Peel away the parchment paper, holding down the meringue as you pull so that it won't break. (If you do break the meringue, it can be patched together when you are assembling the layers.)

Using a serrated bread knife, cut the meringue crosswise (not lengthwise) into 4 even rectangles, each about $4^{1}/_{2}$ by 12 inches (11 by 30 cm). Cover a baking sheet or large rectangular platter with plastic wrap and set one meringue rectangle on top. Spread $^{3}/_{4}$ cup (180 ml) of the chocolate ganache over it in an even layer. Cover and refrigerate the remaining ganache.

Top the ganache layer with a second meringue rectangle and spread evenly with the vanilla cream. Top with a third meringue rectangle and spread evenly with the praline cream. Top with the last meringue rectangle. Wrap the *marjolaine* in plastic wrap and refrigerate it overnight.

To finish the cake, remove the *marjolaine* and the reserved ganache from the refrigerator. Trim the rough edges of the *marjolaine* with the serrated knife. Gently warm the ganache over a small pan of simmering water until it's spreadable, then spread it evenly over the top and sides of the cake.

Using the serrated knife, slice the *marjolaine* crosswise into slabs, dipping the knife blade in hot water and wiping it clean after each cut. Serve at room temperature.

SERVING: *Marjolaine* is flavorful on its own, though you might want to offer some lightly sweetened whipped cream (page 239) alongside.

STORAGE: The assembled unfrosted cake can be stored in the refrigerator for up to 3 days.

Racines Cake

MAKES ONE 9-INCH (23-CM) CAKE; 10 TO 12 SERVINGS

Inspiration can strike at the strangest times and in the most unlikely places. I was in the men's room at Racines, a restaurant in Paris. While I was momentarily preoccupied with other things, my mind wandered and I scanned the wall facing me, which was plastered with poems and drawings from local artists. Much to my surprise, in the midst of it all was a recipe for chocolate cake.

When I returned to my table, I noticed a chocolate cake with the same name on the menu, so I ordered it. It was so delicious that I excused myself again, this time taking a pad of paper and pen with me.

At the restaurant, the cake is baked with a handful of cocoa nibs strewn over the top. Cocoa nibs are unsweetened roasted bits of cocoa beans; they're pretty widely available nowadays. Their slightly bitter chocolate crunch makes a big difference in the flavor and texture of the cake, but you can leave them off if you can't find them.

Cocoa powder, for preparing the pan

10 ounces (280 g) bittersweet or semisweet chocolate, chopped

$^1/_2$ cup (4 ounces/115 g) salted butter, cut into pieces

1 tablespoon freshly brewed espresso

$^1/_2$ teaspoon vanilla extract

6 large eggs, separated, at room temperature

$^1/_4$ cup (50 g) plus 2 tablespoons (30 g) granulated sugar

2 tablespoons (20 g) cocoa nibs (optional)

Powdered sugar, for dusting the cake (optional)

Preheat the oven to 350°F (175°C). Butter the bottom and sides of a 9-inch (23-cm) springform pan, dust it with a bit of cocoa powder, and tap out any excess.

In a large heatproof bowl, combine the chocolate, butter, and espresso. Set the bowl over a pan of simmering water and stir occasionally until the mixture is melted and smooth. Remove the bowl from the heat and stir in the vanilla.

In a stand mixer fitted with the whip attachment, whisk together the egg yolks and the $^1/_4$ cup (50 g) granulated sugar on medium-high speed until the mixture is light and creamy, about 1 minute.

In a clean, dry bowl and with a clean whip attachment, whisk the egg whites on low speed until they begin to hold their shape. Add the remaining 2 tablespoons (30 g) granulated sugar and whisk on high speed until the whites hold soft peaks.

Fold the beaten egg yolks into the melted chocolate mixture, then fold in half of the whipped egg whites. Fold in the remaining whites, mixing just until there are no visible streaks of egg whites. Don't overfold.

Scrape the batter into the prepared pan, sprinkle with cocoa nibs, if using, and bake until the cake feels as though it's just barely set in the center, about 25 minutes. It shouldn't feel too firm. Let cool completely.

Run a knife around the sides of the cake to help loosen it from the pan. Release the sides of the pan and dust the cake with powdered sugar, if using.

SERVING: The suggested accompaniment at Racines was whipped cream scented with orange flower water. But the cake also goes well with a scoop of ice cream and a dousing of Bittersweet Chocolate Sauce (page 243).

STORAGE: The cake is best served the day it's made, although it can be kept for up to 2 days at room temperature.

> TIP: Cocoa nibs can be found in well-stocked markets or purchased by mail order (see Resources, page 270).

Gâteau Victoire

MAKES ONE 9-INCH (23-CM) CAKE; 10 TO 12 SERVINGS

Of all the cakes in the flourless genre, this Gâteau Victoire has the most marvelously creamy texture. Once baked, it's so velvety moist that I recommend you cut it with a length of dental floss instead of a knife—even at the risk of getting some funny looks from your dinner guests who might think that you're preparing to brush your teeth and call it a night.

12 ounces (340 g) bittersweet or semisweet chocolate, chopped

3/4 cup (180 ml) heavy cream

3 tablespoons (45 ml) dark rum, Cognac, or port (ruby or tawny)

6 large eggs, at room temperature

6 tablespoons (75 g) granulated sugar

Pinch of salt

Powdered sugar, for dusting the cake

Preheat the oven to 350°F (175°C). Butter the bottom and sides of a 9-inch (23-cm) springform pan. Wrap a large sheet of aluminum foil around the outside of the pan, making sure it's absolutely watertight. Set the pan in a large roasting pan.

In a large heatproof bowl, combine the chocolate, cream, and rum, Cognac, or port. Set the bowl over a pan of simmering water and stir occasionally until the chocolate is melted and the mixture is smooth. Remove the bowl from the heat.

In a stand mixer fitted with the whip attachment, whisk together the eggs, granulated sugar, and salt on medium speed until the mixture is thick and leaves a well-defined ribbon on the surface when you lift the beater, about 5 minutes.

Fold one-third of the beaten eggs into the chocolate mixture to lighten it. Then, fold in the rest. Scrape the batter into the prepared pan and pour very warm water into the roasting pan to reach halfway up the sides of the springform pan.

Bake until the cake feels just set in the center, about 45 minutes. Remove the cake from the water bath and let cool completely.

Run a knife around the sides of the cake to help loosen it from the pan. Release the sides of the springform pan and dust the cake with powdered sugar.

STORAGE: This cake is best the day it's made, although it can be kept overnight at room temperature.

VARIATION: A colorful cranberry, prune, and kumquat sauce is a lovely winter-season addition to serve alongside this cake during the holidays. Heat 2 cups (500 ml) of ruby or tawny port and 1/2 cup (100 g) of sugar in a small saucepan. Add 12 pitted prunes, quartered, and 2/3 cup (75 g) dried cranberries to the pan and simmer for 4 minutes. Add 12 sliced and seeded kumquats and simmer for 1 minute more.

> TIP: Dental floss pulled taut between your fingers works best for getting neat slices of this delicate cake.

Chocolate-Cherry Fruitcake

MAKES TWO 9-INCH (23-CM) LOAF CAKES

To boost the reputation of the much-maligned fruitcake, I wanted to create a version quite different from those sticky, oversweet loaves riddled with iridescent fruit and soggy pecans. This recipe was my answer: an exceptionally moist loaf, chockablock with freshly toasted nuts, perky dried cherries, and a double wallop of chocolate flavor, courtesy of cocoa powder and lots of chocolate chips.

I was glad that my modern-tasting fruitcake made converts out of those who tried it. But I didn't expect that so many would want to give it a traditional soaking of spirits to preserve the cake. I set to work and experimented a few times, but I had a hunch that something was amiss when I noticed some movement underneath the gauze wrapping. I unwrapped the cake and . . . well, let's just say I discovered I was only one of the many creatures who enjoy this fruitcake. That was the end of my experiments. Instead, I just use with a kirsch-flavored glaze that can be added at the last minute.

FRUITCAKE

$1^1/_2$ cups (180 g) dried sour cherries, coarsely chopped

$1/_3$ cup (80 ml) plus 6 tablespoons (90 ml) kirsch or light rum

$1^1/_4$ cups (175 g) all-purpose flour

$1/_2$ cup (50 g) unsweetened cocoa powder, preferably Dutch-process

1 teaspoon baking powder

$1/_2$ teaspoon baking soda

$1/_2$ teaspoon salt

$1/_2$ cup (4 ounces/115 g) plus 2 tablespoons (1 ounce/30 g) unsalted butter, at room temperature

$1^1/_2$ cups (300 g) granulated sugar

2 large eggs, at room temperature

1 large egg yolk, at room temperature

1 teaspoon vanilla extract

$2/_3$ cup (160 ml) buttermilk or plain yogurt (whole-milk or low-fat)

1 cup (100 g) walnuts or pecans, toasted and finely chopped

$3/_4$ cup (120 g) bittersweet or semisweet chocolate chips

GLAZE

2 cups (225 g) powdered sugar, sifted

6 to 8 tablespoons (90 to 125 ml) kirsch or light rum

To make the fruitcakes, in a small saucepan, bring the dried cherries and $1/_3$ cup (80 ml) kirsch or rum to a boil. Remove from the heat, cover, and set aside to macerate for about 1 hour.

Preheat the oven to 350°F (175°C). Butter the bottom and sides of two 9-inch (23-cm) loaf pans, dust them with flour, and tap out any excess. Line the bottoms with rectangles of parchment paper.

Into a small bowl, sift together the flour, cocoa, baking powder, baking soda, and salt. Set aside.

In a stand mixer fitted with the paddle attachment (or in a bowl by hand), beat together the butter and granulated sugar on medium speed until light and fluffy, 3 to 5 minutes.

In a small bowl, whisk together the eggs, egg yolk, and vanilla, then slowly beat this mixture into the butter mixture. Stir in half of the flour mixture, followed by the buttermilk or yogurt, then mix in the remaining flour mixture. Gently stir in the nuts, chocolate chips, and the macerated cherries along with any unabsorbed liquid.

Divide the batter between the prepared pans and bake until a toothpick inserted into the center of one comes out almost clean, about 45 minutes. (Some chocolate will likely cling to the toothpick.) Let cool for 15 minutes.

Poke each cake about 50 times with a toothpick then slowly drizzle each cake with 3 tablespoons (45 ml) of the remaining kirsch or rum. Let cool 30 minutes, then run a knife around the sides of the cakes to help loosen them from the pans. Invert the cakes onto a wire rack, peel

(continued)

off the parchment paper, turn them right side up, and let cool completely.

To make the glaze, in a medium bowl, whisk together the powdered sugar and 6 tablespoons (90 ml) of the kirsch or rum. If it's too thick to spread (it should have the consistency of melted ice cream), whisk in 1 to 2 tablespoons (15 to 30 ml) more kirsch or rum. Spoon the glaze over the tops of the cakes, letting it run freely down the sides.

Let the glaze set until firm.

STORAGE: You can freeze the loaves after they cool, prior to dousing them with alcohol and applying the glaze. At room temperature, the cakes will keep for up to 5 days, wrapped in plastic. It's preferable to glaze them the day of serving.

VARIATION: Substitute an equal amount of any type of dried fruits, such as cranberries, raisins, or diced prunes, for the dried cherries. Or, $1^{1}/_{2}$ cups (750 g) drained Italian candied cherries make a flavorful substitute, too; because they're packed in syrup, they don't require soaking in kirsch or rum.

TIP: If you're serving the fruitcake to kids, you can soften the dried cherries in cranberry juice. Omit drizzling the cakes with liqueur and use water to make the glaze.

Maple-Walnut Pear Cake

MAKES ONE 9-INCH (23-CM) CAKE; 10 TO 12 SERVINGS

An Italian acquaintance once pleaded, "Please—tell your American friends not to bring us any more maple syrup. *Basta!*" At first, I didn't quite understand. I mean, who doesn't love maple syrup? But then I remembered that while we Americans love to douse everything we can with the sticky stuff, Italians take their infamous 30-second breakfast by downing a quick espresso at their corner *caffè* and never belly up to a stack of pancakes or plate of waffles in the morning. Since I'm not Italian, any gifts of maple syrup are encouraged. And I promise not to save it just for breakfast.

TOPPING

$^1/_3$ cup (80 ml) maple syrup

$^1/_4$ cup (60 g) packed dark or light brown sugar

$^1/_2$ cup (50 g) walnuts, toasted and coarsely chopped

3 ripe Bosc or other firm pears (about 1$^1/_4$ pounds/570 g), peeled, quartered, cored, and cut lengthwise into $^1/_4$-inch (6-mm) slices

CAKE

1$^1/_2$ cups (210 g) all-purpose flour

1 teaspoon baking powder

2 teaspoons ground cinnamon

$^1/_2$ teaspoon salt

$^1/_2$ cup (4 ounces/115 g) unsalted butter, at room temperature

$^1/_2$ cup (100 g) granulated sugar

$^1/_4$ cup (60 g) packed light brown sugar

$^1/_2$ teaspoon vanilla extract

2 large eggs, at room temperature

$^1/_2$ cup (125 ml) whole milk, at room temperature

Preheat the oven to 350°F (175°C).

To make the topping, combine the maple syrup and $^1/_4$ cup (60 g) dark or light brown sugar in a 9-inch (23-cm) round cake pan or cast iron skillet. Set the pan directly on the stovetop over low heat until the mixture begins to bubble. Simmer gently for 1 minute, stirring frequently. Remove the pan from the heat.

Sprinkle the walnuts evenly over the maple mixture in the cake pan and lightly press them in. Arrange the pear slices over the walnuts in the cake pan in an overlapping pinwheel pattern. Set aside.

To make the cake, in a small bowl, whisk together the flour, baking powder, cinnamon, and salt.

In a stand mixer fitted with the paddle attachment (or in a bowl by hand), beat together the butter, granulated sugar, and $^1/_4$ cup (60 g) light brown sugar on medium speed until the mixture is light and fluffy, 3 to 5 minutes. Add the vanilla and eggs, one at a time, beating until completely incorporated. Gradually mix in half of the flour mixture. Stir in the milk followed by the rest of the flour mixture and mix just until combined.

Scrape the batter onto the pears in the cake pan and smooth it into an even layer, being careful not to disturb the arrangement of the pears. Bake until a toothpick inserted into the center of the cake comes out clean, about 50 minutes. Let cool for about 15 minutes.

Run a knife around the sides of the cake to help loosen it from the pan. Invert a serving plate over the pan. Wearing oven mitts, grasp both the pan and the plate and turn them over together. Carefully lift off the pan. Any walnuts that are stuck to the pan can be loosened with a fork and reunited with the cake.

SERVING: Serve the cake warm with whipped cream (page 239) or your favorite flavor of ice cream.

STORAGE: The cake will keep for 2 days at room temperature, but since it's best served warm, you can rewarm the cake, wrapped in aluminum foil, in a low oven, or reheat slices in a microwave oven.

> TIP: Here's a great do-ahead trick: Make the cake, invert it onto a serving platter, and leave the inverted pan over it, which will keep the cake warm for an hour or so until you're ready to serve.

Guinness-Gingerbread Cupcakes

MAKES 12 CUPCAKES

I made a fool of myself when I met Claudia Fleming, who was for many years a noted pastry chef in New York City. But I couldn't help myself—I flipped out whenever I tasted her desserts. Her multiflavored combinations managed to perfectly balance familiar, everyday ingredients with sophisticated presentations. Every time I ran into her, I'd gush about how wonderful her desserts were as I watched her slowly backing away from this clearly unbalanced fan.

I was always intrigued by her combination of gingerbread with rich, malty stout and was inspired to create a cupcake using the same blend of flavors. I add a bright-tasting lime frosting which complements the spicy cake. If you make these, you're likely to have a few deranged fans, too. Consider yourself warned.

CUPCAKES

$1/2$ cup (125 ml) stout beer, such as Guinness

$1/2$ cup (125 ml) mild-flavored molasses

$1/2$ cup (125 ml) vegetable oil

$1/4$ teaspoon baking soda

$3/4$ cup (170 g) packed light brown sugar

$1^1/3$ cups (185 g) all-purpose flour

$1^1/4$ teaspoons baking powder

2 teaspoons ground ginger

1 teaspoon ground cinnamon

$1/4$ teaspoon ground cloves

$1/2$ teaspoon salt

2 large eggs, at room temperature

$1/2$ cup (50 g) finely minced Candied Ginger (page 252)

FROSTING

4 tablespoons (2 ounces/60 g) salted or unsalted butter, at room temperature

$1^1/2$ cups (180 g) powdered sugar, sifted

$2^1/2$ tablespoons (40 ml) freshly squeezed lime juice, or more to taste

1 tablespoon whole milk

Strips of Soft-Candied Citrus Peel (page 253) or Candied Ginger (page 252), for garnish

Preheat the oven to 350°F (175°C). Line a standard 12-cup muffin tin with cupcake liners.

To make the cupcakes, in a very large saucepan, bring the stout, molasses, and oil to a boil over medium-high heat. Remove from the heat and whisk in the baking soda until dissolved. (The mixture will foam up, then settle down.) Stir in the brown sugar, then let cool until tepid.

Into a small bowl, sift together the flour, baking powder, ginger, cinnamon, cloves, and salt.

Whisk the eggs into the stout mixture, then whisk in the flour mixture just until incorporated. Don't overmix. Gently stir in the minced candied ginger.

Divide the batter among the cupcake liners and bake until the cupcakes feel just set in the center, 22 to 24 minutes. Let cool completely.

To make the frosting, in a stand mixer fitted with the paddle attachment, beat the butter on high speed until smooth, about 10 seconds. Decrease the speed to low and, with the mixer running, gradually add half of the powdered sugar. Stop the mixer and scrape down the bowl as needed to make sure the ingredients are being incorporated. Add the lime juice, then add the remaining powdered sugar. Once the sugar is incorporated, add the milk. Beat the frosting on high speed until completely smooth and fluffy, about 3 minutes. Taste, and add a few more drops of lime juice, if desired.

Transfer the frosting to a pastry bag fitted with a star tip. Remove the cupcakes from the muffin tin. Pipe rosettes of frosting in the center of each cupcake. (If you don't have a pastry bag, you can spoon a mound of frosting decoratively in the center.) Garnish each with strips of candied citrus peel or a piece of candied ginger.

STORAGE: The cupcakes can be stored in an airtight container for up to 4 days at room temperature.

VARIATION: For kids, feel free to use apple cider in place of the stout.

Irish Coffee Cupcakes

MAKES 12 CUPCAKES

One of the pitfalls of having a blog is that you leave yourself open to all sorts of questions. The most common are from folks who want to substitute ingredients. I always want to reach through my computer screen, grab hold of their shoulders, and say, "But I worked so hard to develop this recipe. Please make it just as it is!"

When I was working on these cupcakes, I began with the simple idea of individually filled chocolate cakes, similar to the kind I had as a kid, but with an adult sensibility. So I added a pour of Irish cream liqueur to the filling and spiked the ganache icing with a tipple of whiskey, which effectively wiped out the possibility of making these kid-friendly. So please don't ask if you can make them without either, because the bad news is that you can't. But the good news is that you can have them all for yourself and you don't have to share them with the kids.

CUPCAKES

1 1/4 cups (175 g) all-purpose flour

1 teaspoon baking powder

1/4 teaspoon baking soda

1/4 teaspoon salt

1 cup (250 ml) strong brewed coffee

6 tablespoons (50 g) unsweetened Dutch-process cocoa powder

1/2 cup (4 ounces/115 g) unsalted butter, cut into pieces, at room temperature

1 1/4 cups (275 g) packed light brown sugar

2 large eggs, at room temperature

2 teaspoons vanilla extract

FILLING

4 ounces (115 g) cream cheese, at room temperature

4 tablespoons (2 ounces/60 g) salted butter, at room temperature

6 tablespoons (75 g) powdered sugar

1 tablespoon plus 1 teaspoon Irish cream liqueur, such as Bailey's Irish Cream

GLAZE

4 ounces (115 g) bittersweet or semisweet chocolate, chopped

1/4 cup (60 ml) heavy cream

2 teaspoons light corn syrup or agave nectar

2 tablespoons (30 ml) whiskey

Preheat the oven to 350°F (175°C). Line a standard 12-cup muffin tin with cupcake liners.

To make the cupcakes, into a small bowl, sift together the flour, baking powder, baking soda, and salt.

In a medium saucepan, heat the coffee until almost boiling. Remove from the heat and whisk in the cocoa until dissolved, then add the 1/2 cup (4 ounces/115 g) unsalted butter, stirring until melted. Whisk in the brown sugar and let cool until tepid. Whisk in the eggs and vanilla, then stir in the flour mixture, mixing just until incorporated. Don't overmix.

Divide the batter among the cupcake liners and bake until the cupcakes feel just set in the center, 20 to 22 minutes. Let cool completely.

To make the filling, in a stand mixer fitted with the paddle attachment or a food processor fitted with a metal blade, beat together the cream cheese, 4 tablespoons (2 ounces/60 g) salted butter, and powdered sugar until smooth. Beat in the Irish cream liqueur.

To fill the cupcakes, use a sharp knife to cut a 2-inch (5-cm) cone-shaped hole in the center of each cupcake. Remove the plug-like pieces. Trim off the tip of each plug to create a disk-shaped piece that is 1/3 inch (8 mm) thick. Save these disks for capping the filled cupcakes.

Divide the filling among the cupcakes, then gently press the caps into the filling. They won't fit perfectly, which is fine, and some filling may bulge out.

To make the glaze, melt the chocolate with the cream and corn syrup or agave nectar in a small saucepan over low heat, stirring until smooth. Remove from the heat and stir in the whiskey.

Dip the tops of the filled cupcakes in the glaze, completely sealing the tops and generously coating them. Let cool, right side up, until the glaze is firm.

Persimmon Cake with Cream Cheese Icing

MAKES ONE 10-INCH (25-CM) BUNDT CAKE; 12 TO 16 SERVINGS

If you're lucky enough to have a persimmon tree, you're guaranteed to have plenty of gorgeous persimmons come autumn. Or, if you have a neighbor with one, you're bound to find a bag of persimmons on your doorstep one fall day. The prolific trees are especially striking when the leaves drop and the traffic-stopping bright-orange orbs are still clinging to the bare, gnarled branches, silhouetted against a clear autumn sky.

Even if you don't have a tree, or a neighboring one that you can benefit from, you might have seen persimmons at the market. Most likely they were Hachiya persimmons, the most common, elongated-shape variety. It's the one I recommend for this cake. They must be squishy soft before they can be used. If you buy them rock-hard, leave them at room temperature until they feel like water balloons ready to burst. When ready, yank off the stem, slice each persimmon in half, then scoop out the jellylike pulp and purée it in a blender or food processor.

CAKE

3/4 cup (120 g) dried currants

1/4 cup (60 ml) brandy or whiskey

2 cups (280 g) all-purpose flour

2 teaspoons baking soda

1 1/2 teaspoons ground cinnamon

3/4 teaspoon salt

1/2 teaspoon freshly grated nutmeg

1 2/3 cups (355 g) granulated sugar

3/4 cup (6 ounces/170 g) unsalted butter, melted

1 1/2 cups (375 ml) persimmon purée (about 3 Hachiya persimmons)

3 large eggs, at room temperature

2 teaspoons vanilla extract

1 1/2 cups (150g) walnuts or pecans, toasted and finely chopped

ICING

4 ounces (115 g) cream cheese

1 tablespoon salted butter, at room temperature

1/2 teaspoon vanilla extract

1 tablespoon freshly squeezed lemon juice

2/3 cup (90 g) powdered sugar, sifted

4 or 5 teaspoons water

Preheat the oven to 350°F (175°C). Coat a 10-cup (2.5-liter) Bundt cake or tube pan with butter or nonstick cooking spray.

To make the cake, in a small saucepan over medium heat, bring the currants and brandy or whiskey to a boil. Remove from the heat, cover, and let cool.

Into a large bowl, sift together the flour, baking soda, cinnamon, salt, and nutmeg. Stir in the granulated sugar. In a medium bowl, mix together the 3/4 cup (6 ounces/ 170 g) melted butter, persimmon purée, eggs, and 2 teaspoons vanilla.

Make a well in the center of the flour mixture, add the persimmon mixture, and gently stir. Fold in the currants, along with any unabsorbed liquid, and the nuts. Mix just until everything is moistened; don't overmix.

Scrape the batter into the prepared pan and bake until a toothpick inserted into the cake comes out clean, about 1 hour. Remove from the oven and let cool completely. Once cool, invert the cake onto a serving plate.

To make the icing, in a stand mixer fitted with the paddle attachment, beat together the cream cheese and 1 tablespoon butter on high speed until smooth. Beat in the 1/2 teaspoon vanilla and the lemon juice, then gradually add the powdered sugar, beating on high speed until smooth. Add the 4 teaspoons water; the icing should be pourable. If necessary, add 1 more teaspoon water.

Spoon the icing around the top of the cake, then tap the plate on a folded kitchen towel on the countertop to encourage the icing to run down the sides of the cake.

STORAGE: This cake will keep for 4 days at room temperature.

VARIATION: If you don't have persimmons, or if they're not in season, you can substitute unsweetened applesauce or banana purée for the persimmon purée.

Plum-Blueberry Upside-Down Cake

MAKES ONE 9-INCH (23-CM) CAKE; 8 TO 10 SERVINGS

This is the classic upside-down cake that takes advantage of the summer season, when plums and berries are in full swing. I love how the flavor of tart plums contrasts with the toffeelike brown sugar topping. But feel free to swap out other favorite fruits of summer; I offer a few of suggestions in Variations, below.

TOPPING

3 tablespoons (1 1/2 ounces/45 g) unsalted or salted butter

3/4 cup (170 g) packed light brown sugar

1 1/4 cups (6 ounces/170 g) blueberries

6 to 8 plums (1 pound/450 g), halved, pitted, and cut into 1/2-inch (1.5-cm) slices

CAKE

1 1/2 cups (210 g) all-purpose flour

1 1/2 teaspoons baking powder

1/4 teaspoon salt

1/2 cup (4 ounces/115 g) unsalted butter, at room temperature

3/4 cup (150 g) granulated sugar

1 teaspoon vanilla extract

2 large eggs, at room temperature

1/2 cup (125 ml) whole milk, at room temperature

Preheat the oven to 350°F (175°C).

To make the topping, put the 3 tablespoons (1 1/2 ounces/45 g) butter in a 9-inch (23-cm) round cake pan or cast iron skillet. Set the pan directly on the stovetop over low heat until the butter melts. Add the brown sugar and stir until the sugar is thoroughly moistened. Remove from the heat and let cool briefly.

Distribute half of the blueberries evenly over the brown sugar mixture in the pan. Arrange the plum slices over the blueberries in overlapping concentric circles, or just scatter them in an even layer. Strew the remaining blueberries on top of the plums. Set aside.

To make the cake, in a small bowl, whisk together the flour, baking powder, and salt.

In a stand mixer fitted with the paddle attachment (or in a bowl by hand), beat together the 1/2 cup (4 ounces/115 g) butter and the sugar on medium speed until the mixture is light and fluffy, 3 to 5 minutes. Add the vanilla and eggs, one at a time, beating until completely incorporated. Gradually mix in half of the flour mixture. Stir in the milk followed by the rest of the flour mixture and mix just until combined.

Scrape the batter on top of the fruit in the pan and smooth it into an even layer. Bake until golden brown and a toothpick inserted in the center of the cake comes out clean, about 1 hour.

Let cool for about 15 minutes. Run a knife around the sides of the cake to help loosen it from the pan. Invert a serving plate over the pan. Wearing oven mitts, grasp both the pan and the plate and turn them over together. Carefully lift off the pan.

SERVING: Serve the cake warm with whipped cream (page 239) or your favorite flavor of ice cream.

STORAGE: The cake will keep for 2 days at room temperature, but since it's best served warm, you can rewarm the cake, wrapped in aluminum foil, in a low oven, or reheat slices in a microwave oven.

VARIATIONS: You can use fresh apricots instead of plums, and substitute any kind of berries (except strawberries) for the blueberries. In the winter, replace the stone fruit and berries with 2 cups (8 ounces/225 g) fresh or frozen unthawed cranberries.

> TIP: A great do-ahead trick for just about any type of upside-down cake is to make the cake, invert it onto a serving platter, and leave the inverted pan in place. The cake will stay warm for about an hour this way.

Nectarine-Raspberry Upside-Down Gingerbread

MAKES ONE 9-INCH (23-CM) CAKE; 8 TO 10 SERVINGS

As everyone knows, the best part of an upside-down cake is the caramelized bits of topping and batter that get stuck in the bottom of the pan after the cake is unmolded. Instead of eating these bits, the right thing to do is to scrape them out and smear them back onto the warm cake. If you can do that, you're a better person than I.

TOPPING

4 tablespoons (2 ounces/60 g) unsalted or salted butter

$^3/_4$ cup (170 g) packed light brown sugar

$1^1/_4$ cups (6 ounces/170 g) raspberries

4 medium nectarines ($1^1/_2$ pounds/675 g), halved, pitted, and cut into $^1/_2$-inch (1.5-cm) slices

GINGERBREAD

$1^1/_2$ cups (210 g) all-purpose flour

1 teaspoon baking soda

2 teaspoons ground ginger

1 teaspoon ground cinnamon

$^1/_2$ teaspoon ground cloves

$^1/_2$ teaspoon salt

$^1/_2$ cup (4 ounces/115 g) unsalted butter, at room temperature

$^1/_2$ cup (100 g) granulated sugar

$^1/_2$ cup (125 ml) mild-flavored molasses

2 large eggs, at room temperature

$^1/_4$ cup (60 ml) whole milk, at room temperature

Preheat the oven to 350°F (175°C).

To make the topping, put the 4 tablespoons (2 ounces/60 g) butter in a 9-inch (23-cm) round cake pan or cast iron skillet. Set the pan directly on the stovetop over low heat until the butter melts. Add the brown sugar and stir until the sugar is thoroughly moistened. Remove from the heat and let cool briefly.

Distribute the raspberries evenly over the brown sugar mixture in the pan. Arrange the nectarine slices over the raspberries in overlapping concentric circles. Set aside.

To make the gingerbread, in a small bowl, whisk together the flour, baking soda, ginger, cinnamon, cloves, and salt.

In a stand mixer fitted with the paddle attachment (or in a bowl by hand), beat together the $^1/_2$ cup (4 ounces/115 g) butter and the sugar on medium speed until the mixture is light and fluffy, 3 to 5 minutes. Beat in the molasses. (The batter may look curdled, which is fine.) Add the eggs, one at a time, beating until completely incorporated. Gradually mix in half of the flour mixture. Stir in the milk followed by the rest of the flour mixture and mix just until combined.

Scrape the batter on top of the fruit in the pan. Bake until a toothpick inserted into the center of the cake comes out clean, 50 to 55 minutes.

Let cool for about 15 minutes. Run a knife around the sides of the cake to help loosen it from the pan. Invert a serving plate over the pan. Wearing oven mitts, grasp both the pan and the plate and turn them over together. Carefully lift off the pan.

SERVING: Serve the cake warm with whipped cream (page 239) or Vanilla Ice Cream (page 143).

VARIATION: For ORANGE UPSIDE-DOWN GINGERBREAD, add $^1/_2$ teaspoon freshly ground cardamom to the melted butter along with the brown sugar when making the topping. Substitute 4 navel or blood oranges, peeled and sliced crosswise into $^1/_2$-inch (1.5-cm) slices, for the nectarines. You can omit or use the raspberries.

Fresh Ginger Cake

MAKES ONE 9-INCH (23-CM) CAKE; 10 TO 12 SERVINGS

Of all the desserts I've ever made, this cake is the one that is most renowned, drawing acclaim for its incredibly moist texture and its spicy zing from an overload of fresh ginger. Many people have told me this is their all-time favorite dessert. And whenever I make it and take a bite, I'm in agreement: it's one of my favorites as well.

4-ounce (115-g) piece fresh ginger, peeled and
    thinly sliced

1 cup (250 ml) mild-flavored molasses

1 cup (200 g) sugar

1 cup (250 ml) vegetable oil

2 1/2 cups (350 g) all-purpose flour

1 teaspoon ground cinnamon

1/2 teaspoon ground cloves

1/2 teaspoon ground black pepper

1 cup (250 ml) water

2 teaspoons baking soda

2 large eggs, at room temperature

Preheat the oven to 350°F (175°C). Butter the bottom and sides of a 9-inch (23-cm) springform or round cake pan with 2-inch (5-cm) sides and line the bottom with a circle of parchment paper.

In a food processor fitted with the metal blade or with a chef's knife, chop the ginger until very fine. Set aside.

In a large bowl, mix together the molasses, sugar, and oil. In a medium bowl, whisk together the flour, cinnamon, cloves, and pepper.

In a small saucepan, bring the water to a boil, then stir in the baking soda. Whisk the hot water into the molasses mixture, then add the chopped ginger.

Gradually sift the flour mixture over the molasses mixture, whisking to combine. Add the eggs and whisk until thoroughly blended.

Scrape the batter into the prepared springform or cake pan and bake until the top of the cake springs back when lightly pressed with a finger or a toothpick inserted into the center comes out clean, about 1 hour. Let cool completely.

Run a knife around the sides of the cake to help loosen it from the pan. Invert the cake onto a plate, peel off the parchment paper, then re-invert it onto a serving platter.

SERVING: Serve wedges of this cake with whipped cream (page 239), a favorite ice cream, or a fruit compote.

STORAGE: Because this cake is so moist, it keeps well for up to 5 days at room temperature. It can be frozen for up to 1 month.

VARIATION: My favorite complement for this cake is the whipped cream–lightened lemon curd filling used in Lemon Semifreddo (page 65). Another idea is a PLUM-RASPBERRY COMPOTE. Slice 8 pitted plums into 6 wedges. In a medium saucepan, heat 1/4 cup (50 g) sugar, 1 cup (250 ml) water, and half of a vanilla bean, split lengthwise. Add the plum wedges and simmer over low heat until tender, about 10 minutes. Remove from the heat, add 1 1/4 cups (6 ounces/170 g) raspberries and 1 tablespoon kirsch (optional), and let stand for 1 hour. Before serving, remove the vanilla pod (it can be rinsed, dried, and used for another purpose; see page 14).

Buckwheat Cake with Cider-Poached Apples

MAKES ONE 9-INCH (23-CM) CAKE; 8 TO 10 SERVINGS

This cake always reminds me of my trips to Brittany, an exceptionally beautiful region in western France that borders the Atlantic Ocean. The often-blustery weather is the only thing that stands in the way of Brittany becoming a major tourist destination.

Aside from the chilly climate, the region is famous for its hand-harvested sea salt and salted butter caramel, both of which I would travel to the ends of the earth for. And no matter where you go in the region, you'll find buckwheat being served in various guises, from griddled galettes to *kig ha farz*, a local curiosity made by poaching a pasty buckwheat batter in the sleeve of a linen shirt until it's firm. Then it's rolled on the counter until it breaks into tiny bits, like buckwheat couscous. They say it's something that you need to be Breton to enjoy, so I must have some Breton in me since I loved it since the first time I tried it. I'm happy to have this cake in my repertoire because I enjoy the hearty taste of buckwheat in my desserts, too.

CAKE

1^1/$_2$ cups (120 g) sliced unblanched or blanched almonds

^{1}/$_2$ cup (80 g) buckwheat flour

1 teaspoon baking powder

^{3}/$_4$ cup (6 ounces/85 g) unsalted butter, at room temperature

^{1}/$_2$ cup (100 g) plus 6 tablespoons (75 g) sugar

1 teaspoon vanilla extract

4 large eggs, separated, at room temperature

^{1}/$_4$ teaspoon salt

POACHED APPLES

3 very firm medium apples (1^1/$_2$ pounds/675 g), such as Granny Smith or Golden Delicious

3 cups (750 ml) apple cider or unsweetened apple juice

^{1}/$_2$ cup (100 g) sugar

1 cinnamon stick

5 whole cloves

Preheat the oven to 350°F (175°C). Butter the bottom and sides of a 9-inch (23-cm) cake pan and line the bottom with a circle of parchment paper.

To make the cake, in a food processor fitted with the metal blade or in a blender, pulverize the almonds with the buckwheat flour and baking powder until the almonds are powdery and very finely ground.

In a stand mixer fitted with the paddle attachment (or in a bowl by hand), beat together the butter and the ^{1}/$_2$ cup (100 g) sugar on medium speed until very light and fluffy, 3 to 5 minutes. Beat in the vanilla and the egg yolks, one at a time, until combined.

In a clean, dry bowl and with the whip attachment, whisk the egg whites on low speed until frothy. Add the salt and continue to whisk until the whites begin to hold their shape. Increase the speed to high, gradually add the remaining 6 tablespoons (75 g) sugar, and continue whisking on high speed until the whites form soft, shiny peaks.

Add the almond-buckwheat mixture to the creamed butter mixture and stir with a rubber spatula to combine. Stir in about one-third of the whipped egg whites (the batter will be thick, but the egg whites will lighten it up). Carefully fold in the remaining egg whites just until incorporated. Don't overfold.

Scrape the batter into the prepared cake pan and bake until a toothpick inserted into the center of the cake comes out clean, about 45 minutes. Let cool completely.

Run a knife around the sides of the cake to help loosen it from the pan. Invert the cake onto a plate, peel off the parchment paper, and re-invert the cake onto a serving platter.

To poach the apples, peel them and, using a melon baller $^{1}/_{2}$ inch (1.5 cm) in diameter, scoop out balls. Or, cut the peeled apples into $^{1}/_{2}$-inch (1.5-cm) slices.

In a small saucepan, warm the cider, $^{1}/_{2}$ cup (100 g) sugar, the cinnamon stick, and cloves. Drop in the apple balls or slices and simmer gently over medium-low heat until the apple pieces are just tender, about 10 minutes. Serve wedges of the cake with the warm poached apples and a spoonful of their syrup.

STORAGE: The cake will keep for up to 5 days, well wrapped, at room temperature. The poached apples are even better made a day in advance, refrigerated, and rewarmed before serving.

VARIATION: Instead of the cider-poached apples, you might try serving the cake with orange segments drizzled with Tangerine Butterscotch Sauce (page 242) or with slices of fresh peaches or nectarines tossed with a bit of sugar.

Spiced Plum Streusel Cake with Toffee Glaze

MAKES ONE 9-INCH (23-CM) CAKE; 10 SERVINGS

There seems to be an irksome theme in dessert books suggesting that a particular cake or pastry be served "with tea, in the afternoon." I don't know who has time to sit around and sip tea in the middle of the day, but I know at least one person who can usually be found foraging in his kitchen in the late afternoon, on the prowl for something to snack on.

This cake combines everything I crave: tangy plums, toffee with a bit of salt, and buttery cake. If you do take tea in the afternoon, I'm sure it'd be a fine accompaniment. But I'm happy to enjoy it all by itself, whenever I can.

STREUSEL

1 cup (80 g) sliced unblanched or blanched almonds

2 tablespoons (8 g) all-purpose flour

$^1/_3$ cup (70 g) packed light brown sugar

$^1/_2$ teaspoon ground cinnamon

$^1/_2$ teaspoon freshly ground cardamom

$1^1/_2$ tablespoons unsalted or salted butter, melted

CAKE

$1^1/_2$ cups (210 g) all-purpose flour

$^1/_2$ teaspoon baking powder

$^1/_2$ teaspoon baking soda

$1^1/_2$ teaspoons freshly ground cardamom

$^1/_2$ teaspoon ground cinnamon

$^1/_2$ teaspoon salt

$^1/_2$ cup (4 ounces/115 g) unsalted butter, at room temperature

$^3/_4$ cup (150 g) granulated sugar

2 large eggs, at room temperature

1 teaspoon vanilla extract

$^1/_2$ cup (125 ml) buttermilk, at room temperature

5 medium plums (12 ounces/340 g), halved, pitted, and cut into eighths

GLAZE

2 tablespoons (1 ounce/30 g) unsalted or salted butter, cut into pieces

3 tablespoons (45 g) dark brown sugar

3 tablespoons (45 ml) heavy cream

Big pinch of salt

$^1/_4$ teaspoon vanilla extract

Preheat the oven to 350°F (175°C). Butter the bottom and sides of a 9-inch (23-cm) springform pan.

To make the streusel, in a medium bowl, combine the sliced almonds, 2 tablespoons (8 g) flour, the light brown sugar, $^1/_2$ teaspoon cinnamon, $^1/_2$ teaspoon cardamom, and $1^1/_2$ tablespoons melted butter. Toss the mixture with a fork or your fingers until evenly moistened, making sure the almonds are well dispersed. Set aside.

To make the cake, in a small bowl, whisk together the $1^1/_2$ cups (210 g) flour, the baking powder, baking soda, $1^1/_2$ teaspoons cardamom, $^1/_2$ teaspoon cinnamon, and salt.

In a stand mixer fitted with the paddle attachment (or in a bowl by hand), beat together the $^1/_2$ cup (4 ounces/115 g) butter and granulated sugar on medium speed until light and fluffy, 3 to 5 minutes. Add the eggs one at a time, beating until completely incorporated. Stir in half of the flour mixture, followed by the 1 teaspoon vanilla and the buttermilk, and finally, the remaining flour mixture. Mix until just combined.

Scrape the batter into the prepared pan and smooth the top. Arrange the plum slices in an even layer on top of the batter and gently press them in. Sprinkle the streusel over the plums.

Bake until the top is nicely browned and a toothpick inserted into the center of the cake comes out clean, about 55 minutes. Let cool completely.

Run a knife around the sides of the cake to help loosen it from the pan. Release the sides of the springform pan.

To make the glaze, in a small saucepan over medium-low heat, melt the 2 tablespoons (1 ounce/30 g) butter with the dark brown sugar, cream, and salt. Increase the heat to medium-high and bring to a boil, then decrease the heat to medium and simmer gently for 1 minute. Remove from the heat and let cool completely. Once cool, stir in the $1/4$ teaspoon vanilla. Spoon the glaze over the cake, encouraging some to drip down the sides.

Serve slices of the cake warm or at room temperature. Tea alongside is optional.

STORAGE: The cake is best the same day but can be kept at room temperature for up to 4 days well wrapped.

VARIATION: Substitute fresh apricots for the plums. A handful of fresh raspberries can be added with the fruit slices as well.

Cherry Gâteau Basque

MAKES ONE 9-INCH (23-CM) CAKE; 8 TO 10 SERVINGS

The Basque region is an area that spans the border between Spain and France, where a strong sense of nationalism has fueled a desire for independence among some of the Basque people. (I recommend *not* bringing up the topic if you go for a visit.) But one thing that all sides can agree on is that gâteau Basque is one of the region's tastiest achievements and a great source of pride.

I'm an impartial observer, but I am partial to this dessert, which is a cross between a cake and big cookie. But being Basque, it's naturally subject to controversy: some versions have pastry cream sandwiched between the layers and others are filled with cherry jam. While happily tasting my way through various examples in the region, I've enjoyed versions of both, which is a pretty good way to keep the peace.

Don't be too concerned if the dough falls apart as you roll it; it can be pinched together and will still bake up perfectly.

DOUGH

1 1/2 cups (210 g) all-purpose flour

1/2 cup (40 g) sliced blanched almonds

1 teaspoon baking powder

1/4 teaspoon salt

3/4 cup (150 g) sugar

1/2 cup (4 ounces/115 g) unsalted butter, at room temperature

1 large egg

1 large egg yolk

1 teaspoon vanilla extract

1/2 teaspoon almond extract

FILLING

1 cup (240 g) good-quality sour cherry jam (see Tip)

2 teaspoons rum

1 teaspoon brandy

3/4 teaspoon anise-flavored liqueur, such as Pernod or ouzo

1 large egg yolk

1 teaspoon whole milk

> TIP: Use a top-quality sour cherry jam. The less-expensive ones are primarily sugar and are too runny—you want a filling that's plump with flavorful cherries. If you can't find sour cherry jam, add a squirt of lemon juice to regular cherry jam.

To make the dough, in a food processor fitted with the metal blade, process the flour, almonds, baking powder, salt, and sugar until the almonds are ground to a powder. Add the butter and process until the butter is in tiny pieces.

Add the egg, egg yolk, and the vanilla and almond extracts and pulse until the dough comes together. Divide the dough into 2 pieces, one slightly larger than the other, form each into a disk, wrap in plastic wrap, and refrigerate for 1 hour.

Preheat the oven to 350°F (175°C). Butter the bottom and sides of a 9-inch (23-cm) springform pan, dust it with flour, and tap out any excess.

To make the filling, in a small bowl, mix the cherry jam, rum, brandy, and anise-flavored liqueur. Set aside.

Dust the larger disk of dough on both sides with flour and roll it out to a 10-inch (25-cm) circle between 2 sheets of lightly floured plastic wrap. Peel off the top sheet of plastic and invert the dough into the prepared pan. Peel off the sheet of plastic that is now on top and press the dough gently into the bottom of the pan and partially up the sides. Don't worry if the dough tears; it's very forgiving—just patch and press together. Spread the filling over the dough, leaving a 1-inch (3-cm) border.

(continued)

Roll out the second piece of dough between 2 sheets of lightly floured plastic wrap. Peel off the top sheet of plastic and invert the dough over the filling. Peel off the sheet of plastic that's now on top. Gently press the edges together to enclose the filling.

In a small bowl, whisk together the egg yolk and milk and brush it liberally over the top. Rake the tines of a fork 5 or 6 times over the surface in two diagonally opposing directions to create a crosshatch design.

Bake the cake until the top is deep golden brown, about 40 minutes. Let cool for a few minutes, then run a knife around the sides to loosen it from the pan. Release the sides of the springform pan and let cool completely. Cut into wedges and serve.

STORAGE: Gâteau Basque is actually better the second day, after the flavors have had a chance to meld. Wrapped tightly in plastic wrap, it'll keep for about 1 week at room temperature.

VARIATION: A prune filling for gâteau Basque isn't exactly traditional, but since the nearby Gascon region is famous for its prunes, I'll often make a filling with them: Quarter 8 ounces (225 g) of pitted prunes; heat them in a small saucepan with 3 tablespoons (45 ml) brandy, 1 tablespoon rum, 1 tablespoon anise-flavored liqueur, $1/4$ cup (50 g) sugar, and $1/4$ cup (60 ml) water. When the liquid comes to a boil, cover, and remove from the heat. Once cool, process the mixture in a food processor fitted with the metal blade until chunky and use in place of the cherry jam.

Kumquat Sticky Toffee Puddings

MAKES 12 INDIVIDUAL CAKES

During a baking demonstration, I once inadvertently blurted out, "I don't like sweet things," at which point the room erupted with laughter. I didn't quite see what was so funny until someone pointed out that I was making desserts. Well, yes. I was.

But it's true—I don't really like oversweet desserts. I adore caramel and toffee more than anyone, but I like them paired with something to balance the sweetness. Sticky toffee pudding is the Holy Grail for toffee lovers. My version is topped with slices of kumquats as a puckery counterpoint to the gooey-rich sweet toffee.

DATES

4 ounces (115 g) dates, pitted and diced

$^1/_2$ cup (125 ml) water

$^1/_2$ teaspoon baking soda

TOFFEE SAUCE

2 cups (500 ml) heavy cream

$^1/_2$ cup (120 g) packed dark brown sugar

2$^1/_2$ tablespoons (40 ml) mild-flavored molasses

Big pinch of salt

18 large kumquats, sliced and seeded

CAKES

1$^1/_3$ cups (185 g) all-purpose flour

1 teaspoon baking powder

$^1/_2$ teaspoon salt

4 tablespoons (2 ounces/60 g) unsalted butter, at room temperature

$^2/_3$ cup (130 g) granulated sugar

2 large eggs, at room temperature

2 teaspoons vanilla extract

To prepare the dates, in a small saucepan, bring the dates and water to a boil. Remove from the heat and mix in the baking soda. Let stand for 10 minutes, then mash the dates with a fork until they're almost smooth but still a bit lumpy. Set aside.

To make the toffee sauce, in a medium saucepan, bring the cream, brown sugar, molasses, and salt to a boil, stirring to dissolve the sugar. Once boiling, decrease the heat and simmer until the mixture is thick enough to coat a spoon or spatula, about 7 minutes. Remove from the heat and let cool for a few minutes.

Put a scant tablespoon of toffee sauce in each cup of a standard 12-cup nonstick muffin tin (you will have some sauce left over). Arrange the kumquat slices in a pinwheel pattern over the sauce in the muffin tins.

Preheat the oven to 350°F (175°C).

To make the cakes, in a small bowl, whisk together the flour, baking powder, and salt.

In a stand mixer fitted with the paddle attachment (or in a bowl by hand), beat together the butter and granulated sugar on medium speed until light and fluffy, 3 to 5 minutes. Add the eggs one at a time, then add the vanilla and continue to beat until thoroughly combined. Stir in half of the flour mixture until barely mixed in, then stir in the mashed dates. Fold in the remaining flour mixture, stirring just until incorporated. Don't overmix. Divide the batter among the cups of the muffin tin and smooth the tops slightly.

(continued)

Bake until just set, about 25 minutes. Remove the muffin tin from the oven and invert the cakes onto a sturdy nonreactive baking sheet. Push them together so that they're touching each other.

Position the oven rack near the top of the oven and preheat the broiler. While the broiler is heating, ladle the remaining toffee sauce over the cakes, dousing them well.

When the broiler is hot, put the cakes in the oven, leaving the door ajar. Broil until sizzling hot and the sauce is really bubbling, about 5 minutes (the time will vary depending on the strength of your broiler, so keep an eye on the cakes.)

Remove the puddings from the oven and place them on a serving platter or on individual plates. Scrape the sauce from the baking sheet over them.

SERVING: Serve warm with a dollop of whipped cream (page 239) or, better yet, Vanilla Ice Cream (page 143).

STORAGE: Sticky toffee pudding demands to be served warm. The puddings can be made up to 2 days in advance and kept at room temperature, well wrapped; hold off dousing them with the remaining sauce until just before broiling.

VARIATION: If you can't find kumquats, or if they're not in season, you can make the recipe without them for more traditional sticky toffee puddings.

Pumpkin Cheesecake with Pecan Crust and Whiskey-Caramel Topping

MAKES ONE 9-INCH (23-CM) CHEESECAKE; 12 TO 14 SERVINGS

This recipe uses canned pumpkin rather than home-cooked fresh pumpkin simply because the moisture content is consistent and no one wants to take any chances with a cheesecake after spending all that money on cream cheese. This is a fantastic holiday recipe, and as with regular cheesecakes, the secret to great results is to begin with all the ingredients at room temperature and to not overbeat the filling.

CRUST

1^1/$_2$ cups (150 g) pecans, toasted

3 tablespoons (45 g) packed light brown sugar

3 tablespoons (1^1/$_2$ ounces/45 g) unsalted or salted butter, melted

^{1}/$_4$ teaspoon ground cinnamon

FILLING

1^1/$_2$ pounds (675 g) cream cheese, at room temperature

1^1/$_4$ cups (250 g) granulated sugar

Grated zest of ^{1}/$_2$ lemon, preferably organic

4 large eggs, at room temperature

2 tablespoons (15 g) all-purpose flour

^{1}/$_2$ cup (120 g) plain whole-milk yogurt

1 can (15 ounces/425 g) pumpkin purée

1 teaspoon ground cinnamon

^{3}/$_4$ teaspoon ground ginger

^{1}/$_4$ teaspoon freshly ground nutmeg

^{1}/$_4$ teaspoon ground cloves

Large pinch of salt

1 teaspoon vanilla extract

TOPPING

6 tablespoons (3 ounces/85 g) salted butter, cut into small pieces

^{1}/$_2$ cup (125 ml) heavy cream

1 cup (215 g) packed dark brown sugar

^{1}/$_4$ cup (60 ml) light corn syrup or agave nectar

^{1}/$_2$ teaspoon salt

^{1}/$_4$ cup (60 ml) whiskey

1^1/$_2$ cups (150 g) pecan pieces, toasted

1 teaspoon freshly squeezed lemon juice

Preheat the oven to 350°F (175°C). Lightly butter the bottom and sides of a 9-inch (23-cm) springform pan.

To make the crust, in a food processor fitted with the metal blade, pulse the 1^1/$_2$ cups (150 g) pecans, light brown sugar, 3 tablespoons (1^1/$_2$ ounces/45 g) melted butter, and ^{1}/$_4$ teaspoon cinnamon until the nuts are in fine pieces and the mixture begins to hold together. Transfer the mixture to the prepared springform pan and press it evenly into the bottom and a little way up the sides. Bake until deep golden brown, about 15 minutes. Let cool completely.

Wrap a large sheet of aluminum foil around the outside of the springform pan, making sure it's absolutely watertight. Set the pan in a large roasting pan.

To make the filling, in a stand mixer fitted with the paddle attachment (or in a bowl by hand), beat together the cream cheese, granulated sugar, and lemon zest on medium-low speed just until smooth. Add the eggs, one at a time, stopping the mixer and scraping down the sides of the bowl as needed, until completely incorporated. Mix in the yogurt, pumpkin, cinnamon, ginger, nutmeg, cloves, large pinch of salt, and vanilla until combined.

(continued)

Scrape the filling into the crust in the pan. Pour hot water into the roasting pan to reach halfway up the outside of the springform pan. Bake until the edges are just set and the center still quivers, about 1 hour and 15 minutes.

Remove the roasting pan from the oven and let the cheesecake stand in the water bath for 30 minutes. Dip the blade of a sharp knife in hot water and run it around the sides of the cheesecake to loosen it from the sides of the pan, then remove the cheesecake from the water bath. Let cool completely, then cover and refrigerate until chilled.

To make the topping, in a medium saucepan, bring the 6 tablespoons (3 ounces/85 g) salted butter, the cream, dark brown sugar, corn syrup or agave nectar, and $1/2$ teaspoon salt to a gentle but full boil stirring gently until the sugar dissolves. Cook for 2 minutes without stirring. Remove from the heat and stir in the whiskey and $1^1/2$ cups (150 g) pecan pieces. Let cool to room temperature and stir in the lemon juice.

Serve the cheesecake chilled or at room temperature. Cut into wedges and spoon topping over each serving.

STORAGE: The cheesecake can be stored in the refrigerator for up to 3 days. The topping should be made the day of serving; if chilled, it will lose its shine and will need to be rewarmed.

Ricotta Cheesecake with Orange and Aniseed

MAKES ONE 9-INCH (23-CM) CAKE; 12 SERVINGS

American cheesecake is to Italian cheesecake what slouching around the house in a sweatshirt and jeans is to stepping out on the town in a tailored Armani suit. When I stopped comparing Italian cheesecake to its comfy American cousin, I was finally won over. Made with ricotta cheese instead of pounds of cream cheese and sour cream, it's lighter and leaner, and perfectly accompanied by fresh fruit compotes or colorful sauces. For best results, use whole-milk ricotta cheese. Or even better, seek out fresh ricotta from a local producer. And be sure to watch it carefully during baking, taking it out when it is just barely set.

$^1/_2$ cup (80 g) golden raisins

3 tablespoons (45 ml) Marsala or port (ruby or tawny)

2 pounds (1 kg) ricotta cheese

$^2/_3$ cup (130 g) sugar

$^1/_4$ cup (60 ml) heavy cream

5 large eggs, at room temperature

$^3/_4$ teaspoon aniseed

1 tablespoon all-purpose flour

1 teaspoon vanilla extract

Grated zest of 1 orange, preferably organic

Soft-Candied Citrus Peel (page 253) made with oranges, for garnish

In a small saucepan, bring the raisins and Marsala or port to a boil. Remove from the heat, cover, and set aside for about 1 hour.

Preheat the oven to 350°F (175°C). Butter the bottom and sides of a 9-inch (23-cm) springform pan.

In a large bowl, mix together the ricotta, sugar, and cream until well combined. Stir in the eggs one at a time.

Crush the aniseed in a mortar and pestle or seal them inside a sturdy plastic bag and crush them with a rolling pin. Add the crushed seeds to the ricotta mixture and stir to combine. Stir in the raisins and any unabsorbed liquid, along with the flour, vanilla, and orange zest.

Scrape the mixture into the prepared springform pan and bake the cake until it feels barely firm and the top is golden brown, about 1 hour. Remove from the oven and let cool completely.

Run a knife around the sides of the cake to help loosen it from the pan. Release the sides of the springform pan.

Cut into wedges and garnish each serving with strips of candied orange peel.

SERVING: The cake is best served at room temperature. A compote of sweetened fresh peach slices or strawberries, or a drizzle of Bittersweet Chocolate Sauce (page 243) spiked with amaretto is an excellent accompaniment.

STORAGE: Ricotta cheesecake will keep in the refrigerator for up to 3 days.

VARIATION: I also like serving this cake with a **TANGY RHUBARB SAUCE.** Wash and dry 2 stalks of rhubarb, then cut them into $^1/_2$-inch (1.5-cm) pieces. In a small saucepan, simmer the rhubarb in $1^1/_2$ cups (375 ml) water over medium-low heat until tender, about 10 minutes. In a blender, purée the rhubarb along with its cooking liquid, 3 tablespoons (45 g) sugar, and 2 tablespoons (30 ml) Grand Marnier or other orange-flavored liqueur. Taste and add another tablespoon of sugar if you wish.

Date-Nut Torte

MAKES ONE 8-INCH (20-CM) SQUARE CAKE; 8 TO 10 SERVINGS

I've been unable to master Arabic, so I have no idea if there's a translation for the phrase "snack cake." My mother, who was half Syrian (and never mastered Arabic either), often made this cake for me when I was a kid. As an adult, I frequently find myself craving a piece for a snack. Or whatever a between-meal nibble is called.

When I got the recipe from her, I read it through and noticed there wasn't any butter in the cake. I figured it was probably a mistake, but when I baked it up, I found that no butter was necessary—the cake simply didn't need it. It does benefit from a very generous dusting of powdered sugar, which can be a little messy, but part of the fun of Middle Eastern desserts is licking your sugary fingers after you've polished off the last bite.

2 cups (12 ounces/340 g) pitted dates, quartered

1 cup (100 g) walnuts, toasted and coarsely chopped

1 cup (140 g) all-purpose flour

1 teaspoon baking powder

1/4 teaspoon salt

3/4 teaspoon aniseed

3 large eggs, at room temperature

1 cup (200 g) granulated sugar

3 tablespoons (45 ml) orange juice (freshly squeezed or store-bought)

1 teaspoon vanilla extract

Powdered sugar, for dusting the cake

Preheat the oven to 350°F (175°C). Butter the bottom and sides of an 8-inch (20-cm) square cake pan, dust it with flour, and tap out any excess.

In a small bowl, use your fingers to toss together the dates, walnuts, and 1 tablespoon of the flour, breaking up the sticky date pieces.

In another small bowl, whisk together the remaining flour, the baking powder, and salt. Crush the aniseed in a mortar and pestle or seal them inside a sturdy plastic bag and crush with a rolling pin. Add the crushed seeds to the flour mixture and stir to combine.

In a large bowl, whisk together the eggs, granulated sugar, orange juice, and vanilla. Stir in the flour mixture, then the date-nut mixture just until combined.

Scrape the batter into the prepared cake pan and bake until the top is light golden brown and the cake feels just barely firm in the center, about 40 minutes.

Heavily dust the warm or room-temperature cake with powdered sugar. Cut into squares right in the cake pan.

STORAGE: The cake will keep for up to 3 days at room temperature.

Pistachio-Cardamom Cake

MAKES ONE 9-INCH (23-CM) CAKE; 10 TO 12 SERVINGS

At one time, everything I knew about Indian cooking could fit on one *bindi* dot. It wasn't until Niloufer Ichaporia King came to work with us at Chez Panisse, where each year she guided us through the preparation of a traditional Parsi New Year's feast, that I tasted authentic and wonderfully aromatic Indian food. My favorite dish was a cake enrobed in a sheet of gold leaf, a stunning touch that lent the dessert the splendor worthy of a Bollywood musical.

This is my version of that cake, but I left out the gold, since it's not something you're likely to have on hand. I did, however, brighten up the batter with vibrant green pistachios, which should be more easily found in grocery stores than sheets of gold leaf.

TOPPING

2 tablespoons (1 ounce/30 g) unsalted or salted butter

1 teaspoon sugar

$^3/_4$ cup (60 g) sliced almonds, preferably unblanched

CAKE

$^3/_4$ cup (95 g) shelled unsalted pistachios

$^1/_4$ cup (35 g) plus $^3/_4$ cup (110 g) all-purpose flour

2 teaspoons cardamom seeds

$^1/_2$ cup (4 ounces/115 g) unsalted butter, at room temperature

1 cup (200 g) sugar

3 large eggs, at room temperature

1 teaspoon baking powder

Pinch of salt

Preheat the oven to 350°F (175°C).

To make the topping, melt the 2 tablespoons (1 ounce/30 g) butter in a 9-inch (23-cm) round cake pan set directly on the stovetop over low heat. Once melted, remove from the heat and let cool briefly. Sprinkle the 1 teaspoon sugar evenly over the melted butter, then add the almonds, tilting and shaking the pan to distribute them evenly. Set the pan aside.

To make the cake, in a blender or a food processor fitted with the metal blade, pulverize the pistachios with the $^1/_4$ cup (35 g) flour until as finely ground as possible. Transfer to a small bowl.

Crush the cardamom seeds in a mortar and pestle or seal them inside a sturdy plastic bag and crush with a rolling pin. Add the crushed seeds to the pistachio mixture and stir to combine. Set aside.

In a stand mixer fitted with the paddle attachment (or in a bowl by hand), beat together the $^1/_2$ cup (4 ounces/115 g) butter and 1 cup (200 g) sugar on medium speed until very light and fluffy, 3 to 5 minutes. Add the eggs one at a time, beating until completely incorporated.

In a small bowl, whisk together the remaining $^3/_4$ cup (110 g) flour, baking powder, and salt, and stir it into the butter-egg mixture. Stir in the pistachio mixture just until combined.

Spoon the batter into the prepared cake pan by dropping 4 or 5 mounds on top of the almonds. Carefully spread the batter into an even layer, trying not to disturb the almonds. Bake until a toothpick inserted in the center of the cake comes out clean, about 40 minutes. Let cool for 15 minutes.

Run a knife around the sides of the cake to help loosen it from the pan. Invert the cake onto a serving plate. Let cool completely.

SERVING: Although terrific on its own, this cake goes well with a fruit compote or a fresh fruit sorbet. I like to serve it with Tangerine Sorbet (page 159).

STORAGE: This cake will keep for up to 4 days at room temperature, well wrapped. It can be frozen for up to 1 month.

VARIATION: This cake is lovely served with Sauternes-poached apricots: Bring $1^1/_2$ cups (375 ml) water and $^3/_4$ cup (150 g) sugar to a boil in a medium saucepan. Add half a vanilla bean, split lengthwise, and $^3/_4$ cup (180 ml) Sauternes (or other sweet white wine). Decrease the heat to maintain a simmer. Halve and pit 8 apricots. Add the apricot halves to the pan and poach until softened, about 10 minutes. You can also use 8 ounces (225 g) dried apricots, poaching them until tender, 30 to 45 minutes.

Polenta Cake with Olive Oil and Rosemary

MAKES ONE 10-INCH (25-CM) CAKE; 10 TO 12 SERVINGS

Cornmeal is often thought of as purely an American ingredient, probably because of our infatuation with cornbread, but Italians love cornmeal as much as we do. It's not unusual in Italian bakeries to see rows of golden cakes and baskets of crumbly cookies made with polenta and sometimes flavored with a pour of olive oil, just in case you forget you're in Italy.

A bit of minced fresh rosemary infuses this cake with a familiar, yet elusive flavor. I wouldn't dream of leaving the rosemary out. Polenta gives the cake a rustic feel; you can use stone-ground cornmeal instead to make a cake with a more refined texture that retains that agreeable crunch. As for the olive oil, use one that's strong and fruity; its flavor is more important than its provenance.

1 tablespoon plus $^1/_2$ cup (4 ounces/115 g) unsalted butter, at room temperature

2 teaspoons plus 4 teaspoons finely minced fresh rosemary leaves

2 tablespoons (20 g) plus $^3/_4$ cup (130 g) polenta or stone-ground yellow cornmeal

1 cup (140 g) all-purpose flour

2 teaspoons baking powder

1 teaspoon salt

$^1/_2$ cup (125 ml) olive oil

5 large eggs, at room temperature

2 large egg yolks

$^1/_2$ teaspoon almond extract or 1 teaspoon vanilla extract

$1^1/_3$ cups (265 g) sugar

Preheat the oven to 350°F (175°C).

Smear the 1 tablespoon butter all over the inside of a 10-cup (2.5-liter) Bundt cake or tube pan. Sprinkle the 2 teaspoons rosemary evenly into the pan, then dust with the 2 tablespoons (20 g) polenta, tilting the pan to coat the sides.

To make the cake, into a small bowl, sift together the flour, $^3/_4$ cup (130 g) polenta, baking powder, and salt. Set aside. In a separate bowl, whisk together the olive oil, eggs, egg yolks, and almond or vanilla extract.

In a stand mixer fitted with the paddle attachment (or in a bowl by hand), beat together the $^1/_2$ cup (4 ounces/ 115 g) butter and the sugar on medium speed until light and fluffy, 3 to 5 minutes. With the mixer running, slowly dribble in the egg mixture, a little at a time, until completely incorporated. Stir in the flour mixture along

with the 4 teaspoons rosemary just until incorporated. Don't overmix.

Scrape the batter into the prepared cake pan and smooth the top. Bake until a toothpick inserted into the cake comes out clean, about 40 minutes. Let cool for about 30 minutes, then invert the cake onto a serving plate.

SERVING: This cake goes well with whipped cream (page 239) flavored with grappa or Tangy Lemon Frozen Yogurt (page 174).

STORAGE: The cake will keep at room temperature for up to 4 days, well wrapped. It can be frozen for up to 2 months.

VARIATION: You can add $^1/_3$ cup (35 g) finely chopped candied orange peel (page 254) or candied angelica to the dry ingredients. If using angelica, omit the rosemary in the batter but keep the small amount used for the pan preparation.

It's nice to serve slices of peaches or nectarines with the cake when they're in season. During winter months, I'll poach pears with saffron and honey, whose juices mingle nicely with the cake: In a medium nonreactive saucepan, bring $^1/_2$ cup (125 ml) honey and 3 cups (750 ml) water to a boil. Decrease the heat to medium-low to maintain a simmer and add 25 saffron threads and 2 strips lemon zest, each 1 inch (3 cm) wide. Peel, quarter, and core 3 Bosc pears and add them to the poaching liquid. Place a circle of parchment paper over the fruit and simmer gently until a paring knife inserted into the fruit meets no resistance, about 10 minutes.

Coconut Layer Cake

MAKES ONE 9-INCH (23-CM) CAKE; 10 TO 12 SERVINGS

I hate to admit this, but when I was a kid, my all-time favorite snack was those coconut-coated cake-and-cream filled marshmallow snowballs packaged in sticky pairs. Their neon-pink color was so fluorescent and I ate so many that I'm sure my insides are still glowing. Now I'm all grown up and presumably know better, but from time-to-time I still like a coconut-and-cake fix. This recipe is the remedy.

The cake should be assembled at least a few hours before you plan to serve it so the flavors have time to meld. I guarantee that the most memorable thing about this cream-filled coconut cake concoction will be how great it tasted, not its shocking color.

FILLING

$1^1/_4$ cups (310 ml) plus $^1/_4$ cup (60 ml) whole milk

$^1/_2$ cup (100 g) sugar

$^1/_2$ vanilla bean, split lengthwise

2 tablespoons (8 g) cornstarch

5 large egg yolks

1 cup (70 g) dried unsweetened shredded coconut
     (see Tip)

RUM SYRUP

$^2/_3$ cup (160 ml) water

$^1/_2$ cup (100 g) sugar

3 tablespoons (45 ml) dark rum

Sponge cake, 9-inch (23-cm) round (page 233)

WHIPPED CREAM

$1^1/_4$ cups (310 ml) heavy cream

$1^1/_2$ tablespoons sugar

$^1/_4$ teaspoon vanilla extract

$1^1/_4$ cups (90 g) dried unsweetened or sweetened
     shredded or large-flake coconut, toasted

> **TIP:** I prefer to use unsweetened coconut to make the filling, but if you can find only sweetened coconut, reduce the sugar in the filling by 1 tablespoon.

To make the filling, in a medium saucepan over medium heat, warm the $1^1/_4$ cups (310 ml) milk with the $^1/_2$ cup (100 g) sugar. Scrape the seeds from the vanilla bean and add them to the saucepan, then drop in the pod.

In a small bowl, whisk together the cornstarch and the remaining $^1/_4$ cup (60 ml) milk until completely smooth. In a medium bowl, whisk the egg yolks until combined.

When the milk-sugar mixture is hot, stir the cornstarch mixture to recombine, then whisk it into the saucepan. Cook, stirring constantly, until the mixture thickens. While whisking constantly, pour about one-third of the hot thickened milk into the egg yolks, then scrape the yolk mixture into the saucepan. Cook, stirring constantly and scraping the bottom of the pan, just until the mixture begins to boil (it will be very thick). Pour the mixture into a clean bowl and remove the vanilla pod (it can be rinsed, dried, and used for another purpose; see page 14). Stir in the 1 cup (70 g) coconut, cover, and refrigerate until chilled. (To speed up the chilling, you can set the bowl containing the filling in a larger bowl filled with ice water.)

(continued)

To make the syrup, warm the water and $1/2$ cup (100 g) sugar, stirring until the sugar dissolves. Remove from the heat, add the rum, and let cool to room temperature.

To assemble the cake, with a long serrated knife, slice the sponge cake horizontally into 3 equal layers. Place one cake layer on a serving plate and brush evenly with $1/3$ cup (80 ml) rum syrup. Evenly spread half of the filling on top of the soaked cake layer. Cover it with a second cake layer. Brush the second layer with another $1/3$ cup (80 ml) rum syrup. Spread the remaining filling over the second soaked cake layer. Place the final cake layer on top and brush with the remaining rum syrup. Cover with plastic wrap and refrigerate the cake for at least 4 hours or up to overnight.

To make the whipped cream and finish the cake, in a stand mixer fitted with the whip attachment (or in a bowl by hand), whisk the cream until it just beings to hold its shape. Whisk in the $1^1/2$ tablespoons sugar and the vanilla until stiff, but don't overbeat.

Using an icing spatula, spread the whipped cream evenly over the top and sides of the cake. Cover the top and sides of the cake with the toasted coconut by sprinkling coconut on top of the cake and pressing some around the sides with your hands.

SERVING: This cake is delicious on its own. Or, you can make a simple tropical fruit and berry compote to serve alongside: Toss diced mango, papaya, banana, or pineapple (or a mixture); fresh raspberries, blueberries, or sliced strawberries (or a mixture); a few tablespoons of sugar; and a shot of dark rum. Let stand until the sugar dissolves and the mixture is juicy.

STORAGE: This cake will keep in the refrigerator for up to 3 days, unfrosted. Make the whipped cream and finish the cake the same day you plan to serve it.

Passion Fruit Pound Cake

MAKES ONE 9-INCH (23-CM) LOAF CAKE; 10 SERVINGS

For some reason, whenever I'm interviewed, the question always arises: "What would be your last meal?" Or, sometimes it's: "If you were stranded on a deserted island . . ." I find both to be rather morbid questions—who wants to think about their last meal or being stranded on a deserted island?—and I never quite know how to respond.

But if I had to list the things that I couldn't live without, I'd say chocolate and fried chicken. The third food in my holy trinity is passion fruit. If you haven't tasted passion fruit, this pound cake is the perfect introduction. If I'm ever stranded on a deserted tropical island, I might get lucky and find a few vines of passion fruit and perhaps some cocoa pods, but I won't hold out much hope for getting any fried chicken.

CAKE

1¹/₂ cups (210 g) all-purpose flour

1 teaspoon baking powder

¹/₄ teaspoon salt

³/₄ cup (6 ounces/170 g) unsalted butter, at room temperature

1 cup (200 g) sugar

Grated zest of 2 oranges, preferably organic

3 large eggs, at room temperature

1 teaspoon vanilla extract

GLAZE

¹/₂ cup (125 ml) strained fresh passion fruit pulp (from about 6 passion fruits) or thawed frozen purée (see Tip)

¹/₃ cup (65 g) sugar

Preheat the oven to 350°F (175°C). Butter the bottom and sides of a 9-inch (23-cm) loaf pan, dust it with flour, and tap out any excess. Line the bottom with a rectangle of parchment paper.

To make the cake, in a small bowl, whisk together the flour, baking powder, and salt. Set aside.

In a stand mixer fitted with the paddle attachment (or in a bowl by hand), beat together the butter, 1 cup (200 g) sugar, and the orange zest on medium speed until light and fluffy, 3 to 5 minutes.

In a small bowl, beat together the eggs and vanilla. With the mixer running, slowly dribble the egg mixture into the butter mixture, stopping the mixer and scraping down the sides of the bowl as needed, until the eggs are completely incorporated. (The mixture may look curdled, which is normal.)

Using a rubber spatula, stir the flour mixture into the butter-sugar mixture by hand just until combined. Don't

overmix. Scrape the batter into the prepared loaf pan and smooth the top. Bake until a toothpick inserted into the center of the cake comes out clean, about 1 hour. Let cool about 15 minutes.

While the cake is cooling, prepare the glaze. In a small bowl, very gently stir together the passion fruit juice and ¹/₃ cup (65 g) sugar. Don't let the sugar dissolve.

Loosen the cake from the loaf pan by running a knife around the sides of the cake. Invert the warm cake out of the pan, peel off the parchment paper, and turn it right side up onto a plate.

Using a wooden skewer, pierce the top of the cake all the way through to the bottom about 50 times. Spoon half of the glaze over the top of the cake. Turn the cake on each of its sides, spooning the rest of the glaze over so that the cake is evenly coated. Sop up the glaze that collects in the plate by rubbing the bottom and sides of the cake in it.

SERVING: Serve the sliced cake just as it is or with a compote of fresh tropical fruit or berries.

STORAGE: Store the cake loosely wrapped in plastic wrap, to keep the glaze crisp.

VARIATION: To make **ORANGE POUND CAKE**, replace the passion fruit juice in the glaze with ¹/₂ cup (125 ml) freshly squeezed orange juice.

> **TIP:** To strain fresh passion fruit pulp, halve the fruits, scoop the pulp into a mesh strainer set over a bowl, and press the pulp to separate the seeds from the juice. You can find frozen passion fruit purée in Latin markets as well as online (see Resources, page 270).

Banana Cake with Mocha Frosting and Salted Candied Peanuts

MAKES ONE 9-INCH (23-CM) CAKE; 12 TO 16 SERVINGS

This is one big, tall, scrumptious dessert: layers of moist banana cake topped with a mocha ganachelike frosting, and crowned with handfuls of salted candied peanuts.

Speaking of tall and scrumptious, I made this cake for a friend who's a showgirl at the Lido in Paris as a thank you for allowing me a behind-the-scenes visit. She shared it with her colleagues between high kicks on stage and she assured me that even though those women are leggy and lean, their cake-eating capacity knew no limits.

The next morning, I read an email, sent at 3 A.M., undoubtedly just after the last curtain call, giving the cake quite a few thumbs up. Or, should I say, a few legs up?

CAKE

2 1/2 cups (350 g) all-purpose flour

1 1/2 teaspoons ground cinnamon

1 1/2 teaspoons baking powder

3/4 teaspoon baking soda

1/2 teaspoon salt

1 cup (8 ounces/230 g) unsalted butter, at room temperature

1 1/2 cups (300 g) sugar

1 teaspoon vanilla extract

1 tablespoon instant espresso or coffee powder

2 large eggs, at room temperature

6 tablespoons (90 ml) buttermilk, yogurt, or sour cream (regular or low-fat), at room temperature

2 cups (500 ml) banana purée (3 to 4 very ripe bananas)

1 1/4 cups (125 g) pecans or walnuts, toasted and coarsely chopped

CANDIED PEANUTS

1 cup (150 g) raw or unsalted lightly roasted peanuts (see Tip, page 64)

1/2 cup (100 g) sugar

3 tablespoons (45 ml) water

1/2 teaspoon flaky sea salt

1/8 teaspoon ground cinnamon

FROSTING

10 ounces (280 g) bittersweet or semisweet chocolate, coarsely chopped

1/2 cup (125 ml) strong brewed coffee or espresso

10 tablespoons (5 ounces/140 g) unsalted or salted butter, cut into pieces, at room temperature

Preheat the oven to 350°F (175°C). Butter the bottom and sides of two 9-inch (23-cm) round cake pans and line the bottoms with circles of parchment paper.

To make the cake, in a medium bowl, whisk together the flour, 1 1/2 teaspoons cinnamon, the baking powder, baking soda, and salt.

In a stand mixer fitted with the paddle attachment (or in a bowl by hand), beat together the 1 cup (8 ounces/ 230 g) butter and 1 1/2 cups (300 g) sugar on medium speed until light and fluffy, 3 to 5 minutes. Add the vanilla and instant espresso or coffee powder, then beat in the eggs one at a time, mixing until completely incorporated. Mix in half of the flour mixture, followed by the buttermilk and banana purée. Stir in the remaining flour mixture, then stir in the pecans or walnuts just until combined. Don't overmix.

Divide the batter evenly among the 2 prepared pans. Bake until golden brown and a toothpick inserted into the center of the cakes comes out clean, about 40 minutes. Remove from the oven and let cool completely.

To prepare the peanuts, in a medium heavy-bottomed skillet over medium heat, combine the peanuts, 1/2 cup (100 g) sugar, and the water. When the sugar begins to liquefy, begin stirring. Continue cooking, stirring frequently, until the sugar crystallizes. Decrease the heat to medium-low and continue to cook, stirring, letting the crystallized sugar on the bottom melt and brown slightly. Then, use a heatproof spatula to scrape up the liquefied sugar and continuously coat the peanuts with it, tilting the pan to help the sugar coat the nuts evenly.

(continued, page 64)

Once the peanuts are a bit glossy and coated with syrup (there will be some sugary crystals on them still, which is normal), sprinkle the sea salt and $^{1}/_{8}$ teaspoon cinnamon over them. Stir the peanuts a couple of times, then scrape the candied peanuts onto a baking sheet and let cool completely.

To make the frosting, combine the chocolate and coffee in a medium heatproof bowl set over a pan of simmering water, stirring occasionally until the chocolate is melted and the mixture is smooth. Remove the bowl from the heat and whisk in the 10 tablespoons (5 ounces/ 140 g) butter until combined.

TIP: If you can't find raw peanuts (I buy them in Asian markets), you can use unsalted roasted peanuts that aren't too darkly roasted. You can also replace the peanuts with raw almonds. The recipe makes more candied peanuts than you'll need for the cake—leftovers are great sprinkled over ice cream or just eaten out of hand. If you wish, you can use 1 cup store-bought honey-roasted peanuts in lieu of making your own salted candied peanuts.

To assemble the cake, run a knife around the sides of the cakes to help them loosen from the pans. Invert one cake onto a serving plate and peel off the parchment. Spread about $^{3}/_{4}$ cup (180 ml) of the mocha frosting over the surface of the cake. Invert the second cake layer out of its pan, peel off the parchment, and place it over the frosted cake layer. Spread the remaining frosting evenly over the top and sides of the cake.

Coarsely chop 1 cup (100 g) of the candied peanuts and sprinkle them over the top of the cake.

STORAGE: The cake will keep for up to 3 days, at room temperature. Because of its height, the cake is best stored under a cake dome.

VARIATION: If you're serving the cake to kids, you can replace the coffee in the frosting with water or decaffeinated coffee.

Lemon Semifreddo

This is *the* dessert for lemon lovers. It's light, but supersaturated with lemon flavor. *Semifreddo* usually refers to a dessert that's partially frozen, but this cake layered with lightened lemon curd was christened "semifreddo" by the Italian American chef at the time at Chez Panisse. I don't know about you, but I find it pretty hard to win an argument with an Italian, so I let the name stick.

I based this recipe on the lemon semifreddo that one of my colleagues, Linda Zagula, made at the restaurant. It was not only popular with the customers, but with me, too—I couldn't resist sneaking a mouthful every so often. And from the scraped-clean spoons I'd find hidden in the pastry fridge after all the guests had gone home, I knew I wasn't the only one.

LEMON CURD

$^1/_2$ cup (125 ml) freshly squeezed lemon juice

$^1/_2$ cup (100 g) sugar

6 tablespoons (3 ounces/85 g) unsalted or salted butter, cut into pieces

2 large eggs

2 large egg yolks

LEMON SYRUP

$^3/_4$ cup (180 ml) water

$^1/_3$ cup (65 g) sugar

$^1/_4$ cup (60 ml) freshly squeezed lemon juice

2 tablespoons (30 ml) kirsch (optional)

Sponge cake, 12 by 18-inch (30 by 46-cm) sheet (page 233)

1 cup (250 ml) heavy cream

$^2/_3$ cup (75 g) crushed amaretti (about 25 cookies; page 215)

> TIP: Rather than make your own amaretti cookies, you can purchase them in stores specializing in Italian products and well-stocked supermarkets. The most popular brand is Amaretti di Saronno, packaged in a distinctive red tin.

To make the lemon curd, in a medium nonreactive saucepan over low heat, combine the $^1/_2$ cup (125 ml) lemon juice, $^1/_2$ cup (100 g) sugar, and the butter. Set a mesh strainer over a medium bowl.

In another medium bowl, briefly whisk together the eggs and egg yolks. When the butter has melted, whisk some of the warm liquid from the saucepan into the eggs, whisking constantly as you pour, then stir the egg mixture into the saucepan. Cook, whisking constantly, until the curd starts to thicken and looks slightly jelled. Don't let the mixture boil.

Pour the lemon curd through the strainer set over the bowl. Cover, let cool, then refrigerate until chilled.

To make the lemon syrup, in a small nonreactive saucepan, warm the water and $^1/_3$ cup (65 g) sugar, stirring until the sugar dissolves. Remove from the heat, then stir in the $^1/_4$ cup (60 ml) lemon juice and the kirsch. Let cool completely.

To assemble the semifreddo, remove the parchment paper from the sponge cake and cut out 2 pieces of cake that will each fit in the bottom of a 2-quart (2-liter) baking dish. (You will have extra sponge cake left over that can be frozen for future use.)

In a stand mixer fitted with the whip attachment (or in a bowl by hand), whisk the cream until it forms soft peaks. Fold the whipped cream into the chilled lemon curd.

Spread 1 cup (250 ml) of the lemon cream mixture evenly in the bottom of the baking dish. Place one of the cake pieces on top and brush evenly with about $^1/_2$ cup (125 ml) of the lemon syrup.

(continued)

Spread 1 cup (250 ml) of the lemon cream evenly on top of the first cake layer and sprinkle with two-thirds of the amaretti crumbs. Lay the second piece of cake on top and brush evenly with the remaining lemon syrup. Spread the remaining lemon cream in an even layer over the top and refrigerate, uncovered, for about 30 minutes to firm up the top layer of lemon cream. Cover with plastic wrap and refrigerate until chilled.

When ready to serve, sprinkle the remaining amaretti crumbs over the top. Cut the semifreddo into neat rectangles.

SERVING: Set individual servings of semifreddo in a pool of Raspberry Sauce (page 246), Blackberry Sauce (page 248), or Strawberry Sauce (page 248). Or, accompany with a mixture of your favorite berries, lightly sugared and left to sit for a while until juicy.

STORAGE: The semifreddo is best served the next day, which gives the flavors time to meld. It will keep for up to 3 days in the refrigerator. You can make the lemon curd up to 5 days in advance and keep it chilled until ready to use.

VARIATION: You can use Meyer lemons, which are sweeter than regular lemons, but decrease the amount of sugar in the lemon curd by $1/4$ cup (50 g). If time-pressed, substitute store-bought ladyfingers for the sponge cake.

Peach-Mascarpone Semifreddo

Here's a superb dessert for highlighting summer peaches when they are at their peak of flavor and so juicy that you struggle to pick up the slippery slices that elude your grasp. This is an ideal dessert to bring to a summertime picnic or barbecue: it's easy to assemble in advance and even easier to eat.

KIRSCH SYRUP

1 cup (250 ml) water

$^1/_3$ cup (65 g) sugar

$^1/_3$ cup (80 ml) kirsch

PEACH FILLING

6 to 8 peaches (about 2 pounds/1 kg) , peeled, pitted, and cut into $^1/_2$-inch (1.5-cm) dice

3 tablespoons (45 g) sugar

MASCARPONE FILLING

2 cups (450 g) mascarpone cheese

$^1/_4$ cup (60 ml) heavy cream, if needed to thin the mascarpone

$^1/_4$ cup (50 g) sugar

1 teaspoon vanilla extract

Sponge cake, 12 by 18-inch (30 by 46-cm) sheet (page 233)

3 peaches (about 1 pound/450 g), peeled, pitted, and cut into $^1/_2$-inch (1.5-cm) slices

1 tablespoon sugar

$^3/_4$ cup (75 g) crushed amaretti (about 25 cookies; page 215)

To make the kirsch syrup, in a small saucepan, warm the water and $^1/_3$ cup (65 g) sugar, stirring until the sugar dissolves. Remove from the heat, then stir in the kirsch. Let cool completely.

To make the peach filling, in a small bowl, toss the diced peaches with the 3 tablespoons (45 g) sugar and let stand until juicy.

To make the mascarpone filling, put the mascarpone in a medium bowl; if it is very thick straight out of the container, add the cream. Whisk until the mascarpone begins to hold its shape and has the consistency of but-tercream frosting. Stir in the $^1/_4$ cup (50 g) sugar and vanilla. Set aside.

To assemble the semifreddo, remove the parchment paper from the sponge cake and cut out 2 pieces of cake that will each fit in the bottom of a 2-quart (2-liter) baking dish. (You will have extra sponge cake left over that can be frozen for future use.)

Spread $^1/_2$ cup (125 ml) of the mascarpone filling evenly in the bottom of the baking dish. Place one of the cake pieces on top and brush evenly with about half of the kirsch syrup (it may seem like a lot, but it will all soak in).

Spread the peach filling over the cake. Spread $1^1/_4$ cups (310 g) mascarpone filling over the peaches. Add the second cake layer and soak it with the remaining syrup. Spread the remaining mascarpone over the cake and refrigerate, uncovered, for about 30 minutes to firm up the top layer of mascarpone. Cover with plastic wrap and refrigerate until chilled.

Just before serving, in a small bowl, toss the sliced peaches with the 1 tablespoon sugar. Let stand until the sugar dissolves and the peaches are juicy. Scatter the peach slices over the semifreddo and sprinkle with the crushed amaretti. Cut the semifreddo into neat rect-angles and serve.

STORAGE: The semifreddo can be made up to 1 day ahead and refrigerated.

VARIATION: If you wish to make this dessert without the kirsch, add a teaspoon of almond extract to the syrup in place of the kirsch.

> TIP: Instead of making your own amaretti cookies, you can use store-bought ones. Purchased amaretti are tiny, so you'll need a few more than indicated to get the right amount of crumbs.

Bahamian Rum Cake

MAKES ONE 10-INCH (25-CM) CAKE; 10 TO 12 SERVINGS

I had a cake crisis at Club Med in the Bahamas. A round yellow tin was waiting in my room when I arrived, and when I pried off the lid, inside was a small rum cake. Curious, I sliced off a small wedge, and then another, and then another. It took every bit of willpower in me not the finish the entire cake right then and there. But I thought that I should I save half to share with my partner who'd gone for a swim.

We went to lunch, and when we returned to the room, the other half of the cake was missing, apparently the work of an overzealous housekeeper, or one who liked the cake as much as I did.

When I got home from that trip, I set to work recreating that lovely golden cake with island flavor courtesy of a little dose of coconut milk and a lot of dark rum. I added a tasty coconut-rum glaze for good measure, although you can skip it if swimsuit season is around the corner. If you make this cake, be sure to keep an eye on any leftovers.

CAKE

3 cups (420 g) all-purpose flour

$^1/_2$ teaspoon baking powder

$^1/_2$ teaspoon baking soda

$^3/_4$ teaspoon salt

$^1/_4$ teaspoon freshly grated nutmeg

1 cup (8 ounces/225 g) unsalted butter, at room temperature

2 cups (400 g) granulated sugar

3 large eggs, at room temperature

2 large egg yolks, at room temperature

1 tablespoon vanilla extract

$^3/_4$ cup (180 ml) canned Thai coconut milk

COCONUT-RUM SYRUP

$^3/_4$ cup (180 ml) canned Thai coconut milk

6 tablespoons (75 g) granulated sugar

$^1/_2$ cup (125 ml) dark rum

GLAZE

4 tablespoons (2 ounces/60 g) unsalted or salted butter, cut into pieces

6 tablespoons (90 ml) heavy cream

6 tablespoons (90 g) dark brown sugar

Pinch of salt

1 tablespoon dark rum

$^1/_2$ cup (40 g) dried large-flake coconut (unsweetened or sweetened), toasted

Preheat the oven to 350°F (175°C). Coat a 10-cup (2.5-liter) Bundt cake or tube pan with butter or nonstick cooking spray, dust it with flour, and tap out any excess.

To make the cake, into a medium bowl, sift together the flour, baking powder, baking soda, $^3/_4$ teaspoon salt, and the nutmeg.

In a stand mixer fitted with the paddle attachment (or in a bowl by hand), beat together the 1 cup (8 ounces/225 g) butter and 2 cups (400 g) granulated sugar on medium speed until light and fluffy, 3 to 5 minutes.

In a small bowl, beat together the eggs, egg yolks, and vanilla. With the mixer running, slowly dribble the egg mixture into the butter mixture, stopping the mixer and scraping down the sides of the bowl as needed, until the eggs are completely incorporated. (The mixture may look curdled, which is normal.) Gently stir in one-third of the flour mixture, then about half of the $^3/_4$ cup (180 ml) coconut milk. Mix in about half of the remaining flour mixture, followed by the remaining coconut milk. Finally, gently stir in the remaining flour mixture just until combined.

Scrape the batter into the prepared pan and bake until the cakes feels just set in the center, 55 to 60 minutes.

While the cake is baking, make the coconut-rum syrup. In a medium saucepan, warm the $^3/_4$ cup (180 ml) coconut milk and the 6 tablespoons (75 g) granulated sugar, stirring until the sugar dissolves. Remove from the heat and add the $^1/_2$ cup (125 ml) rum.

When the cake comes out of the oven, leave it in the pan and poke it with a wooden skewer about 60 times. Spoon about two-thirds of the coconut-rum syrup over the cake, letting it soak in gradually. Let the cake cool completely.

Invert the cake onto a cake plate. Brush or spoon the remaining coconut-rum syrup over the cake.

To make the glaze, in a small saucepan over high heat, bring the 4 tablespoons (2 ounces/60 g) butter, the cream, brown sugar, and pinch of salt to a boil. Cook, stirring to dissolve the sugar, for $1^1/_2$ minutes. Remove from the heat, stir in the 1 tablespoon rum, and let cool completely. Once cool, stir in the toasted coconut.

Spoon the glaze over the top of the cake, encouraging it to run down the sides of the cake (if the glaze seems too thick, rewarm it slightly).

STORAGE: The cake can be stored at room temperature for up to 4 days, preferably under a cake dome.

Coconut and Tropical Fruit Trifle

MAKES 8 SERVINGS

I've found that as I get older, I tend to forget about the things that aren't all that important to me, like paying bills, what day it is, and so on. But I never, ever forget a dessert. A few decades ago, some friends who had lived in Brazil for a few years invited me for dinner and served *bien me sabe*, a moist concoction of sponge cake and coconut cream. And I never got it out of my head how fantastic that simple combination tasted. Years later, when I was the pastry chef at a restaurant that specialized in Asian cooking, I had the opportunity to seek out and use all sorts of tropical fruit, many of which I hadn't ever seen before. And I thought *bien me sabe* would be the perfect backdrop for a jumble of exotic flavors.

Although I've used the types of tropical fruit that are the most widely available, feel free to add or use others in place of what I've suggested. But just be sure to heat them through, as most tropical fruits contain a heat-sensitive enzyme that causes custards to break down. I learned this the hard way.

I like the way large shreds of fresh coconut look on top of this dessert. If you have the inclination, crack one open, shave off large shards, and toast them to use as garnish.

COCONUT CUSTARD

$1^1/4$ cups (310 ml) whole milk

$1/2$ cup (100 g) sugar

$1/2$ vanilla bean, split lengthwise

3 tablespoons (25 g) cornstarch

$1/2$ cup (125 ml) canned Thai coconut milk

4 large egg yolks

1 cup (70 g) dried unsweetened shredded coconut
(see Tip)

FRUIT FILLING

1 pineapple, peeled, eyes removed, cored, and cut into
1-inch (3-cm) pieces

$2^1/2$ cups (1 pound/450 g) strawberries, hulled and sliced

1 medium mango, peeled, pitted, and cut into $1/2$-inch
(1.5-cm) cubes

6 tablespoons (75 g) sugar

Juice of $1/2$ lime

$1/2$ cup (125 ml) dark rum

Sponge Cake, 12 by 18-inch (30 by 46-cm) sheet
(page 233)

Fresh or dried unsweetened shredded coconut, toasted,
for garnish

> TIP: I prefer to use unsweetened coconut, but if you can only find sweetened coconut, reduce the sugar in the custard by $1^1/2$ tablespoons.

To make the coconut custard, in a medium saucepan over medium heat, warm the milk with the $1/2$ cup (100 g) sugar. Scrape the seeds from the vanilla bean and add them to the saucepan, then drop in the pod.

In a small bowl, whisk together the cornstarch and coconut milk until completely smooth. In another small bowl, whisk the egg yolks until combined.

When the milk mixture is hot, stir the cornstarch mixture to recombine, then whisk it into the saucepan. Cook, stirring constantly, until the mixture thickens. While whisking constantly, pour about one-third of the hot thickened milk into the egg yolks, then scrape the yolk mixture into the saucepan. Cook, stirring constantly and scraping the bottom of the pan, just until the mixture begins to boil (it will be very thick). Remove from the heat and strain into a clean bowl. (The vanilla pod can be rinsed, dried, and used for another purpose; see page 14.) Stir in the 1 cup (70 g) coconut, and refrigerate until chilled. (To speed up the chilling, you can set the bowl containing the custard in a larger bowl filled with ice water.)

To make the fruit filling, in a nonreactive skillet, gently cook the pineapple until it is heated through, 3 to 5 minutes. Transfer to a medium bowl and let cool completely.

Add the strawberries, mango, 6 tablespoons (75 g) sugar, lime juice, and rum to the pineapple and toss gently.

To assemble the trifle, use a 2-quart (2-liter) rectangular baking dish with at least 3-inch (8-cm) sides. Remove the parchment paper from the sponge cake and cut out 2 pieces that each fit in the bottom of the baking dish. (You'll need the cake trimmings, so don't eat them!)

Spread $^1/_2$ cup (125 ml) of the coconut custard evenly in the bottom of the dish. Place one of the cake pieces on top. Spread half of the fruit filling and some of their juice over the cake.

Spread about 1 cup (250 ml) of the coconut custard over the fruit, then place the second cake piece on top. Cover the cake with the remaining fruit filling and juice. Spread another 1 cup (250 ml) of the coconut custard over the fruit, and cover with the cake trimmings, fitting them in a single layer.

Finally, spread the remaining coconut custard over the top and refrigerate, uncovered, for about 30 minutes to firm up the top layer of custard. Cover with plastic wrap and refrigerate until chilled.

SERVING: Scoop out big spoonfuls of the trifle so all the layers of fruit, cake, and custard can be seen. Strew toasted coconut over the top of each serving. The dessert is delicious by served all by itself, but even better in a pool of Raspberry Sauce (page 246), Mango Sauce (page 246), or Strawberry Sauce (page 248).

STORAGE: This trifle will keep overnight, but if stored any longer, the juices from the fruit will make the cake too soggy.

Pies, Tarts, and Fruit Desserts

Being an avid baker keeps me in intimately connected with the seasons because I'm always on the lookout for seasonal gems to turn into desserts. Sure, you can find ordinary apples in the spring and decent oranges in the summer, but fruits that are in season are not only plentiful and inexpensive (which appeals to my frugal side), they're also at their peak of ripeness and flavor (which appeals to my palate).

Fall, of course, means apples. Bins and bins of apples. And the good thing is that no matter where you live, it's pretty easy to find good-tasting local varieties. While supermarkets carry an impressive selection of shiny specimens that probably traveled a long way to get there, I like prowling the stalls at the farmers' market and seeing the wooden baskets piled with that week's haul. Even better is learning about some the old-fashioned varieties being revived by growers, many having been anointed with heirloom status.

Like apples, oranges are seasonal, although since we see them year-round, it's easy to forget that the best tangerines, lemons, and grapefruits shine their brightest during the winter. Their abundance is a good thing, since those juicy, colorful fruits can be a ray of sunshine during an otherwise bleak season—a reason why many European royals maintained *orangeries*, which kept their spirits bright when the temperatures dropped.

I know spring is here when I see crimson rhubarb stalks nudging winter's oranges and tangerines aside, clearing the way for the cascade of stone fruits that are ready to burst forward. Rhubarb was the first fruit (vegetable, actually) I learned to eat right from the earth: as a kid, I'd strip off the leaves and dip the stalks in a cup of sugar stolen from my mother's pantry and munch on the raw, puckery stalks. Now, I often bake with rhubarb, usually mixing it with the first berries of the year.

The summer's eventual cavalcade of peaches, nectarines, cherries, and berries soon arrive to the relief of all. From the moment I spy summer's first apricots until late-season plums are pushed aside by fall's earliest apples and pears, I'm always revved up for baking season by season.

···

Though most fresh fruits are wonderful eaten out of hand (I'll concede that uncooked rhubarb is an acquired taste), cooking intensifies and deepens their flavors. Depending on the season, you'll find me pulling an apple-pear crisp (page 101) with an especially crunchy polenta topping, a bubbling nectarine-berry cobbler (page 104) topped with big, fluffy biscuits, or a golden-crusted mixed berry pie (page 80) out of my oven.

Because produce varies, I've given fruit measurements in number and weight, and I've specified size as well. Most fruits and berries aren't grown in uniform sizes, nor is each one exactly like the other. If they are, they're likely not the kinds of fruits you want to be eating. It's hard to say what exactly is a "large apple," so when in doubt, use the weight measurement for a more accurate indication of how many or how much to use. Similarly, the peaches and plums that I use may be more, or less, sweet than the ones you're using, so feel free to add a sprinkle more sugar or hold back a spoonful as you see fit.

BERRY MEASUREMENTS: When shopping for berries for recipes in this book, keep in mind that a half-pint container of raspberries, blackberries, or blueberries contains about 1¼ cups of fruit and weighs about 6 ounces (170 g). Strawberries are usually sold in pint baskets that hold about 2½ cups of whole berries (2¼ cups sliced) and weigh close to 1 pound (450 g) each.

Banana Butterscotch Cream Pie

MAKES ONE 10-INCH (25-CM) PIE; 8 SERVINGS

I've been accused of peeling bananas incorrectly. Several people have pointed out that I, who always peel bananas from the stem end, do it wrong, and they advised me to peel them like monkeys do: by grasping the bottom of the fruit and pinching the banana open. To be honest, I found that it doesn't make all that much difference, especially when using the bananas in a dessert.

Peeling technique aside, this pie does differ from the usual butterscotch cream pie. I use homemade chocolate-cookie crumbs in the crust and make the filling with lots of dark brown sugar, which gives it a toffee-like creaminess that separates it from the jungle of other pies out there.

CRUST

1¹/₂ cups (180 g) crushed chocolate cookie crumbs (about 15 Flo's Chocolate Snaps, page 191)

3 tablespoons (45 g) sugar

4 tablespoons (2 ounces/60 g) unsalted or salted butter, melted

FILLING

1 cup (215 g) packed dark brown sugar

2 tablespoons (1 ounce/30 g) unsalted or salted butter

3 tablespoons (25 g) cornstarch

1¹/₂ cups (375 ml) whole milk

¹/₂ teaspoon salt

3 large egg yolks

2 teaspoons dark rum

¹/₂ teaspoon vanilla extract

3 ripe medium bananas

TOPPING

1 cup (250 ml) heavy cream

1 tablespoon sugar

2 tablespoons (30 ml) dark rum

¹/₂ teaspoon vanilla extract

Chocolate curls, for garnish (see page 8)

Preheat the oven to 350°F (175°C).

To make the crust, generously butter a 10-inch (25-cm) pie plate. In a medium bowl, mix together the chocolate cookie crumbs, the 3 tablespoons (45 g) sugar, and 4 tablespoons (2 ounces/60 g) melted butter until evenly moistened. Pat the mixture in an even layer into the bottom and up the sides of the buttered pie plate. Refrigerate or freeze for 30 minutes.

Bake the crust until if feels slightly firm, about 10 minutes. Let cool completely.

To make the filling, in a small saucepan, heat the brown sugar and the 2 tablespoons (1 ounce/30 g) butter, stirring, until the butter is melted. Pour into a large bowl, set a mesh strainer across the top, and set aside.

In a small bowl, whisk the cornstarch with just enough of the milk to make a smooth slurry. In a medium saucepan over medium heat, warm the remaining milk and the salt. When the milk is hot, stir the cornstarch mixture to recombine, then whisk it into the milk in the saucepan. Cook over medium heat, stirring constantly, until the mixture begins to boil and thickens. Whisk the egg yolks in a small bowl, then whisk a small amount of the hot thickened milk mixture into the yolks. Whisk the warmed egg-yolk mixture into the saucepan. Cook, stirring constantly, until the mixture returns to a boil and is as thick as mayonnaise. Pour it through the strainer into the butter–brown sugar mixture. Add the 2 teaspoons rum and ¹/₂ teaspoon vanilla and whisk until combined.

Peel and cut the bananas into slices ¹/₄ inch (6 mm) thick and scatter them in the bottom of the cooled crust. Pour the filling into the crust, cover with plastic wrap, and refrigerate until chilled, about 2 hours.

To make the topping, in a stand mixer fitted with the whip attachment (or in a bowl by hand), whisk the cream on high speed until it begins to mound softly. Add the 1 tablespoon sugar and 2 tablespoons rum and continue whisking until the cream holds peaks. Spread or pipe the topping over the pie. Garnish with chocolate curls.

STORAGE: The baked or unbaked crust can be refrigerated for up to 4 days, or frozen for up to 1 month. The pie can be refrigerated for up to 2 days, but whip the cream and top the pie with it a few hours before serving.

Lime-Marshmallow Pie

MAKES ONE 9-INCH (23-CM) PIE; 8 SERVINGS

When you have your own website, you develop a thick skin and come to expect all sorts of questions, including being asked advice about marketing $4,000 keepsake boxes for storing chocolate truffles ("Don't do it," I responded) to inquiries about preferred styles and brands of undergarments (that one didn't get answered).

This recipe was a topic in an online forum that I came across, and some fellow remarked, "Why would anyone make their own marshmallows? Or graham crackers?" While I wanted to respond, "Well, why would anyone make a hamburger from scratch? Or a salad?" I thought that not getting to taste this pie himself was punishment enough.

Personally, I can't think of anything more fun than making marshmallows and graham crackers, but if you'd prefer to take a few shortcuts, I've offered suggestions in Variation (page 78).

CRUST

1¼ cups (175 g) whole wheat flour

¾ teaspoon ground cinnamon

½ teaspoon ground ginger

⅛ teaspoon salt

5 tablespoons (2½ ounces/70 g) unsalted butter, cut into ½-inch (1.5-cm) pieces and chilled, plus 3 tablespoons (1½ ounces/45 g) unsalted butter, melted

2½ tablespoons (40 ml) honey

2 tablespoons (30 g) sugar

FILLING

½ cup (125 ml) freshly squeezed lime juice

½ cup (100 g) sugar

Pinch of salt

3 large eggs

2 large egg yolks

6 tablespoons (3 ounces/85 g) unsalted butter, cut into pieces

Grated zest of 2 limes, preferably organic

TOPPING

1 envelope (7 g) unflavored gelatin

¼ cup (60 ml) plus ⅓ cup (80 ml) cold water

⅓ cup (80 ml) light corn syrup

½ cup (100 g) sugar

3 large egg whites

1 teaspoon vanilla extract

Preheat the oven to 375°F (190°C). Line a baking sheet with parchment paper or a silicone baking mat. Generously butter a 9-inch (23-cm) pie plate.

To make the crust, in a stand mixer fitted with the paddle attachment (or in a bowl by hand), mix together the whole wheat flour, cinnamon, ginger, and ⅛ teaspoon salt on low speed until combined. Add the 5 tablespoons (2½ ounces/70 g) chilled butter pieces and mix on medium speed (or cut them in with a pastry blender) until the butter is in very small pieces about the size of grains of rice. Mix in the honey until the dough is smooth.

Transfer the dough to the prepared baking sheet and pat it into a circle about ⅛ inch (3 mm) thick. Bake until the cracker is golden brown and slightly firm to the touch, about 15 minutes. Let cool completely.

In a food processor fitted with the metal blade, process about three-quarters of the cracker to fine crumbs, or crush in a sturdy plastic bag with a rolling pin. Measure 1½ cups (180 g) crumbs into a small bowl. (You can snack on the rest of the cracker.)

Add the 2 tablespoons (30 g) sugar and 3 tablespoons (1½ ounces/45 g) melted butter to the cracker crumbs in the bowl and mix until evenly moistened. Pat the mixture evenly into the bottom and halfway up the sides of the buttered pie plate. Bake just until set, about 10 minutes. Let cool completely.

To make the filling, in a medium nonreactive saucepan, whisk together the lime juice, ½ cup (100 g) sugar, pinch of salt, eggs, egg yolks, 6 tablespoons (3 ounces/ 85 g) butter, and the lime zest. Cook over medium heat, stirring constantly, until the mixture thickens and the

(continued)

edges just barely begin to bubble. Don't let it boil. Pour the mixture through a mesh strainer into the crust. Bake until the filling is just set, about 8 minutes.

Remove the pie from the oven. Position a rack in the upper third of the oven and increase the oven temperature to 450°F (230°C).

To make the topping, in a small bowl, sprinkle the gelatin evenly over the $^1/_4$ cup (60 ml) cold water and allow it to soften and swell for 5 minutes.

In a small saucepan fitted with a candy thermometer, heat the remaining $^1/_3$ cup (80 ml) water with the corn syrup and $^1/_2$ cup (100 g) sugar over medium-high heat. When the sugar syrup reaches about 210°F (99°C), in a stand mixer fitter with the whip attachment, start whipping the egg whites. When the egg whites are frothy and the syrup temperature has climbed to 245°F (118°C), increase the speed to high and, with the mixer running, slowly dribble the syrup into the whites, being careful to avoid pouring hot syrup on the beater (the beater will fling the syrup onto the sides of the bowl, where it will stick).

Scrape the softened gelatin into the still-warm saucepan used to make the sugar syrup and stir until melted. With the mixer running, slowly drizzle the gelatin into the egg whites. Add the vanilla and continue to beat until the mixture is cooled to room temperature, 5 to 10 minutes.

Using a spatula, spread the topping over the filling, creating swirls and billowy peaks. Bake until the topping is golden brown, 2 to 4 minutes.

Serve at room temperature or chilled.

STORAGE: The graham cracker crumbs can be made up to 2 weeks in advance. The lime filling can be made up to 4 days in advance, and chilled.

VARIATION: You can also use store-bought graham crackers for the crumbs in the crust; you'll need $1^1/_2$ cups (180 g) crumbs. If you don't want to make your own marshmallow topping, top this pie with 2 cups of whipped cream (page 239).

> **TIP:** To cut clean slices of the pie, use a sharp serrated knife dipped in warm water and wiped dry after each cut.

Butternut Squash Pie

MAKES ONE 9- OR 10-INCH (23- OR 25-CM) PIE; 8 SERVINGS

Growing up in New England, I stayed as far away from pumpkin pie as possible. I did whatever I could to keep my distance from those dubious wedges of orangey-brown filling. For some reason, I just couldn't bring myself to try it. But when I did, later in my life, I mourned for all those opportunities I missed. (I wouldn't eat lobster either, which was cheap and plentiful back then. Talk about regrets!)

One thing I don't regret, though, is trying butternut squash in place of pumpkin in my pie. The cooked squash is naturally sweeter and thicker than pumpkin, and makes for a silkier pie. Note that in this recipe, the filling is added while still warm to the prebaked pie shell. This reduces the baking time for the pie and eliminates the problem of the crust burning while the filling bakes. You can make the filling in advance, but be sure to rewarm it gently before pouring it into the crust.

2 pounds (1 kg) butternut squash (1 medium or 2 small squashes), halved lengthwise, seeds and strings removed

1 cup (250 ml) heavy cream

$^1/_2$ cup (125 ml) whole milk

4 large eggs

$^3/_4$ cup (170 g) packed light or dark brown sugar

1 teaspoon ground ginger

1 teaspoon ground cinnamon

$^1/_4$ teaspoon ground cloves

$^1/_4$ teaspoon freshly ground black pepper

$^1/_4$ teaspoon freshly grated nutmeg

Pinch of salt

$^1/_2$ teaspoon vanilla extract

1 tablespoon Cognac or brandy

Pie dough, prebaked into a 9- or 10-inch single-crust pie shell (page 230)

Preheat the oven to 400°F (200°C). Line a baking sheet with parchment paper and smear the parchment generously with butter.

Place the squash halves cut sides down on the prepared baking sheet. Bake until the squash is fully tender and a sharp paring knife inserted into the thickest part meets no resistance, about 45 minutes. Remove from the oven and decrease the oven temperature to 375°F (190°C).

In a food processor fitted with a metal blade or in a blender, process the cream, milk, eggs, brown sugar, ginger, cinnamon, cloves, pepper, nutmeg, salt, vanilla, and Cognac or brandy until combined. Scoop out the warm squash pulp from the skin, measure out 2 cups (500 ml), and add it to the food processor or blender. Process until the mixture is smooth.

Pour the warm filling into the prebaked pie shell and bake until the filling is just barely set in the center (it should be slightly jiggly), 30 to 35 minutes. Don't over-bake the pie, as overbaking will cause the filling to crack while cooling.

SERVING: Some people like this pie warm, but I prefer it cold served with whipped cream (page 239) that's been spiced or flavored with brandy.

VARIATION: If you want to substitute canned pumpkin purée, use 2 cups (425 g) or one 15-ounce can. If you wish to use pumpkin that you cook and purée yourself, for the best results, choose a variety like sugar pumpkin that is low in moisture.

> TIP: Any extra butternut squash purée can be frozen and used for another recipe.

Mixed Berry Pie

MAKES ONE 9-INCH (23-CM) PIE; 8 SERVINGS

If you're as wild about berries as I am, you'll find that this pie is the height of luxury and one of the season's greatest treats. It's a dessert that I make only in the summer, at the moment when berries are abundant and at their peak. When I lived in San Francisco, I'd drive east across the bay to Monterey Market in Berkeley where flats of berries were so plentiful—and so inexpensive—that I found it impossible *not* to come home with at least a few piled up in my trunk. In addition to turning the berries into jams, compotes, and sorbets, I'd always bake this pie.

A total of 6 cups of berries makes up the filling—use whichever types you prefer. Unless you buy berries by the flat, like I did, most berries are sold in half-pint or pint baskets, so expect to have some leftover fruit, which I know you'll put to good use. I always did.

Pie dough (page 230)

2 cups (13 ounces/360 g) hulled and sliced strawberries

2 cups (10 ounces/270 g) blueberries

2 cups (10 ounces/270 g) blackberries

1/2 cup (100 g) sugar

2 tablespoons (20 g) tapioca flour or cornstarch

1 tablespoon freshly squeezed lemon juice or kirsch

1 large egg yolk

1 teaspoon whole milk or cream

1 tablespoon coarse-crystal or granulated sugar

Preheat the oven to 400°F (200°C).

Lightly flour a work surface and roll out one disk of dough into a 14-inch (36-cm) circle. Drape it into a 9-inch (23-cm) pie plate. Trim away the excess dough, leaving a slight overhang.

In a large bowl, gently mix the berries with the 1/2 cup (100 g) sugar, tapioca flour or cornstarch, and lemon juice or kirsch. Transfer the berry mixture to the dough-lined pie plate and distribute in an even layer.

Roll out the second dough disk into a 14-inch (36-cm) circle. Moisten the exposed edges of the dough in the pie plate with water, then drape the second dough circle over the top. Working all the way around the pie, tuck the upper dough edges under the lower dough edges and crimp to seal.

In a small bowl, whisk together the egg yolk and milk or cream. Brush the top crust generously with the egg wash and sprinkle with the 1 tablespoon coarse-crystal or granulated sugar. Pierce the top crust with a paring knife in 6 places.

Bake until the top crust is browned and the filling juices are thick and bubbling, 50 to 60 minutes. If the crust is browning too quickly, loosely drape a sheet of aluminum foil over the top during baking.

Let the pie cool for about 1 hour before serving.

SERVING: The pie is lovely with Vanilla Ice Cream (page 143) or Frozen Sour Cream (page 173).

> TIP: Have a sheet of foil on the lower rack in the oven during baking to help catch any dripping juices.

Concord Grape Pie

MAKES ONE 9-INCH (23-CM) PIE, 8 SERVINGS

The first time my parents took me to Disneyland, they probably assumed that they'd be spending the day racing after an energetic tyke who'd try to get on as many rides as possible. Instead of hitting all the main attractions, I discovered the Welch's grape-colored pavilion and begged my parents to let me spend the day there, chugging inky-purple Concord grape juice. I doubt the pavilion is still there, but it was the start of my lifelong love affair with this native American grape.

You might think seeding the quantity of grapes for this recipe would require a considerable amount of time. But I timed myself, and it took less than 30 minutes. Simply slice each grape in half and pluck out the seeds. If you have kids, you can get them to assist, although don't hold me responsible if any of them develops a grape addiction as a result.

4 cups (2 pounds/1 kg) Concord grapes, washed, stemmed, halved, and seeded

$1/2$ cup (100 g) granulated sugar

$3 1/2$ tablespoons (30 g) tapioca flour

Pie Dough (page 230)

1 large egg yolk

1 teaspoon whole milk or cream

2 tablespoons (30 g) coarse-crystal or granulated sugar

Preheat the oven to 400°F (200°C).

In a medium bowl, mix together the grapes, granulated sugar, and tapioca flour. Set aside.

Lightly flour a work surface and roll out one disk of dough into a 14-inch (36-cm) circle. Drape it into a 9-inch (23-cm) pie plate. Trim away the excess dough, leaving a slight overhang and distribute the grape mixture in the dough-lined pie plate.

Roll out the second dough disk into a 14-inch (36-cm) circle. Moisten the exposed edges of the dough in the pie plate with water, then drape the second dough circle over the top. Working all the way around the pie, tuck the upper dough edges under the lower dough edges and crimp to seal.

In a small bowl, whisk together the egg yolk and milk or cream. Brush the top crust generously with the egg wash and sprinkle with the coarse-crystal or granulated sugar. Pierce the top crust with a paring knife in 6 places.

Bake until the top crust is browned and the filling juices are thick and bubbling, 50 to 60 minutes. If the crust is browning too quickly, loosely drape a sheet of aluminum foil over the top during baking.

Let the pie cool for about 1 hour before serving.

SERVING: Don't expect to cut neat wedges of this pie. Vanilla Ice Cream (page 143) or whipped cream (page 239) are lovely accompaniments.

VARIATION: If you come across seedless Concord-style grapes at greenmarkets, you can use them, but be sure to halve them anyway, which breaks the skin and helps them soften during baking.

TIP: Tapioca flour is available at Asian markets or by mail order (see Resources, page 270). It makes a clear, glossy pie filling. Substitute an equal amount of cornstarch if tapioca flour is unavailable.

Peanut, Butter, and Jelly Linzertorte

MAKES ONE 9-INCH (23-CM) TART; 12 SERVINGS

I don't have an Austrian bone in my body, but there was just something about the beloved linzertorte, Austria's cross between a tart and a cake, that seemed ripe for an all-American adaptation. Traditionally, the crust is made with almonds and the filling is raspberry jam. But mine is made with peanuts and is filled with peanuts' natural partner: grape jelly. Delicious on its own, linzertorte needs no accompaniment.

1¹/₂ cups (210 g) all-purpose flour

1¹/₂ cups (225 g) roasted unsalted peanuts

³/₄ cup (150 g) sugar

1 teaspoon baking powder

1 teaspoon ground cinnamon

¹/₂ teaspoon salt

³/₄ cup (6 ounces/170 g) unsalted butter, cut into ¹/₂-inch (1.5-cm) pieces and chilled

1 large egg

1 large egg yolk

1¹/₄ cups (320 g) Concord grape jelly

Preheat the oven to 350°F (175°C). Butter the bottom of a 9-inch (23-cm) springform pan.

In a food processor fitted with the metal blade, pulse the flour, peanuts, sugar, baking powder, cinnamon, and salt until the peanuts are coarsely ground, but still slightly chunky. Add the butter pieces and continue to pulse until the mixture resembles coarse cornmeal. Add the egg and egg yolk and process until the dough comes together in a ball.

Transfer two-thirds of the dough to the prepared springform pan. Using your hands, press the dough evenly into the bottom and about 1¹/₂ inches (4 cm) up the sides of the pan. (If the dough is very sticky, lightly dampen your hands with water to help prevent the dough from sticking to them.) Spread the grape jelly evenly over the dough.

Lightly flour a work surface. Divide the remaining dough into 4 pieces and use your hands to roll each piece into a rope about 16 inches (40 cm) long. Cut the ropes into lengths to span the surface of the tart and arrange them on the jam filling, spacing them about 1 inch (3 cm) apart. Pinch off the ends of the ropes where they meet the sides of the pan. (Dough scraps can be rerolled into more ropes.) Arrange a second set of ropes on the tart, positioning them diagonally across the first ones, to create a lattice top. (It's not necessary to be too fussy or exact when forming the lattice; the dough will spread quite a lot during baking and flaws will disappear.)

Bake the linzertorte until the pastry is deep golden brown, about 40 minutes. Let cool completely. Run a knife around the sides of the linzertorte to help loosen it from the pan. Release the sides of the springform pan.

STORAGE: Linzertorte is actually better the second day and can be stored at room temperature for up to 1 week wrapped well in plastic wrap.

VARIATION: Substitute any kind of jam or jelly that you like. For those avoiding peanuts, almonds and hazelnuts are good substitutes in the crust.

Apple Tart with Whole Wheat Puff Pastry and Maple-Walnut Sauce

MAKES 8 SERVINGS

If you've never had whole wheat puff pastry before, you're in for a treat. While many people love the taste of the buttery layers of traditional puff pastry, adding whole wheat flour gives it a hearty, nutty taste that I find especially appealing when paired with apples. I also reason that the whole wheat balances out what some might consider an injudicious amount of butter in the dough.

This is a quick puff pastry, adapted from a technique I learned from Linda Zagula, that takes a fraction of the time and work required to make the traditional kind. It still takes six turns to roll it out, but you do the first four all at once, then the last two later. And the pastry recipe makes enough for two tarts, so you can wrap the extra piece and stash it away in the freezer, ready for the next tart.

PUFF PASTRY

2 cups (1 pound/450 g) unsalted butter, cut into
$^1/_2$-inch (1.5-cm) cubes

2 cups (280 g) all-purpose flour

$^3/_4$ cup (110 g) whole wheat flour

1 teaspoon salt

$^3/_4$ cup (180 ml) ice water

FILLING

3 medium apples ($1^1/_2$ pounds/675 g)

$1^1/_2$ tablespoons unsalted or salted butter, melted

2 tablespoons (30 g) granulated or coarse-crystal sugar

SAUCE

2 tablespoons (1 ounce/30 g) salted butter

$^1/_2$ cup (120 g) packed light brown sugar

$^1/_3$ cup (80 ml) maple syrup

2 tablespoons (30 ml) water

$^1/_2$ cup (50 g) walnuts, toasted and chopped

$^1/_4$ teaspoon ground cinnamon

1 teaspoon bourbon, or more to taste

To make the puff pastry, distribute the 2 cups (1 pound/450 g) unsalted butter cubes evenly onto a dinner plate or small baking sheet, separating them with your fingers, and freeze until cold and firm, at least 1 hour.

In a stand mixer fitted with the paddle attachment (or in a bowl by hand), mix together the all-purpose and whole wheat flours and the salt. Add the frozen butter pieces and mix on low speed (or with a pastry blender) until the edges of the butter pieces just begin to lose their sharpness, about 1 minute. Add the ice water and mix until the flour absorbs the water; the dough will look very ragged, with large pieces of butter relatively intact.

Turn the dough out onto a lightly floured work surface and knead with your hands a few times. Using your hands or a rolling pin, shape the dough into a 10 by 15-inch (25 by 38-cm) rectangle. The dough will not be at all smooth at this point, which is normal—and don't expect a perfect rectangle.

For the first turn, with the long side of the dough rectangle parallel with the counter's edge, fold the dough into thirds: the right third over the center, then fold the left third over to cover it. Rotate the dough clockwise one quarter turn so that the seam is closest to you. Lightly flour the work surface and again roll out the dough into a 10 by 15-inch (25 by 38-cm) rectangle.

For the second turn, again with the long side of the dough rectangle parallel with the counter's edge, fold the dough into thirds: the right third over the center, then fold the left third over to cover it. The edges of the dough should be close to being aligned; if they aren't, unfold the dough and refold it so they're parallel. Again rotate the dough clockwise one quarter turn so the seam is closest to you. Lightly flour the work surface and roll the dough into a 10 by 15-inch (25 by 38-cm) rectangle.

For the third and fourth turns, fold, rotate, roll out, then again fold the dough. Wrap the dough in plastic wrap and refrigerate for at least 2 hours.

Remove the dough from the refrigerator. For the fifth and sixth turns, roll out, fold, and rotate the dough two more times. Wrap the dough in plastic wrap, and refrigerate for at least 2 hours.

Preheat the oven to 400°F (200°C). Line a baking sheet with parchment paper.

To make the filling and assemble the tart, cut the chilled dough in half crosswise (you need only one half; see Storage for tips on keeping the remaining half). Lightly flour the work surface and roll out the dough half into a 12 by 15-inch (30 by 38-cm) rectangle. Transfer the dough rectangle to the prepared baking sheet. Brush water around the border, then fold in the edges and crimp by pressing down with a fork to make a decorative edge. Prick the bottom of the dough about 25 times with the fork.

Peel, quarter, and core the apples, and cut them into $1/4$-inch (6-mm) slices. Arrange the apple slices on the puff pastry in overlapping rows. Brush the apples with the $1^1/_2$ tablespoons melted butter and sprinkle them, and the crust, with the granulated or coarse-crystal sugar. Bake the tart until the apples are tender and beginning to brown, about 35 minutes.

While the tart bakes, make the sauce. In a small saucepan, bring the 2 tablespoons (1 ounce/30 g) salted butter, brown sugar, maple syrup, and water to a boil. Boil for 30 seconds, then remove from the heat. Mix in the walnuts, cinnamon, and bourbon. Taste and add more bourbon, if desired.

When the tart is ready, slide it off the parchment paper and onto a wire rack.

Cut the tart into squares and serve warm with generous spoonfuls of the sauce.

STORAGE: The tart is best the day it's made. The reserved puff pastry can be frozen for up to 2 months, if well wrapped. Defrost it, still wrapped, in the refrigerator overnight before rolling it out. Or, keep the dough in the refrigerator, but for no more than a day or two—any longer and it starts to discolor.

VARIATION: Instead of the maple-walnut sauce, try serving the tart with Cider Sabayon (page 238).

Apple-Quince Tarte Tatin

MAKES ONE 10-INCH (25-CM) TART; 8 SERVINGS

I love a good, classic version of tarte Tatin, the famed French caramelized-apple tart, as much as the next guy—probably even more. But adding slices of quince makes this variation extra inviting to me. If you're unfamiliar with quince, a cousin of the apple, it's likely because they're inedible in their raw state, so they tend to get neglected by folks who don't know about the seductive, beguiling flavor that's coaxed out of them by cooking.

Like apples, quince are in season in the fall, and they're easy to find by following your nose; when they're ripe, their scent is rather intoxicating. I often keep a bowl of them on my dining table to perfume my entire apartment.

TARTE TATIN DOUGH

1 cup (140 g) all-purpose flour

2 teaspoons sugar

$1/4$ teaspoon salt

4 tablespoons (2 ounces/60 g) unsalted butter cut into $1/2$-inch (1.5-cm) pieces and chilled

3 tablespoons (45 ml) ice water

FRUIT

8 medium apples (4 pounds/2 kg)

2 medium quinces (1 pound/450 g)

3 tablespoons ($1^1/2$ ounces/45 g) unsalted butter

$3/4$ cup (150 g) sugar

> TIP: Use a full-flavored apple, one that won't turn to mush during cooking. Winesap, Granny Smith, Northern Spy, Pippin, and Jonagold work well.

To make the dough, in a stand mixer fitted with the paddle attachment (or in a bowl with a pastry blender), mix together the flour, the 2 teaspoons sugar, and the salt. Add the 4 tablespoons (2 ounces/60 g) chilled butter pieces and keep mixing until the butter pieces are about the size of corn kernels. Add the ice water and mix until the dough comes together. Gather the dough and shape it into a disk, wrap it in plastic wrap, and refrigerate for at least 30 minutes.

To prepare the fruit and assemble the tart, peel, quarter, and core the apples. Peel, quarter, and core the quinces, then cut them into $1/4$-inch (6-mm) slices. Melt the 3 tablespoons ($1^1/2$ ounces/145 g) butter in a 10-inch (25-cm) cast iron skillet. Sprinkle the $3/4$ cup (150 g) sugar over the bottom of the pan and remove from the heat.

Pack the apples tightly in the pan, standing them on end, with the cored sides facing inward. It may seem like a lot of fruit, but they'll cook down considerably. Insert the quince slices between the apples.

Place the skillet on the stovetop and cook over medium heat until the juices thicken and become lightly caramelized, about 25 minutes. While they're cooking, press down on the apples to ease them into the pan and promote caramelization.

Preheat the oven to 375°F (190°C).

Lightly flour a work surface and roll out the dough into a 12-inch (30-cm) circle. Drape the dough over the apples in the skillet and tuck the edges down between the sides of the skillet and the apples.

Bake the tart until the pastry has browned, about 40 minutes. Remove from the oven and invert a serving plate over the skillet. Wearing long oven mitts, grasp both the skillet and the plate and turn them over together, away from you, to unmold the tart. Be careful of any hot juices that may spill out!

SERVING: Although purists say tarte Tatin is best served on its own, others appreciate a spoonful of crème fraîche or Vanilla Ice Cream (page 143) on top or alongside.

STORAGE: The dough can be made up to 2 days ahead and refrigerated, or frozen for up to 1 month. Tarte Tatin should be served warm the day it's made. You can make it an hour or so in advance and leave it on the serving plate, under the overturned skillet, to keep it warm after baking. It can also be rewarmed in a low oven.

VARIATION: Poaching the quince before assembling the tart will turn them a lovely ruby-red color and bring out even more flavor: In a medium saucepan, bring $1/2$ cup (100 g) sugar, $1^1/_2$ cups (375 ml) water, and a 2-inch (5-cm) piece of vanilla bean, split lengthwise, stirring to dissolve the sugar, then decrease the heat to maintain a simmer.

Peel, core, and cut the quinces into eighths. Put the pieces in the saucepan, cover with a circle of parchment paper cut to fit inside the pan, and simmer gently, covered, until tender, 30 to 60 minutes. Once poached, the quince can be kept in the refrigerator in the poaching liquid for up to 1 week. When assembling the tart, tuck the poached quince pieces between the apples. The poaching liquid can be reduced in a skillet until thick and syrupy, cooled slightly, and used as a sauce, if desired.

Apple-Frangipane Galette

MAKES 8 SERVINGS

A thin layer of frangipane, a rich almond pastry cream, elevates this simple, classic French dessert into something special. It's made in the style of many French fruit tarts: thin-crusted and only lightly sweetened to let the fruit truly shine.

Americans have eagerly adopted French-inspired freeform tarts, even giving them a French name, *galette*, a word that the French generally use to describe a round, squat pastry, cookie, or buckwheat crêpe. The most famous galette is *Galette des Rois*, two disks of puff pastry filled with frangipane and eaten on Epiphany. I considered calling this dessert a *tart*, but decided against it because that term can put off people who are worried about dealing with fussy doughs and trying to achieve picture-perfect results. This pastry is intended to be rustic, and for that reason, it's often my go-to galette. Or tart.

Speaking of tart, if your apples are particularly tart, you could sprinkle a bit more sugar on top of them before baking, but if you serve a sweet accompaniment alongside, as I usually do, additional sugar probably won't be necessary.

6 medium apples (3 pounds/1.5 kg)

Galette dough (page 231)

Frangipane (page 234)

2 tablespoons (1 ounce/30 g) unsalted or salted butter, melted

4 tablespoons (60 g) granulated or coarse-crystal sugar

Preheat the oven to 375°F (190°C). Line a baking sheet with parchment paper or a silicone baking mat.

Peel, core, and cut the apples into $1/2$-inch (1.5-cm) slices.

Lightly flour a work surface and roll out the dough into a circle about 14 inches (36 cm) in diameter. Transfer it to the prepared baking sheet.

Smear the frangipane over the dough, leaving a 2-inch (5-cm) border. Arrange the apple slices in concentric circles over the frangipane, or simply scatter them in an even layer. Fold the border of the dough over the apples and brush the crust with some of the melted butter, then lightly brush or dribble the rest of the butter over the apples. Sprinkle half of the sugar over the crust, and the remaining half over the apples.

Bake the galette until the apples are tender and the crust has browned, about 1 hour. Slide the galette off the parchment paper and onto a wire rack.

SERVING: Serve warm or at room temperature. You can drizzle the galette with warm honey or glaze it with strained apricot jam, thinned with just enough water to make it spreadable. Vanilla Ice Cream (page 143), Cider Sabayon (page 238), or crème fraîche are all fine accompaniments.

STORAGE: The dough can be made up to 3 days in advance and refrigerated. The tart should be served the day it's baked.

VARIATION: For a NECTARINE-FRANGIPANE GALETTE, substitute 3 large nectarines ($1^3/4$ pounds/ 795 g), pitted and cut in $1/2$-inch (1.5-cm) slices, for the apples. (If you want the nectarines to have a very pronounced flavor in the tart, decrease the amount of frangipane; you can use as little as one-half the quantity, or about $1/2$ cup/125 ml). Arrange the necctarine slices in barely overlapping concentric circles. You can use peeled peaches in place of the nectarines.

Apple–Red Wine Tart

MAKES ONE 10-INCH (25-CM) TART; 8 SERVINGS

This is an unusual tart. Not just for its brilliant red color, but for how it takes people by surprise when it's turned out onto a serving platter. Be sure to plan in advance, as the apples really benefit from marinating in the red wine for at least one day, although two days of steeping gives them the best color. You'll find the tart worth the wait.

8 firm medium apples (4 pounds/2 kg), such as Pippin, Granny Smith, or Golden Delicious

3/4 cup (150 g) sugar

1 bottle (750 ml) fruity red wine, such as Zinfandel or Merlot

Tarte Tatin Dough (page 86)

Peel, core, and cut the apples into 3/4-inch (2-cm) slices. In a large nonreactive bowl or container, toss the apple slices with the sugar. Pour the red wine over, cover, and refrigerate for 24 to 48 hours. During that time, stir the mixture a few times so that all the slices get evenly saturated with the wine.

Drain the red wine from the apples into a 10-inch (25-cm) nonreactive skillet (don't use cast iron). Simmer the wine over medium-high heat until thickened and reduced to about 1/3 cup (80 ml). Remove from the heat and measure out a few tablespoons of the wine syrup into a small bowl and reserve for glazing the baked tart. Heap the apples in the skillet with the remaining wine syrup and press them down to even them out.

Preheat the oven to 375°F (190°C).

Lightly flour a work surface and roll out the dough into a 12-inch (30-cm) circle. Drape the dough over the apples in the skillet and tuck the edges down between the skillet and the apples.

Bake until the pastry has browned and the apples are tender when poked with a paring knife through the pastry, about 1 hour. Let cool about 10 minutes. If there appears to be an excessive amount of liquid, carefully tilt the pan over a bowl to drain some of it off (you can reduce it to a syrupy consistency for additional sauce or glaze).

Invert a serving plate over the skillet. Wearing long oven mitts, grasp both the skillet and the plate and turn them over together, away from you, to unmold the tart. Be careful of any hot juices that may spill out! Brush the tart with the reserved wine syrup.

SERVING: Serve warm with crème fraîche or Vanilla Ice Cream (page 143).

STORAGE: The dough can be made up to 2 days ahead and refrigerated, or frozen up to 2 months. The tart should be served warm, the same day it's made. You can make it and leave it on the serving plate, under the overturned skillet, to keep it warm for about 1 hour before serving. It can also be rewarmed in a low oven. In either case, the tart should be glazed right before it is presented.

Pear Tart with Brown Butter, Rum, and Pecans

MAKES ONE 9-INCH (23-CM) TART; 8 TO 10 SERVINGS

If you've never made brown butter, it's simple. You put butter in a pan and cook it until it develops the wonderful nutty aroma for which the French named it: *beurre noisette*, or hazelnut butter. Here, custard flavored with brown butter provides a rich background for a tart filled with dark rum–spiked pears and toasted pecans.

CUSTARD

3 large eggs

$1/4$ cup (35 g) all-purpose flour

$3/4$ cup (150 g) granulated sugar

$1/4$ teaspoon salt

$1/2$ teaspoon vanilla extract

3 tablespoons (45 ml) dark rum

10 tablespoons (5 ounces/140 g) unsalted butter, cut into pieces

$1/2$ cup pecans (50 g), toasted and very coarsely chopped

PEARS

2 medium pears (1 pound/450 g)

2 tablespoons (30 g) packed dark or light brown sugar

1 tablespoon dark rum

Prebaked tart shell (page 229)

To make the custard, in a medium bowl, whisk together the eggs, flour, granulated sugar, salt, vanilla, and the 3 tablespoons (45 ml) rum.

In a large skillet, warm the butter over low heat. It will bubble and sizzle for a while before it settles down. Continue to cook over low heat until the butter darkens to the color of maple syrup and smells toasty but not burnt. Quickly and vigorously whisk it into the egg mixture, leaving behind any black sediment in the pan. Stir in the pecans. Refrigerate the custard mixture until chilled and thickened, about 1 hour.

To prepare the pears, peel, quarter, and core the pears, then cut them into slices $1/4$ inch (6 mm) thick. In a medium bowl, toss the pear slices with the brown sugar and the 1 tablespoon dark rum and let macerate for 15 minutes, tossing frequently to coat the slices.

Preheat the oven to 375°F (190°C).

To assemble the tart, set the prebaked tart shell on a baking sheet. Arrange the pear slices in concentric circles in the tart shell. Pour the custard over the pears, filling the tart to the rim, but don't overfill it.

Bake the tart on the baking sheet until browned, about 30 minutes. Let cool completely.

Remove the tart pan sides by setting the tart on an overturned bowl or other tall, wide surface (a large can of tomatoes works well). Gently press down on the outer ring and let the ring fall to the countertop. Set the tart on a flat surface. Release the tart from the pan bottom by sliding the blade of a knife between the crust and the pan bottom, then slip the tart onto a serving plate. (If it doesn't release cleanly, simply serve the tart on the pan bottom.)

SERVING: This tart can be served on its own or with whipped cream (page 239) flavored with pear eau-de-vie or dark rum. I sometimes serve slices with a scribble of Bittersweet Chocolate Sauce (page 243) or with a scoop of Chocolate Gelato (page 146).

STORAGE: The custard can be made up to 3 days ahead and refrigerated. The tart is best the day it's made, though it will keep for up to 2 days in the refrigerator. Let it come to room temperature before serving.

> TIP: To protect yourself from splatters, invert a strainer or colander over the butter while it's browning.

Brazil Nut, Date, and Fresh Ginger Tart

MAKES ONE 9-INCH (23-CM) TART; 8 SERVINGS

I tried to explain to some French pals what a "treehugger" is, a term that we Americans jokingly use to refer to a person who participates in well-intentioned earth-saving activities. Judging from my friends' baffled expressions, the meaning got lost in translation. There are now a few French people wandering around scratching their heads, puzzled about nutty Americans with a penchant for wrapping their arms around tree trunks.

I'm guilty of hugging a few trees myself. I read that using Brazil nuts is something positive that we can do to help sustain the rain forests, so I came up with this tart, which is packed full of them. I can't say you'll feel better about saving the planet if you make it, but anyone who doesn't give it a try is, in my opinion, definitely nuts.

4 large egg yolks

1¹/₂ cups (335 g) packed light brown sugar

4 tablespoons (2 ounces/60 g) unsalted butter, melted

¹/₄ cup (60 ml) heavy cream or whole milk

1 tablespoon all-purpose flour

1¹/₂ tablespoons peeled and grated fresh ginger

¹/₄ teaspoon salt

12 large dates, pitted and quartered

1¹/₂ cups (225 g) Brazil nuts, toasted and coarsely chopped

Prebaked tart shell (page 229)

Preheat the oven to 350°F (175°C).

In a medium bowl, whisk together the egg yolks, brown sugar, butter, cream or milk, flour, ginger, and salt until smooth. Stir in the date pieces and Brazil nuts until combined.

Set the prebaked tart shell on a baking sheet and pour in the filling. Bake the tart on the baking sheet until the top is uniformly deep brown and the filling is set (it shouldn't jiggle when you gently shake the tart), 35 to 40 minutes. Let cool completely.

Remove the tart pan sides by setting the tart on an overturned bowl or other tall, wide surface (a large can of tomatoes works well). Gently press down on the outer ring and let the ring fall to the countertop. Set the tart on a flat surface. Release the tart from the pan bottom by sliding the blade of a knife between the crust and the pan bottom, then slip the tart onto a serving plate. (If it doesn't release cleanly, simply serve the tart on the pan bottom.)

SERVING: Serve with whipped cream (page 239) or a drizzle of Bittersweet Chocolate Sauce (page 243) spiked with rum.

STORAGE: The filling can be made up to 4 days in advance and refrigerated.

VARIATION: To add coconut flavor to this tart, substitute 1¹/₂ cups (340 g) softened or grated palm sugar (available in Asian markets) for the brown sugar and replace the cream or whole milk with Thai coconut milk.

Easy Marmalade Tart

MAKES ONE 9-INCH (23-CM TART); 10 SERVINGS

I once found a long-forgotten jar of homemade quince marmalade in the back of my refrigerator. Rather than throw it out, I took it with me to a friend's house out in the country with the hope that one morning I could slip it onto the breakfast table and no one would be the wiser. But I was so mesmerized by the gorgeous rosy hue of the quince preserves that, instead, I used the marmalade as a filling for this amazingly easy-to-make jam tart.

The tart is easy for a couple of reasons. The first is that there is no filling to make or fruit to cut up—any type of thick jam or marmalade, homemade or otherwise, is all you'll need. The second is that the dough doesn't require rolling: two-thirds of it is pressed into the tart pan, and the rest is formed into a log, sliced like refrigerator cookie dough, then layered onto the tart to create the top crust.

Truly a piece of cake to make, this tart serves as a wonderful breakfast pastry. In the end, the marmalade did indeed make an early (well, not *too* early) morning appearance on the table, and I didn't have to be sneaky about it.

1^1/$_2$ cups (210 g) all-purpose flour

^{1}/$_2$ cup (70 g) stone-ground cornmeal or polenta

2 teaspoons baking powder

^{1}/$_2$ teaspoon salt

9 tablespoons (4^1/$_2$ ounces/130 g) unsalted butter, at room temperature

^{1}/$_2$ cup (100 g) granulated sugar

1 large egg

1 large egg yolk

^{1}/$_8$ teaspoon almond extract

1^3/$_4$ cups (450 g) Quince Marmalade (page 260) or other marmalade or jam

2 tablespoons (30 g) coarse-crystal or granulated sugar

In a small bowl, whisk together the flour, cornmeal or polenta, baking powder, and salt.

In a stand mixer fitted with the paddle attachment (or in a bowl by hand), beat together the butter and ^{1}/$_2$ cup (100 g) granulated sugar on medium speed just until smooth. Add the egg, egg yolk, and almond extract and beat until combined. With the mixer running, gradually add the flour mixture and mix just until the dough comes together.

Transfer about one-third of the dough to a lightly floured work surface and shape it into a log about 2 inches (5 cm) in diameter. Wrap it in plastic wrap and refrigerate until needed.

Transfer the remaining dough to a 9-inch (23-cm) tart pan with a removable bottom or a 9-inch (23-cm) spring-form pan. Using your hands, press the dough evenly into the bottom. If using a tart pan, press the dough up the sides to the rim of the pan and set the tart pan on a baking sheet; if using a springform pan, press the dough about ^{3}/$_4$ inch (2 cm) up the sides of the pan. Refrigerate the dough-lined pan until firm, at least 1 hour.

Preheat the oven to 375°F (190°C).

Spread the marmalade or jam evenly over the dough in the pan. Cut the chilled dough log into disks ^{1}/$_3$ inch (8 mm) thick and lay them in an even layer over the jam to form a top crust. Sprinkle evenly with the 2 table-spoons (30 g) coarse-crystal or granulated sugar. Bake until the top crust is golden brown, about 25 minutes. Let cool completely.

If you've used a tart pan, remove the tart pan sides by setting the cooled tart on an overturned bowl or other tall, wide surface (a large can of tomatoes works well). Gently press down on the outer ring and let the ring fall to the countertop. Set the tart on a flat surface. Release the tart from the pan bottom by sliding the blade of a knife between the crust and the pan bottom, then slip the tart onto a serving plate. (If it doesn't release cleanly, simply serve the tart on the pan bottom.) If you've used a springform pan, simply release the sides.

STORAGE: This tart keeps beautifully for up to 3 days if well wrapped. It's pretty sturdy, so it'd be perfect to take along on a picnic.

Freestyle Lemon Tartlets with White Chocolate Sauce

MAKES SIX 5-INCH (12-CM) TARTLETS

I never would have thought of pairing white chocolate with lemon. My first taste of the combination was in the form of a slice of a towering lemon pie with white chocolate sauce at a restaurant in San Francisco. The second was in a filling made of the two enrobed as a neat square of chocolate at Theo Chocolate in Seattle. I didn't need any more convincing that the pair is delicious match. My third experience with the combination was making these tartlets, and they were a charm as well.

Although I'm happy to share my recipes, I'm not so big on sharing desserts, so I made these tartlets in individual portions. You can swirl each plate with the white chocolate sauce or, if you're better at sharing than I am, you can pass a bowl of it at the table.

FILLING

$1/2$ cup (125 ml) freshly squeezed lemon juice

$1/3$ cup (65 g) sugar

6 tablespoons (3 ounces/85 g) unsalted or salted butter, cut into pieces

Grated zest of 2 lemons, preferably organic

2 large eggs

2 large egg yolks

DOUGH

$1^1/4$ cups (175 g) all-purpose flour

2 teaspoons sugar

$1/2$ teaspoon salt

5 tablespoons ($2^1/2$ ounces/70 g) unsalted butter cut into $1/2$-inch (1.5-cm) pieces and chilled

$1/4$ cup (60 ml) ice water

MERINGUE

5 large egg whites

$1/4$ teaspoon cream of tartar (optional)

Pinch of salt

10 tablespoons (135 g) sugar

1 teaspoon vanilla extract

White Chocolate Sauce (page 244)

To make the filling, set a mesh strainer over a medium bowl or container. In a medium nonreactive saucepan, whisk together the lemon juice, 1/3 cup (65 g) sugar, 6 tablespoons (3 ounces/85 g) butter, lemon zest, eggs, and egg yolks. Cook over medium heat, stirring constantly, until the mixture thickens and the edges just barely begin to bubble. Don't let the mixture boil. Pour the filling through the strainer. Let cool, then cover and refrigerate until chilled.

To make the dough, in a stand mixer fitted with the paddle attachment, mix together the flour, 2 teaspoons sugar, and 1/2 teaspoon salt on low speed until combined. Add the 5 tablespoons (2 1/2 ounces/70 g) chilled butter pieces and beat on medium speed until the butter pieces are about the size of corn kernels. Add the ice water and mix until the dough just begins to hold together.

Transfer the dough to a work surface, form it into log about 5 inches (12 cm) long, wrap in plastic wrap, and refrigerate until firm, at least 30 minutes.

Preheat the oven to 350°F (175°C). Line a baking sheet with parchment paper or a silicone baking mat.

Slice the chilled dough log into 6 equal pieces. Lightly flour a work surface and roll out each piece into a 5-inch (12-cm) circle. Place the circles on the prepared baking sheet, spacing them evenly. Bake until golden brown, 20 to 25 minutes. Let cool completely.

Increase the oven temperature to 450°F (230°C).

To make the meringue, in a clean, dry bowl of the stand mixer fitted with the whip attachment, whisk the egg whites on low speed until frothy. Add the cream of tartar, if using, and the pinch of salt, then increase the speed to high and continue to whisk until the whites begin to form soft, drooping peaks when the beater is lifted. With the mixer running, gradually add the 10 tablespoons (135 g) sugar, then the vanilla, and continue to whisk until the meringue forms stiff peaks.

To finish the tartlets, divide the lemon filling evenly among the baked pastry disks, mounding it in the center and leaving a 1-inch (3-cm) border around the edges. Spoon the meringue onto the tartlets, dividing it evenly and covering the filling, then create decorative swirls and peaks. Bake until the meringue is golden brown, about 5 minutes.

Serve the tarts warm from the oven or at room temperature, with the white chocolate sauce drizzled onto individual plates or passed in a bowl on the side.

STORAGE: The filling and the dough can both be made up to 4 days in advance and refrigerated until needed. The tarts should be served the same day they're made.

Fresh Fig and Raspberry Tart with Honey

MAKES ONE 9-INCH (23-CM) TART; 8 SERVINGS

The first time I saw a fresh fig was nearly three decades ago when I was living in upstate New York. I had no idea what it was. Then I moved to California and saw them everywhere. I can't say for sure that fresh figs were the reason I stayed put there for so long, but they certainly were one of them.

DOUGH

1 cup (140 g) all-purpose flour

$^1/_2$ cup (40 g) sliced blanched almonds

$^1/_2$ cup (100 g) sugar

$^1/_2$ teaspoon salt

6 tablespoons (3 ounces/85 g) unsalted butter, cut into $^1/_2$-inch (1.5-cm) pieces and chilled

2 large egg yolks

$^3/_4$ teaspoon almond extract

FILLING

$^1/_4$ cup (65 g) raspberry jam (with seeds or seedless)

12 ripe fresh figs

$1^1/_4$ cups (6 ounces/170 g) raspberries

3 tablespoons (45 ml) honey, warmed

To make the dough, in a food processor fitted with the metal blade, grind the flour, almonds, sugar, and salt until the almonds are very fine and powdery. Add the butter and pulse until the butter is in very small pieces about the size of grains of rice. Add the egg yolks and the almond extract, then let the machine run until the dough starts to come together. Transfer the dough to a work surface, knead it briefly with your hands until smooth, press the dough into a disk.

Very lightly butter a 9-inch (23-cm) tart pan with a removable bottom, or use one with a nonstick coating. Transfer the dough disk to the pan. Using your hands, press the dough as evenly as possible into the bottom and up the sides of the pan. Freeze the dough-lined tart pan for at least 30 minutes.

Preheat the oven to 375°F (190°C).

Set the tart pan on a baking sheet and prick the frozen tart dough about 10 times with a fork. Line the dough with a sheet of aluminum foil and fill with pie weights or dried beans. Bake the tart shell on the baking sheet until the dough is set, about 20 minutes. Remove the foil and pie weights and continue to bake until the tart shell is deep golden brown, about 10 minutes more. Let cool completely.

To fill the tart, spread the raspberry jam in an even layer in the bottom of the cooled tart shell. Trim the hard stem ends from the figs and quarter them lengthwise. Arrange the figs in the tart shell in 2 concentric circles, cut sides up, fitting them snugly against the sides of the tart shell and each other. Arrange the raspberries snugly in the center. Drizzle the warm honey over the tart.

Remove the tart pan sides by setting the tart on an overturned bowl or other tall, wide surface (a large can of tomatoes works well). Gently press down on the outer ring and let the ring fall to the countertop. Set the tart on a flat surface. Release the tart from the pan bottom by sliding the blade of a knife between the crust and the pan bottom, then slip the tart onto a serving plate. (If it doesn't release cleanly, simply serve the tart on the pan bottom.)

SERVING: Serve the tart in wedges, just as it is, or with Frozen Nougat (page 177) or Champagne Sabayon (page 238).

STORAGE: This tart is best the day it is assembled.

> TIP: Buy only fresh figs that are positively ripe, as they don't ripen once they're picked. The best-tasting, ripest figs will be splitting at the seams with a bit of sap-like nectar exuding from the blossom end.

Apricot-Marzipan Tart

MAKES ONE 9-INCH (23-CM) TART; 8 SERVINGS

Friend and fellow baker Dede Wilson presented me with a slice of this tart after she made it on television. Believe me, if every viewer could have tasted it, ratings would've gone through the roof!

The name of this tart is a little deceptive, just as television sometimes is. The recipe calls for almond paste, not marzipan, as the title suggests. (Marzipan is almond paste's sweeter cousin that's used for molding and modeling.) Yes, Dede took some liberties when she named her creation, but no matter what it's called, this tart is renewed season after season in my kitchen.

DOUGH

1 cup (140 g) flour

$^{1}/_{2}$ cup (40 g) sliced unblanched almonds

$^{1}/_{4}$ cup (50 g) granulated sugar

$^{1}/_{8}$ teaspoon salt

$^{1}/_{2}$ cup (4 ounces/115 g) unsalted butter, cut into $^{1}/_{2}$-inch (1.5-cm) pieces and chilled

1 large egg yolk

FILLING

$^{1}/_{2}$ cup (70 g) flour

$^{1}/_{3}$ cup (70 g) packed light brown sugar

3 ounces (85 g) almond paste, crumbled

$^{1}/_{4}$ cup (20 g) sliced unblanched or blanched almonds

4 tablespoons (2 ounces/60 g) unsalted butter, cut into $^{1}/_{2}$-inch (1.5-cm) pieces and chilled

12 to 14 fresh apricots (about $1^{1}/_{4}$ pounds/565 g)

1 tablespoon cornstarch

$^{1}/_{4}$ cup (50 g) granulated sugar

To make the dough, in a food processor fitted with the metal blade, pulse the 1 cup (140 g) flour, $^{1}/_{2}$ cup (40 g) sliced almonds, $^{1}/_{4}$ cup (50 g) granulated sugar, and the salt until the nuts are finely ground. Add the chilled butter pieces and pulse until the mixture resembles coarse meal. Add the egg yolk and process until the dough comes together.

Transfer the dough to a 9-inch (23-cm) tart pan with a removable bottom. (There's no need to wash the bowl of the food processor—you'll need it again to make the filling.) Using your hands, press the dough as evenly as possible into the bottom and up the sides of the pan. Refrigerate the dough-lined tart pan until the dough is firm, at least 1 hour.

Preheat the oven to 400°F (200°C).

Set the tart pan on a baking sheet and prick the dough about a dozen times with a fork. Bake the tart shell on the baking sheet until deep golden brown, about 20 minutes. If it puffs up during baking, press it down with the back of a metal spatula. Let cool while making the filling. Decrease the oven temperature to 375°F (190°C).

To make the filling, in a food processor fitted with the metal blade, pulse together the $^{1}/_{2}$ cup (70 g) flour, brown sugar, almond paste, and $^{1}/_{4}$ cup (20 g) sliced almonds until the almond paste is broken into fine pieces. Add the 4 tablespoons (2 ounces/60 g) chilled butter and pulse until the butter pieces are about the size of corn kernels. Set aside.

Halve, pit, and cut the apricots into $^{1}/_{2}$-inch (1.5-cm) slices. In a large bowl, toss the apricots with the cornstarch and $^{1}/_{4}$ cup (50 g) sugar. Distribute the apricot slices in the tart shell and sprinkle them evenly with the almond mixture. Bake until the fruit is bubbling and the topping is golden brown, about 30 minutes.

Serve the tart warm or at room temperature.

VARIATIONS: For **RASPBERRY, APRICOT, AND MARZIPAN TART**, add 1 cup (5 ounces/135 g) raspberries to the apricots. To make **PLUM-MARZIPAN TART**, substitute plums for the apricots and increase the cornstarch to 1 tablespoon plus 1 teaspoon.

Cherry-Almond Cobbler

MAKES 6 TO 8 SERVINGS

My friend Cindy Meyers, who tested many of the recipes in this book and my two previous ones, wrote me, excitedly, that this dessert was her favorite of all that she tested. "The almond topping is so fluffy!" she commented. Considering she's someone that I look to for criticism, when praise comes forth, I'm flattered.

FILLING

6 cups (2^1/$_4$ pounds/1 kg) sweet cherries, pitted

2 tablespoons (30 g) sugar

Juice of ^{1}/$_2$ lemon

TOPPING

1 cup (140 g) all-purpose flour

1^1/$_2$ teaspoons baking powder

^{1}/$_2$ teaspoon salt

7 ounces (200 g) almond paste, crumbled

^{1}/$_3$ cup (65 g) sugar

^{1}/$_2$ cup (4 ounces/115 g) unsalted butter,
    at room temperature

1 large egg, at room temperature

^{1}/$_2$ teaspoon vanilla or almond extract

^{1}/$_2$ cup (125 ml) whole milk

Preheat the oven to 350°F (175°C).

To make the filling, in a shallow 2-quart (2-liter) baking dish, toss the pitted cherries with the 2 tablespoons (30 g) sugar and the lemon juice.

To make the topping, in a small bowl, whisk together the flour, baking powder, and salt.

In a stand mixer fitted with the paddle attachment, beat together the almond paste and ^{1}/$_3$ cup (65 g) sugar on medium speed until the almond paste is broken into fine pieces. Beat in the butter, then the egg and vanilla or almond extract. Add half of the flour mixture, followed by the milk, then the remaining flour mixture, mixing just until combined.

Spoon the batter evenly over the cherries in the baking dish. Bake until the topping is golden brown and a toothpick inserted into the center of the topping comes out clean, about 45 minutes.

SERVING: Serve the cobbler warm or at room temperature with whipped cream (page 239), Vanilla Ice Cream (page 143), or White Chocolate–Ginger Ice Cream (page 149).

VARIATIONS: For MANGO, BLACKBERRY, AND ALMOND COBBLER; make a filling with 5 pounds (2.5 kg) mangoes, peeled, pitted, and cubed; 2^1/$_2$ cups (12 ounces/340 g) blackberries; 2 tablespoons (30 g) packed light or dark brown sugar; ^{1}/$_2$ teaspoon vanilla extract; and the juice of 1 lemon. To Make MIXED BERRY–ALMOND COBBLER; substitute 6 cups (about 1^3/$_4$ pounds/795 g) mixed berries for the cherries. For CHERRY, APRICOT, AND ALMOND COBBLER; substitute 1 pound (450 g) apricots, pitted and cut into eighths, for half of the cherries.

Apple-Pear Crisp with Grappa-Soaked Raisins and Polenta Topping

MAKES 8 SERVINGS

I'm a big fan of fruit crisps. When I worked at Chez Panisse, I learned I wasn't alone—they were more popular than our signature dark chocolate cake. But I'm not entirely convinced that I'd choose a fruit crisp over chocolate cake. Maybe I'd order both in the name of research.

This fruit crisp topping, made with crunchy polenta, stands up well to the juiciest mélange of fruits. Here, I mix apples and pears, and it may seem like a lot of fruit when you're doing all that peeling and slicing, but it cooks down considerably during baking. Use a good baking apple, such as Gravenstein, Winesap, Pippin, Northern Spy, or Cortland.

FILLING

$^3/_4$ cup (120 g) raisins

3 tablespoons (45 ml) grappa

4 medium apples (about 2 pounds/1 kg)

6 medium ripe pears (about 2 pounds/1 kg)

$^1/_3$ cup (65 g) granulated sugar

$1^1/_2$ teaspoons vanilla extract

TOPPING

$^3/_4$ cup (110 g) all-purpose flour

$^1/_2$ cup (50 g) walnuts, almonds, or pecans, toasted

$^1/_2$ cup (120 g) packed light brown sugar

$^2/_3$ cup (100 g) polenta or stone-ground cornmeal

1 teaspoon ground cinnamon

$^1/_2$ cup (4 ounces/115 g) unsalted or salted butter, cut into pieces and chilled

To make the filling, in a large bowl, combine the raisins and grappa and let stand until most of the grappa has been absorbed, about 1 hour.

Preheat the oven to 375°F (190°C).

Peel and core the apples and pears and cut them into $^1/_3$-inch (8-mm) slices. Add the apple and pear slices to the grappa-soaked raisins along with the granulated sugar and vanilla. Toss well, then pack the mixture firmly into a 2-quart (2-liter) baking dish.

To make the topping, in a food processor fitted with the metal blade, pulse the flour, nuts, brown sugar, polenta or cornmeal, and cinnamon a few times to combine. Add the butter pieces and pulse until the butter is finely broken up. Continue to pulse until the mixture just begins to clump together.

Scatter the topping evenly over the fruit. Bake until the topping is nicely browned and the fruit is tender (a sharp paring knife inserted into the center meets no resistance), about 50 minutes.

SERVING: Serve the crisp warm with a pitcher of cold heavy cream or scoops of Vanilla Ice Cream (page 143).

STORAGE: The polenta topping can be made ahead and refrigerated for up to 1 week or frozen for up to 2 months.

VARIATIONS: If you're avoiding alcohol, you can skip macerating the raisins. You can substitute dried cranberries or diced prunes for the raisins.

To make an **APPLE-BLACKBERRY CRISP**, in place of the grappa-soaked raisins, use $1^1/_4$ cups (6 ounces/170 g) blackberries; increase the apples to 8 medium (4 pounds/2 kg); omit the pears; and use $^1/_4$ cup (50 g) granulated sugar and 1 teaspoon vanilla extract.

> **TIP:** While the crisp bakes, have a sheet of aluminum foil on the oven rack below the crisp to catch any overflow of juices.

Peach-Amaretti Crisp

MAKES 8 SERVINGS

With such a strong almond-like flavor, it makes sense to think that authentic Italian amaretti cookies are made with almonds. But, in fact, it's apricot kernels that give them their robust, nutlike bite. Whatever the source of their flavor, amaretti cookies have a remarkable affinity for stone fruits such as peaches. I often double (or triple) the recipe for this topping and freeze the leftover in a zippered plastic bag. That way, I have some on hand and can bake up a crisp at a moment's notice.

FILLING

8 medium peaches (about 3 pounds/1.5 kg)

2 tablespoons (30 g) granulated sugar

1 tablespoon all-purpose flour

1 teaspoon vanilla extract or $^1/_2$ teaspoon almond extract

TOPPING

$^3/_4$ cup (110 g) all-purpose flour

$^1/_4$ cup (50 g) granulated sugar

$^1/_2$ cup (120 g) packed light brown sugar

$^3/_4$ cup (90 g) crushed amaretti (about 16 cookies; page 215)

1 teaspoon ground cinnamon

$^1/_2$ cup (65 g) almonds, toasted

$^1/_2$ cup (4 ounces/115 g) unsalted butter, cut into $^1/_2$-inch (1.5-cm) pieces and chilled

Preheat the oven to 375°F (190°C).

To make the filling, peel, pit, and cut the peaches into $^1/_2$-inch (1.5-cm) slices. In a large bowl, toss the peaches with the 2 tablespoons (30 g) granulated sugar, 1 tablespoon flour, and vanilla or almond extract. Transfer the peaches to a shallow 2-quart (2-liter) baking dish. Set aside.

To make the topping, in a food processor fitted with the metal blade, pulse together the $^3/_4$ cup (110 g) flour, $^1/_4$ cup (50 g) granulated sugar, brown sugar, amaretti crumbs, cinnamon, and almonds until the almonds are in small bits but with chunks still visible. Add the chilled butter pieces and pulse until the topping no longer looks sandy and is just beginning to hold together.

Distribute the topping evenly over the peaches. Bake until the filling is bubbling around the edges and a sharp paring knife inserted into the center of the cobbler meets no resistance, 40 to 50 minutes.

SERVING: Serve warm or at room temperature with Vanilla Ice Cream (page 143) or just a pour of fresh, cold cream.

VARIATION: For a MIXED BERRY CRISP, make the filling using 6 cups ($1^3/_4$ pounds/795 g) mixed berries (raspberries, blackberries, blueberries, and quartered strawberries) with $^1/_3$ cup (65 g) granulated sugar, 2 tablespoons (15 g) all-purpose flour, and 2 teaspoons kirsch or lemon juice.

TIPS: If using store-bought amaretti, which are usually tiny, you'll need a few more than indicated in the recipe to make the right amount of crumbs.

Have a sheet of aluminum foil on the lower rack of the oven during baking to catch any overflow of fruit juices.

Pineapple, Rhubarb, and Raspberry Cobbler

MAKES 8 SERVINGS

I was in line at an outdoor market in Paris and *une dame d'un certain âge* in front of me was getting a lesson on preparing rhubarb from *la vendeuse*, who insisted that rhubarb absolutely, positively had to be peeled before cooking. Having prepared quite a bit of rhubarb, often in a professional capacity, I figured I could add my *deux centimes*, so I spoke up, telling them that I'd never done that and that it really wasn't necessary. Immediately, the line of French housewives erupted, insisting that yes, you simply must peel rhubarb. Seeing as I was outnumbered, I decided to not argue the point.

Safely back at home, I'll admit with confidence that I've never found the need to peel rhubarb for a recipe, but I have experimented with using it in unconventional ways and found that it has a remarkable affinity for pineapple and raspberries, a mix that makes a delicious fruit cobbler—which no one should have any quibbles with.

FILLING

7 cups diced rhubarb (2 pounds/1 kg stalks)

2 cups (300 g) cubed pineapple (from $^1/_2$ pineapple, peeled, eyes removed, and cored)

$2^1/_2$ cups (12 ounces/340 g) raspberries

$^3/_4$ cup (150 g) sugar

2 tablespoons (15 g) all-purpose flour

1 teaspoon vanilla extract

1 tablespoon kirsch (optional)

BISCUITS

3 cups (420 g) all-purpose flour

2 tablespoons (30 g) sugar

1 tablespoon baking powder

$1^1/_2$ teaspoons salt

10 tablespoons (5 ounces/135 g) unsalted butter, cut into $^1/_2$-inch (1.5-cm) pieces and chilled

$^3/_4$ cup (180 ml) heavy cream or buttermilk, plus more as needed

1 large egg yolk

1 teaspoon heavy cream or whole milk

Preheat the oven to 400°F (200°C).

To make the filling, in a large bowl, mix together the rhubarb, pineapple, raspberries, the $^3/_4$ cup (150 g) sugar, 2 tablespoons (15 g) flour, vanilla, and kirsch, if using, until combined. Transfer the mixture to a shallow 2-quart (2-liter) baking dish and bake until the fruit is heated through, about 40 minutes, stirring several times during baking.

While the filling bakes, make the biscuits. Into the bowl of a stand mixer (or a large bowl if making by hand), sift together the 3 cups (420 g) flour, 2 tablespoons (30 g) sugar, baking powder, and salt. Add the butter pieces to the flour mixture. Mix briefly in a stand mixer fitted with the paddle attachment (or by hand with a pastry blender) until the butter is mostly incorporated, but small chunks are still visible. Stir in $^3/_4$ cup (180 ml) cream or buttermilk and mix until the dough begins to come together. Gather the dough into a ball with your hands; if the dough is too dry to hold together, gradually mix in additional cream or buttermilk until it does.

Lightly flour a work surface and roll out the dough until it is $^3/_4$ inch (2 cm) thick. Using a 3-inch (8-cm) round biscuit cutter dipped in flour, cut out 8 biscuits. (You may need to gather the dough scraps and roll them out again in order to make 8 biscuits.) Set the biscuits aside until needed. In a small bowl, whisk together the egg yolk and cream or milk to make an egg wash.

When the filling is ready, remove the baking dish from the oven and arrange the biscuits on top of the filling. Brush the tops of the biscuits with the egg wash. Return the baking dish to the oven and continue baking until the biscuits are golden brown, 15 to 20 minutes.

SERVING: Serve warm with Vanilla Ice Cream (page 143).

> TIP: Have a sheet of aluminum foil on the lower rack of the oven during baking since this cobbler is quite juicy and the foil will catch any spills.

Nectarine-Berry Cobbler with Fluffy Biscuits

MAKES 6 SERVINGS

If you're starting to feel a little, um, bulky as summer approaches, keep this fruity cobbler in mind because it's a lean, but delicious, dessert. The biscuits are moistened by a healthy pour of buttermilk, and the modest amount of butter provides flavor without weighing the biscuits (or you) down.

The other great thing is that the biscuits are made in a bowl and simply spooned over the fruit, rather than rolled out and cut, making this a no-sweat dessert (another plus in summer).

FILLING

8 medium nectarines (about 3 pounds/1.5 kg)

6 tablespoons (75 g) sugar

2 teaspoons kirsch or lemon juice

2 teaspoons all-purpose flour

1 teaspoon vanilla extract

$1^1/_4$ cups (6 ounces/170 g) blueberries, raspberries, or blackberries

BISCUITS

$1^1/_2$ cups (210 g) all-purpose flour

1 teaspoon baking powder

$^1/_4$ teaspoon baking soda

2 teaspoons sugar

$^1/_4$ teaspoon salt

4 tablespoons (2 ounces/60 g) unsalted butter, frozen in 1 piece

$^2/_3$ cup (160 ml) buttermilk

1 large egg yolk

1 teaspoon whole milk or cream

Coarse-crystal or granulated sugar, for sprinkling

Preheat the oven to 375°F (190°C).

Halve, pit, and cut the nectarines into $^1/_2$-inch (1.5-cm) slices. In a large bowl, toss the nectarines with the 6 tablespoons (75 g) sugar, the kirsch or lemon juice, the 2 teaspoons flour, the vanilla, and berries. Divide the mixture evenly among six shallow individual baking dishes or transfer to a shallow 2-quart (2-liter) baking dish. Bake, stirring once, until the fruit is heated through, about 20 to 25 minutes for individual dishes or 40 minutes for a large baking dish. Remove from the oven.

To make the biscuits, in a large bowl, whisk together the $1^1/_2$ cups (210 g) flour, the baking powder, baking soda, the 2 teaspoons sugar, and the salt. Grate the frozen butter on the largest holes of a box grater into the flour mixture. Stir in the buttermilk just until an evenly moistened batter forms.

Using a large spoon, divide the batter evenly among the individual dishes, dropping it in mounds over the partially baked fruit, or drop 6 equal-size mounds of batter over the fruit in the large baking dish.

In a small bowl, whisk together the egg yolk and milk or cream. Dab the top of each biscuit liberally with the egg wash and sprinkle with coarse-crystal or granulated sugar. Bake until the biscuits are golden brown, 20 to 25 minutes.

SERVING: This cobbler is great served warm with a favorite ice cream or, if you're counting calories, frozen yogurt.

VARIATION: To make **NECTARINE-CHERRY COBBLER**, substitute $1^1/_2$ cups (8 ounces/225 g) pitted sweet cherries for the blackberries.

> TIP: Have a sheet of aluminum foil on the lower rack of the oven during baking to catch any overflow of fruit juices.

Baked Apples with Ginger, Dates, and Walnuts

MAKES 4 SERVINGS

There are a lot of rather timid recipes for baked apples out there, but this one, packed with spicy ginger and sweet dates, is a twist on the usual homey fare. It's a dessert that pleads to be topped with a scoop of ice cream that will melt from the warmth of the fruit.

These apples also make an eye-opening breakfast when you're weary of the same old eggs-and-toast routine. If you're anything like me, you're not at your peak in the morning, so bake them the night before, then rewarm them while the coffee is brewing. At breakfast, ice cream is optional.

$^1/_2$ cup (125 ml) white wine or unsweetened apple juice

$^1/_2$ cup (120 g) packed light brown sugar

$1^1/_2$ tablespoons plus 2 tablespoons (1 ounce/30 g) unsalted or salted butter, melted

2 teaspoons all-purpose flour

$^1/_4$ teaspoon ground cinnamon

$1^1/_2$ tablespoons peeled and minced fresh ginger

2 large egg yolks

Grated zest of $^1/_2$ lemon, preferably organic

$^1/_2$ cup (50 g) walnuts, toasted and chopped

8 to 10 dates, pitted and cut into $^1/_2$-inch (1.5-cm) pieces

4 medium apples (2 pounds/1 kg)

> TIP: Use a firm-fleshed apple, one that will resist falling apart during baking, such as Golden Delicious, Granny Smith, Pippin, Rome Beauty, or Winesap.

Preheat the oven to 350°F (175°C). Liberally butter a baking dish that will hold the apples in a single layer without a lot of extra room. Pour in the white wine or apple juice.

In a small bowl, stir together the brown sugar, the $1^1/_2$ tablespoons melted butter, the flour, cinnamon, ginger, egg yolks, and lemon zest. Mash in the walnuts and dates.

Using a melon baller, remove the stem end of the apple, then dig out the core, making sure to remove all the tough bits and seeds, but don't cut through the bottom. With a vegetable peeler, remove a 1-inch (3-cm) ring of the skin from around the top of the cavity. Stuff the apples with the walnut-date mixture, but do not overfill. Brush the exposed flesh of the apples with the 2 tablespoons (1 ounce/30 g) melted butter.

Arrange the apples in the baking dish and bake until a sharp paring knife inserted into the apples meets no resistance, 30 to 45 minutes, basting occasionally with the liquid in the dish. If the filling is browning too quickly, drape the apples loosely with aluminum foil as they bake.

SERVING: These apples beg to be served warm, drizzled with the pan juices and topped with a scoop of Vanilla Ice Cream (page 143), White Chocolate–Ginger Ice Cream (page 149), frothy Cider Sabayon (page 238), or simply on their own.

STORAGE: Baked apples can be cooked in advance then covered loosely with foil and rewarmed in a moderate oven before serving.

VARIATION: Vary the pan juices by using $^1/_4$ cup (60 ml) rum or whiskey with $^1/_4$ cup (60 ml) apple juice.

Very Spicy Baked Pears with Caramel

MAKES 4 TO 6 SERVINGS

I've been living with a kitchen a fraction of the size of a normal kitchen for a number of years, so I'm always looking out for desserts that can be made with a minimum of fuss. And I'm happy when a dessert requires a minimal amount of counter space because between my imposing stand mixer and the half-eaten chocolate bars and other edibles scattered around my kitchen (and on my desk, and in my living room, and, I'm not embarrassed to say, sometimes even in the bathroom), I'm lucky to have enough space to peel a few pears. That's a good thing, actually, because it means I can make this dessert all winter long, no matter what shape my kitchen counter is in.

Once peeled, just pop the pears in the oven, and when they come out, strain out the liquid and use it as a base for one of the best—and easiest—caramel sauces imaginable.

15 whole cloves

2 star anise

2 cinnamon sticks

$^1/_2$ teaspoon whole black peppercorns

4 firm, ripe medium pears ($1^1/_2$ pounds/680 g), such as Bosc, Winter Nellis, or d'Anjou

4 tablespoons (2 ounces/60 g) unsalted or salted butter, melted

$^1/_2$ cup (120 g) packed dark or light brown sugar

$^1/_4$ cup (60 ml) Cognac, brandy, or rum

$^1/_4$ cup (60 ml) heavy cream

Preheat the oven to 400°F (200°C).

Coarsely crush the cloves, star anise, cinnamon sticks, and peppercorns in a mortar and pestle or seal them inside a sturdy plastic bag and crush them with a rolling pin.

Peel, quarter, and core the pears. Pour the butter into a large, shallow baking dish that will hold all the pear quarters in a single layer. Add the pears to the baking dish along with the crushed spices, brown sugar, and cognac, brandy, or rum and toss to combine.

Cover the baking dish with aluminum foil and bake until the pears are tender (a sharp paring knife inserted into the center meets no resistance), 30 to 45 minutes, stirring the pears a few times during baking. (The baking time will vary depending on the variety and ripeness of the pears.)

Using a slotted spoon, transfer the pears to individual plates. Scrape the juices and spices from the baking dish into a skillet. Pour the cream into the skillet and cook over medium heat until the mixture deepens in color, thickens, and caramelizes. Strain the caramel and drizzle it over the pears.

SERVING: These pears are delicious with Frozen Sour Cream (page 173) or served as an accompaniment to slices of Fresh Ginger Cake (page 42).

VARIATION: You can use a softer pear, such as Comice, Bartlett, or French butter pear, but watch them while baking as they'll cook quickly—in about 30 minutes or less. The pears can also be replaced with good, firm baking apples—Golden Delicious, Granny Smith, Pippin, Rome Beauty, or Winesap—peeled, cored, and cut into eighths, and baked for about 25 minutes.

> **TIP:** If you don't mind the spices in the caramel, it's not necessary to strain them out.

Blackberry–Brown Butter Financiers

MAKES 12 SMALL CAKES

The almond-scented French cakes known as *financiers* are traditionally baked in small rectangular shapes meant to resemble bars of gold. Unless you're loaded, you likely don't have 12 fancy, expensive French rectangular baking molds lying around, so I've adapted this recipe for baking in a standard-size muffin tin, which works beautifully—and won't lead you to finanicial ruin.

7 tablespoons (3 1/2 ounces/105 g) unsalted butter

1 3/4 cups (140 g) sliced almonds, preferably blanched

1/2 cup (100 g) granulated sugar

1/2 cup (70 g) powdered sugar

5 tablespoons (45 g) all-purpose flour

1/8 teaspoon salt

4 large egg whites

1/2 teaspoon almond extract

1 1/4 cups (6 ounces/170 g) blackberries

Preheat the oven to 400°F (200°C). Butter a standard 12-cup muffin tin.

In a medium skillet, warm the butter over low heat. It will bubble and sizzle for a while before it settles down. Continue to cook over low heat until the butter darkens to the color of maple syrup and smells toasty but not burnt. Remove from the heat and set aside.

In a food processor fitted with the metal blade or in a blender, grind the almonds with the granulated and powdered sugars, flour, and salt. With the motor running, gradually pour in the egg whites and almond extract. Pour in the warm brown butter, leaving behind any blackened bits in the pan, and mix until the batter is smooth.

Divide the batter evenly among the muffin cups. Press 3 or 4 blackberries into the batter in each cup. Bake until the cakes are puffy and deep golden brown, about 18 minutes.

Let cool for 10 minutes, then tip the cakes out onto a wire rack. Let cool completely.

SERVING: *Financiers* are mostly enoyed as snack cakes. To dress them up as desserts, serve them with a bit of Blackberry Sauce (page 248) or Mango Sauce (page 246) and dollops of crème fraîche.

STORAGE: Some folks swear that *financier* batter is best if refrigerated overnight before baking. I've tested that theory and haven't noticed any difference. But if you'd like to try it for yourself, the batter can be kept for up to 5 days in the refrigerator. Store the cooled baked *financiers* in an airtight container for up to 1 week.

VARIATIONS: Substitute peach, nectarine, or plum slices for the blackberries (you may want to peel the peaches first). Cut the fruit into 1/2-inch (1.5-cm) slices and press a few into the batter in each muffin cup before baking.

Peaches in Red Wine

MAKES 4 SERVINGS

I once worked with a French waiter known for a fierce scowl that could cause even the most self-assured chef and diner to wither. He tasted one spoonful of these peaches and told me that this was his idea of the perfect dessert. It was one of the few times I saw him smile. But what's not to like? Icy peaches floating in sweet red wine is pretty close to perfection, if I do say so myself. His good mood didn't last very long. But after that, every time we passed each other, I knew from the tiny gleam in his eye that I'd won the admiration of my toughest customer.

$^3/_4$ cup (150 g) sugar

2 cups (500 ml) fruity red wine, such as Merlot, Zinfandel, or Beaujolais

4 ripe yellow or white medium peaches ($1^1/_2$ pounds/675 g)

In a large nonreactive bowl, whisk together the sugar and wine until the sugar is completely dissolved.

Peel the peaches, halve them, and remove the pits. Cut each peach half into slices 1 inch (3 cm) thick and submerge them in the wine. Taste and add more sugar if desired. Cover and chill until cold, at least 4 hours.

SERVING: The peaches should be enjoyed as cold as possible. Serve them right from the refrigerator in well-chilled bowls with lots of the cold sweetened wine. Crisp cookies, such as Pecan-Butterscotch Tuiles (page 214) or Croquants (page 211), are great served alongside.

STORAGE: You can make the recipe up to 8 hours in advance and keep the mixture chilled until ready to serve. You can also chill the sweetened wine a few days in advance and add the peaches the day you plan to serve them.

VARIATION: Use yellow and white nectarines instead of peaches (there's no need to peel the nectarines).

> **TIP:** Superfine or baker's sugar dissolves much more quickly than regular granulated sugar. To make you own superfine sugar, pulse granulated sugar in a blender or a food processor a few times until the texture is very fine.

Pavlova

MAKES 4 SERVINGS

I've become famous—or infamous—for not wanting people to dip their forks into a dish that I'm eating so that they can get a taste. I'm sorry, but I find nothing more unnerving than having to stop eating and pass something that I'm enjoying around the table. And it seems that the more I like whatever it is, the more it never quite makes it back to me.

Traditionally, Pavlova is a jumbo meringue topped with whipped cream and tropical fruit. But to avoid conflict, I opt to make individual ones so that everyone gets their fair share and forks don't wander at the table. Individual Pavlovas are also easier to serve.

You can vary the types of tropical fruit that you use, but really try to search out fresh passion fruit. The vibrant orange pulp and seeds spilling over everything will make it instantly clear why this is one dessert you'd not want to share either.

3 large egg whites, at room temperature

Pinch of cream of tartar (optional)

$^2/_3$ cup (130 g) sugar

$^1/_2$ teaspoon vanilla extract

1 teaspoon distilled white vinegar

1 teaspoon cornstarch

Blood Orange Sorbet (page 157), Strawberry-Mango Sorbet (page 166), or Toasted Coconut Sherbet (page 152)

2 to 3 cups (500 to 750 g) mixed tropical fruit (a combination of diced pineapple, mango, papaya, kiwifruit, and banana)

Whipped cream (page 239)

2 fresh ripe passion fruits

Preheat the oven to 200°F (100°C). Line a baking sheet with parchment paper or a silicone baking mat.

In a stand mixer fitted with the whip attachment (or in a bowl by hand), whisk the egg whites on low speed until frothy. Add the cream of tartar, if using, increase the speed to high, and continue whisking until the whites begin to hold their shape and form soft, drooping peaks when you lift the beater. With the mixer running, gradually add the sugar, then the vanilla, vinegar, and cornstarch and continue whisking until the meringue is shiny and holds stiff peaks.

Drop the meringue in 5 equal mounds (you'll have an extra meringue in case one breaks), spaced equally apart, on the prepared baking sheet. Dip a soup spoon in

water and use the back of it to flatten each mound into a disk 4 to 5 inches (10 to 12 cm) in diameter. With the spoon, make a depression in the center of each meringue that will eventually hold the cream and fruits.

Bake the meringues for $1^1/_2$ hours. Turn off the heat and leave the meringues in the oven to dry for at least 1 hour. Remove from the oven and let cool completely.

Place a meringue on each of 4 individual plates. Scoop some sorbet into the centers of the meringues. Pile the fruits on top and around the sorbet, then spoon on a dollop of whipped cream. Halve the passion fruits and spoon the pulp and seeds over each Pavlova.

STORAGE: The meringues can be made up to 1 week in advance and kept in an airtight container at room temperature in a cool, dry spot.

VARIATIONS: The classic Pavlova is meringue topped with whipped cream and fruit. I like a scoop of sorbet nestled in there, too, but if you prefer it without, spread whipped cream over each meringue and top with the tropical fruits.

If you can't find fresh passion fruit or frozen purée, add a spoonful of Raspberry Sauce (page 246) or Blackberry Sauce (page 248) over each Pavlova instead.

> TIP: All ovens are different, and that difference is never more apparent than when baking meringues. If your oven appears to be browning the meringues too fast, prop the oven door open with a wooden spoon to allow the temperature to cool.

Summer Pudding

There was an expression—"too good to use"—at a certain well-known restaurant where I used to work. One of the cooks coined the phrase to describe what we, the pastry people, would do: hoard beautiful fruits and berries, buying much more than we could possibly use. We considered the fruits so precious that we'd hold off using them, waiting for something very special or just the right moment. Eventually, though, we'd find ourselves with a glut on our hands and had to scramble to use up our stash before it went bad.

If you find yourself in a similar position or if you're just looking for the great summer dessert loaded with lots of juicy berries, this is it. And if anyone says your summer pudding looks too good to eat, don't believe them. Just dig right in.

5 cups (1^1/$_2$ pounds/680 g) raspberries

5 cups (1^1/$_2$ pounds/680 g) blackberries

1^1/$_2$ cups (12 ounces/340 g) red currants, stemmed

1 cup (200 g) sugar

2 teaspoons kirsch or freshly squeezed lemon juice

1 loaf (1 pound/450 g) firm-textured white bread (such as *pain de mie*), crust removed and cut into ^{1}/$_2$-inch (1.5-cm) slices

> TIP: You can use frozen unsweetened berries in place of the fresh ones.

In a large saucepan over low heat, gently warm the berries, red currants, and sugar. Cook until the berries soften and release their juices, about 10 minutes. Remove from the heat and stir in the kirsch or lemon juice. Let cool, stirring occasionally to encourage juiciness.

Line a 1^1/$_2$-quart (1.5-liter) soufflé dish or a deep bowl of similar size with plastic wrap. Line the bottom and sides with a single layer of bread slices, trimming the slices as needed to fit snugly against each other. Ladle half of the berries and their juice into the bread-lined dish and distribute them evenly.

Arrange a single layer of bread slices over the berries, trimming to fit. Add the remaining berries and juice, then cover with a final layer of bread.

Cover with plastic wrap pressed directly on the surface of the pudding, cover with a plate slightly smaller in diameter than the dish, and place a fairly heavy object (such as a large can of tomatoes) on the plate to weigh the pudding down. Refrigerate overnight.

The next day, remove the plastic wrap and invert the pudding onto a plate. Lift off the dish or bowl and the plastic used to line it.

SERVING: Serve with whipped cream (page 239). Depending on how juicy the berries were that you used to make the pudding, you may wish to have some additional lightly sweetened berries or Raspberry Sauce (page 246) on hand to douse any unsoaked areas.

STORAGE: The pudding, in its mold, will keep in the refrigerator for up to 2 days.

VARIATION: Because red currants add a distinctive bit of tang, they are an important addition to this dessert and they're worth seeking out. But they can be difficult to find. If so, use another pint of raspberries in their place.

Tropical Fruit Soup with Coconut Sherbet and Meringue

MAKES 4 SERVINGS

One of the questions I'm often asked is "How do you stay so thin?" I want to respond by saying that I'm about average for my height and age, but instead I tell people that I eat only my own desserts. I'm not just being a salesman, it's close to the truth. Aside from the occasional treat, for everyday meals, I prefer to make desserts that are well balanced rather than outrageously rich. I'll often serve small slivers of cake, a plate of cookies, or scoops of icy sorbet along with a fresh fruit compote and have never met with resistance from any of my guests. When it comes to this virtuous fruit soup, the thin sheet of crackly coconut meringue always seals the deal for those who are doubtful that lean can taste luxurious.

SOUP BASE

2 cups (500 ml) water

$^2/_3$ cup (130 g) sugar

1 small cinnamon stick

$^1/_2$ star anise

8 whole cloves

8 black peppercorns

$^1/_2$ vanilla bean, split lengthwise

Grated zest of 2 oranges, preferably organic

2 (2-inch/5-cm) pieces lemongrass, white parts only from the bulb end, sliced

4 slices fresh ginger

1 tablespoon dark rum

MERINGUE

1 large egg white, at room temperature

Pinch of salt

$^1/_4$ cup (50 g) sugar

$^1/_2$ cup (35 g) dried unsweetened shredded coconut

FRUIT AND GARNISH

2 to 3 cups (500 to 750 g) mixed tropical fruit (a combination of diced pineapple, mango, kiwifruit, and banana, and passion fruit pulp with seeds)

A sprinkle of sugar

Fresh mint leaves, for garnish

Toasted Coconut Sherbet (page 152)

To make the soup base, in a medium saucepan over medium-high heat, bring the water and $^2/_3$ cup (130 g) sugar to a boil. Meanwhile, coarsely crush the cinnamon, star anise, cloves, and black peppercorns in a mortar and pestle or seal them in a sturdy plastic bag and crush them with a rolling pin. Add the spices to the boiling syrup and turn off the heat. Scrape the seeds from the vanilla bean and add them to the saucepan, then drop in the pod along with the orange zest, lemongrass, and ginger. Cover the pan, and let the mixture steep to allow the flavors to infuse, at least 1 hour.

Pour the soup base through a mesh strainer into a medium bowl. (The vanilla pod can be rinsed, dried, and used for another purpose; see page 14.) Stir in the rum, cover, and refrigerate until icy cold.

Preheat the oven to 350°F (175°C). Line a baking sheet with parchment paper or a silicone baking mat.

To make the meringue, in a stand mixer fitted with the whip attachment (or in a bowl by hand), whisk together the egg white and salt on low speed until frothy. Increase the speed to high and continue whisking until the white begins to hold its shape. With the mixer running, gradually sprinkle in the $^1/_4$ cup (50 g) sugar and continue whisking until the meringue is shiny and holds stiff peaks. Fold in the coconut.

Using an offset icing spatula, spread the meringue into a very thin circle about 12 inches (30 cm) in diameter on the prepared baking sheet. Bake until the meringue is deep golden brown, about 10 minutes. Let cool completely.

Slide the icing spatula under the meringue to release it from the parchment paper or silicone mat. Break the meringue into large shards.

In a large bowl, toss the fruit with a sprinkling of sugar.

To assemble, divide the fruit evenly among four chilled wide soup bowls, then ladle the cold soup base over. Finely chop some mint leaves and scatter them over the soup. Place a scoop of the coconut sherbet in the center and stick a shard of the coconut meringue, pointing upward, into the sherbet.

> **TIP:** I like to use flat soup bowls for serving so guests can see all the tropical fruit floating in the spiced syrup. Put the bowls in the refrigerator or freezer before assembling the dessert to make sure they're very cold.

STORAGE: The soup base can be made up to 1 day in advance of serving and the coconut meringues shards can be kept in an airtight container at room temperature for up to 1 week.

VARIATIONS: Sliced kumquats, sliced strawberries, and orange segments are nice additions to the mixture of tropical fruits. You can use any other tropical-flavored sorbet in place of the Toasted Coconut Sherbet, such Passion Fruit–Tangerine Sorbet (page 159) or Strawberry-Mango Sorbet (page 166).

Champagne Gelée with Kumquats, Grapefruits, and Blood Oranges

Not all gelatin desserts are squidgy, old-fashioned jelled rings studded with oversweetened canned fruits. Take this thoroughly modern dessert, for example. You'll see why it won top honors from a national food magazine that called it one of the "Top Ten Desserts of All Time."

GELÉE

1/2 cup (125 ml) plus 1/2 cup (125 ml) cold water

2 envelopes (7 g each) unflavored gelatin

1 cup (200 g) sugar

1 bottle (750 ml) Champagne or other sparkling wine

Juice of 1/2 lime, plus more to taste

FRUITS

12 kumquats

2 tablespoons (30 g) sugar

1/2 cup (125 ml) water

3 pink grapefruits

4 blood or navel oranges

Soft-Candied Citrus Peel (page 253)

To make the gelée, into a large bowl, pour 1/2 cup (125 ml) of the water. Sprinkle the gelatin evenly over the water and allow it to soften and swell for 5 minutes.

Meanwhile, in a small saucepan, warm the remaining 1/2 cup (125 ml) water with the 1 cup (200 g) sugar, stirring until the sugar dissolves.

Pour the warm sugar syrup over the gelatin and stir until the gelatin completely dissolves. Add the Champagne or other sparkling wine (it will foam up; hence the large bowl) and the lime juice. Taste and add additional lime juice, if desired. Cover and refrigerate until jelled, at least 6 hours.

To prepare the fruits, slice and seed the kumquats. In a small saucepan, warm the 2 tablespoons (30 g) sugar and 1/2 cup (125 ml) water, stirring to dissolve the sugar. Remove from the heat and add the kumquats. Let them soak in the sugar syrup for 15 minutes. Meanwhile, peel, section, and seed the grapefruits and oranges.

To assemble, spoon some of the chilled gelée into 6 wine glasses or goblets. Add a few sections of fruit and a few strips of citrus peel. Spoon in more gelée. Continue to layer in the fruit, citrus peel, and gelée until each glass is full. Serve immediately or chill until ready to serve.

STORAGE: The gelée mixture will keep for up to 5 days in the refrigerator. Assemble the dessert the day of serving.

VARIATION: Feel free to vary the fruit according to what's in season. In the summer, slightly sweetened peaches or nectarines are perfect, along with a few types of berries tossed in for good measure and color.

> TIP: If you're in a bit of a rush, you can speed up the jelling. Divide the still-liquid gelée mixture among 6 goblets or wine glasses and chill for a couple of hours until firm. When ready to serve, top each with a mixture of the fruits and citrus peel.

Custards, Soufflés, and Puddings

Eggs show up in a lot of dessert recipes, but nowhere are they held in higher esteem or have a greater purpose than in custards and soufflés. I remember digging into bright-yellow baked egg custards when I was young, and the thrill of my spoon busting through the layer of chewy, almost-burnt skin—a large part of the overall appeal—to get to the smooth custard scented faintly of nutmeg just below.

Now that I'm grown up, and presumably more sophisticated, I still like custard skin, but my taste has broadened to include other egg-rich desserts like mousse, crème caramel, and soufflé. In fact, my baking career began with a chocolate soufflé made in a Pyrex measuring cup. It was the first night my parents left me home alone without a babysitter and I made dinner and dessert for myself. (Even back then, I chose a dark chocolate dessert.) The soufflé came out of the oven high and crusty—and surprisingly delicious, proving that soufflés are so simple that even a kid can make one and that you don't need an arsenal of fancy equipment to create impressive dessert. From that soufflé on, I was hooked.

A majority of the desserts in this chapter are made in individual portions. Not only are they easier to bake and serve, but you're certain to get your fair share of crust when you've got your very own soufflé. With flan and crème brûlée, the burnt sugar is yours and yours alone. Bread pudding, on the other hand, is meant to be shared.

Porcelain ramekins—French-style custard cups—are what I use for baking custards and soufflés because I like their clean look, but regular oven-proof glass custard cups work equally well. And for those who spend their weekends scouring flea markets (or nowadays, the Internet), you can find lovely vintage custard cups in sets, or individual ones that can be mixed and matched.

Custards need a wide window of baking times, much more so than any other dessert. A slew of factors can affect how quickly they cook, from the temperature of the unbaked custard mixture, to the temperature of the water bath, to the weight and thickness of the ramekins or custard cups, so it's best to be vigilant during baking. Use the times only as guidelines and begin checking for doneness about 10 minutes before the indicated cooking time. It's easy to bake something a little longer, but as far as I'm aware, once something is baked, it's impossible to bake it less.

I remove individual custards from the oven when they're set around the perimeter, yet a small area in the center, about the size of a bottle cap, still quivers when you gently jiggle the ramekins. One strategy that I sometimes employ is to take the custards out of the oven when they're quite shy of being done, and let them sit in the water bath in the pan, tightly covered with the aluminum foil; the residual heat from the water bath gently guides them to a perfectly cooked conclusion.

WATER BATHS

In order to obtain their signature smooth, silky texture, custards are gently baked in a water bath that allows them to cook slowly and evenly. The filled ramekins or custard cups are placed in a roasting pan or deep baking dish (the sides should be higher than the rims of the ramekins) and enough warm water is added to the pan or dish so that it reaches halfway up the sides of the custard cups. Then the pan is covered tightly with foil.

When transferring the pan to the oven, you want to avoid splashing water into the ramekins. If you're not the steady type, you can set the roasting pan on the oven rack, place the custards in the pan, add the water, and then cover with foil. If you do this, the oven door will be open for a good amount of time, which will cause the oven temperature to drop quite a bit, so you'll likely need to increase the baking time by several minutes.

Coffee-Caramel Custards

Even before the recent coffee-caramel craze, I was proudly baking up these custards because they bring together two of my favorite flavors. Although I'd love to take responsibility for starting the trend, the only thing I can say with certainty is that I'm unabashedly crazy for the combination.

For best results, use very strong espresso because you want to make sure that the coffee flavor is bold enough to stand up to the deep, dark caramel. I think the custards are best served chilled, like some of those barista drinks.

$1^1/_4$ cups (250 g) sugar

$2^1/_2$ cups (625 ml) heavy cream

$^1/_2$ vanilla bean, split lengthwise

7 large egg yolks

$^1/_4$ cup (60 ml) freshly brewed espresso (see Tip)

$^1/_2$ teaspoon vanilla extract

Pinch of salt

Before preparing this recipe, see Caramelization Guidelines, page 265.

Preheat the oven to 350°F (175°C). Set six 4- to 6-ounce (125- to 180-ml) ramekins or custard cups in a roasting pan or deep baking dish.

Spread the sugar in an even layer in a large, heavy-bottomed saucepan and cook over medium heat without stirring until the sugar begins to melt around the edges. Using a heatproof utensil, slowly drag the liquified sugar to the center and stir gently until all the sugar is melted. Continue to cook, stirring infrequently, until the caramel turns dark amber in color and begins to foam a bit. Quickly remove the pan from the heat and immediately add the cream. The mixture will steam and bubble up vigorously, then the bubbling will subside. Scrape the seeds from the vanilla bean and add them to the saucepan, then drop in the pod. Stir the mixture over low heat until the caramel is smooth.

In a large bowl, whisk the egg yolks. Gradually whisk in about one-quarter of the warm caramel mixture, whisking constantly as you pour to prevent the yolks from cooking. Gradually whisk in the remaining caramel mixture, the espresso, vanilla, and salt. Pour the mixture through a mesh strainer into a large measuring cup or pitcher. (The vanilla pod can be rinsed, dried, and used for another purpose; see page 14.) Divide the custard mixture evenly among the ramekins.

Fill the roasting pan or baking dish with warm water to reach halfway up the sides of the ramekins. Cover the pan tightly with aluminum foil and bake until the perimeters of the custards are just set and the centers are still slightly jiggly, about 35 minutes.

Transfer the custards from the water bath to a wire rack and let cool completely. Cover with plastic wrap and refrigerate until ready to serve.

SERVING: Top the custards with dollops of whipped cream (page 239), if you wish, and sprinkle with chocolate shavings (see page 8), crushed coffee beans, or a bit of finely ground espresso.

STORAGE: The baked custards will keep for up to 2 days in the refrigerator.

TIP: If you can't get your hands on freshly made espresso, substitute 1 rounded tablespoon of instant espresso powder dissolved in $^1/_4$ cup (60 ml) water.

Chocolate Pots de Crème

MAKES 6 SERVINGS

This is the French classic that everyone knows and loves. I've resisted doing anything to change it, except be more generous with the chocolate than the pastry chef in the average Parisian bistro. *Excusez-moi*, but I like chocolate so much that I just couldn't help myself.

This recipe is a good place to use top-notch chocolate, French or otherwise. You won't regret it when your spoon cuts through the glossy surface and dives into the smooth custard below. For best results, use a high-percentage dark chocolate, one that's 60 to 70 percent cacao.

7 ounces (200 g) bittersweet or semisweet chocolate, chopped

2 cups (500 ml) half-and-half

3 tablespoons (45 g) sugar

1 teaspoon instant espresso or coffee powder (optional)

Pinch of salt

6 large egg yolks

1 teaspoon vanilla extract

Preheat the oven to 350°F (175°C). Set six 4- to 6-ounce (125- to 180-ml) ramekins or custard cups in a roasting pan or deep baking dish.

Put the chocolate in a large heatproof bowl. In a medium saucepan, heat the half-and-half, sugar, instant espresso or coffee powder, if using, and salt until quite hot, stirring to dissolve the sugar. Pour the hot half-and-half mixture over the chocolate and whisk until the chocolate is completely melted and smooth. Let cool until tepid, then whisk in the egg yolks and the vanilla. (If the mixture looks at all grainy, whisk well or purée in a blender until smooth.)

Transfer the custard mixture to a large measuring cup or pitcher and divide evenly among the ramekins.

Fill the roasting pan or baking dish with warm water to reach halfway up the sides of the ramekins. Cover the pan tightly with aluminum foil and bake until the perimeters of the custards are just set and the centers are still slightly jiggly, about 35 minutes.

Transfer the custards from the water bath to a wire rack and let cool.

SERVING: Serve slightly warm or at room temperature, garnished with small mounds of whipped cream (page 239) and chocolate shavings (see page 8).

STORAGE: The custard mixture can be stored in the refrigerator for up to 3 days before baking. Once baked, the custards can be chilled for up to 2 days (although they're much better when they haven't been refrigerated). Bring them to room temperature before serving.

Bittersweet Chocolate Mousse
with Pear and Fig Chutney

MAKES 8 TO 10 SERVINGS

The surprising zip of fruit chutney counters the richness of *mousse au chocolat* and adds a whole other dimension to this unconventional dessert. I don't know if it's a combination the French would approve of, but when I made it as a pastry chef on a cruise line, a few thousand people gave their consent. Each plate that came back to the kitchen was scraped clean. Unlike traditional chocolate mousse that uses uncooked eggs, this one has a cooked custard base. So, there's no reason for anyone with concerns about consuming raw eggs to jump ship rather than dive into this dessert full-steam ahead.

CHUTNEY

10 dried pear halves (10 ounces/280 g), cut into
    $^1/_2$-inch (1.5-cm) dice

8 to 12 dried figs (12 ounces/340 g), stemmed, halved,
    and cut into $^1/_4$-inch (6-mm) slices

1 cup (250 ml) water

$^2/_3$ cup (140 g) packed light or dark brown sugar

2 tablespoons (30 ml) apple cider vinegar

Four 1-inch (3-cm) strips lemon zest, preferably organic

1 cinnamon stick

Pinch of ground cloves

1 vanilla bean, split lengthwise

2 tablespoons (30 ml) whiskey or Cognac

MOUSSE

10 ounces (280 g) bittersweet or semisweet chocolate,
    chopped

$^3/_4$ cups (180 ml) whole milk

2 tablespoons (30 g) granulated sugar

4 large egg yolks

2 teaspoons rum or Cognac

$^1/_2$ cup (125 ml) heavy cream

To make the chutney, combine the pears, figs, water, brown sugar, vinegar, lemon peel, cinnamon stick, and cloves in a medium saucepan. Scrape the seeds from the vanilla bean and add them to the saucepan, then drop in

> TIP: You can transfer the mousse to a wide, shallow container before chilling, which will help it firm up faster.

the pod. Bring to a boil over high heat, then decrease the heat to medium-low and simmer until most of the liquid is absorbed, about 8 minutes.

Remove from the heat and stir in the whiskey or Cognac. Remove the vanilla pod and lemon peel. (The vanilla pod can be rinsed, dried, and used for another purpose; see page 14.) Let cool to room temperature.

To make the mousse, put the chocolate in a large heatproof bowl and set a mesh strainer across the top.

In a medium saucepan, heat the milk and granulated sugar, stirring to dissolve the sugar. In a medium bowl, whisk the egg yolks. Gradually whisk in about one-quarter of the warm milk, whisking constantly as you pour to prevent the yolks from cooking. Scrape the mixture back into the saucepan and cook over low heat, stirring constantly, until the custard is thick enough to coat the back of a spoon. Immediately pour the custard through the strainer into the chocolate. Whisk gently until the chocolate has melted and the mixture is smooth, then stir in the rum or Cognac. Let cool completely, cover with plastic wrap, and refrigerate until chilled.

In a stand mixer fitted with the whip attachment or in a bowl by hand, whisk the cream until it forms soft peaks. Fold about one-third of the chilled chocolate mixture into the whipped cream, then add this mixture to the remaining chocolate and fold just until there are no streaks of cream. Cover with plastic wrap and chill for at least 2 hours.

Serve the mousse in individual glasses or dishes with big spoonfuls of the chutney on top.

STORAGE: The chutney will keep in the refrigerator for up to 1 month. The mousse will keep in the refrigerator for up to 3 days.

Chocolate Ganache Custard Tart

MAKES ONE 9-INCH (23-CM) TART; 8 TO 10 SERVINGS

This tart exemplifies what the French do best: combine just a few top-quality ingredients, doing as little to them as possible. Ganache is a mélange of cream and chocolate, reportedly named after a young baker who accidentally spilled some cream into the chocolate the chef was melting. The chef called him a *ganache*, which is slang for "idiot," but when he stirred in the cream, they realized the mistake was probably one of the most brilliant things to ever happen to chocolate.

10 ounces (280 g) bittersweet or semisweet chocolate, chopped

1 cup (250 ml) heavy cream or half-and-half

1 large egg

1 large egg yolk

2 teaspoons Cognac

Prebaked tart shell (page 229)

Preheat the oven to 350°F (175°C).

In a large heatproof bowl, combine the chocolate and cream or half-and-half. Set the bowl over a pan of simmering water, stirring occasionally until the chocolate is melted and the mixture is smooth.

Remove the bowl from the saucepan and whisk in the egg, egg yolk, and Cognac. Pour the mixture into the prebaked tart shell, tilting and shaking it very gently to even out the filling.

Set the tart pan on a baking sheet and bake until the filling looks almost set but still quivers when the tart is gently jiggled, about 20 minutes. Don't overbake. Let cool completely.

Remove the tart pan sides by setting the tart on an overturned bowl or other tall, wide surface (a large can of tomatoes works well). Gently press down on the outer ring and let the ring fall to the countertop. Set the tart on a flat surface. Release the tart from the pan bottom by sliding the blade of a knife between the crust and the pan bottom, then slip the tart onto a serving plate. (If it doesn't release cleanly, simply serve the tart on the pan bottom.)

SERVING: Whipped cream (page 239) is one possible accompaniment to a wedge of this delectable tart, but Caramel Ice Cream (page 144) dials up the richness. Or, a scribble of Orange Caramel Sauce (page 242) will add a pleasant citrusy note.

STORAGE: The tart should be served the same day it's made. Keep it at room temperature until ready to serve.

Orange-Cardamom Flan

MAKES 8 SERVINGS

Many countries have a version of caramelized custard turned out of its mold for serving—from Mexico's flan to France's *crème renversée*. No border seems to be a barrier to the migration of this universally popular dessert.

Cardamom is rather an exotic spice, but it is sometimes used in classic American coffee cakes and other familiar baked goods. Do not buy preground cardamom because its flavor dissipates quickly and you'll miss the wonderful aroma released by cracking the seeds yourself. Oftentimes, cardamom seeds are sold still in their papery husks or pods, which should be peeled away to reveal the seeds within.

CUSTARD

1 teaspoon cardamom seeds

3 cups (750 ml) whole milk

Grated zest of 2 oranges, preferably organic

3/4 cup (150 g) sugar

3 large eggs

3 large egg yolks

CARAMEL

3/4 cup (150 g) sugar

1/4 cup (60 ml) plus 1/4 cup (60 ml) water

Pinch of cream of tartar or a few drops of lemon juice

> Before preparing this recipe, see Caramelization Guidelines, page 265.

To make the custard, lightly crush the cardamom seeds in a mortar and pestle or seal them inside a sturdy plastic bag and crush them with a rolling pin.

In a medium saucepan, heat the milk, crushed cardamom seeds, orange zest, and 3/4 cup (150 g) sugar, stirring to dissolve the sugar. Once warm, remove from the heat, cover, and let steep for 1 hour.

Set eight 4- to 6-ounce (125- to 180-ml) ramekins or custard cups in a roasting pan or deep baking dish.

To make the caramel, spread the 3/4 cup (150 g) sugar in an even layer in a medium heavy-bottomed skillet or saucepan. Pour 1/4 cup (60 ml) water evenly over the sugar to dampen it, but don't stir. Cook over medium heat until the sugar dissolves, then add the cream of tartar or lemon juice. Continue to cook without stirring, but swirl the pan if the sugar begins to brown unevenly. When the caramel turns dark amber in color and begins to foam a bit, remove from the heat and immediately add the remaining 1/4 cup (60 ml) water. The caramel will bubble up vigorously, then the bubbling will subside. Stir with a heatproof utensil until any hardened bits of caramel completely dissolve. Divide the hot caramel evenly among the 8 ramekins, then carefully swirl each ramekin so that the caramel coats the sides halfway up. Let cool completely.

Preheat the oven to 325°F (160°C).

To finish the custard, reheat the milk mixture until it's quite warm. In a medium bowl, whisk together the eggs and egg yolks, then gradually whisk the warm milk into the eggs, whisking constantly as you pour to prevent the eggs from cooking (don't whisk too vigorously, which will create air bubbles). Pour the mixture through a mesh strainer into a large measuring cup or pitcher.

Divide the custard mixture evenly among the caramel-lined ramekins. Fill the roasting pan or baking dish with warm water to reach halfway up the sides of the ramekins. Cover the pan tightly with aluminum foil and bake until the perimeters of the custards are just set and the centers are still slightly jiggly, 25 to 35 minutes.

Transfer the custards from the water bath to a wire rack and let cool completely. Cover with plastic wrap and refrigerate until chilled.

To unmold, run a sharp knife around the inside of each ramekin to loosen the custard, invert a serving plate or bowl over the ramekin, and turn them over together. Shake a few times to release the custard, then lift off the ramekin. (If the custard is stubborn, using a finger, gently pull it away from the side of the ramekin and invert again; it should slide out easily.) Pour any caramel remaining in the ramekin over the flan.

Serve the flans cold.

STORAGE: The baked custards will keep for up to 3 days in the refrigerator.

VARIATION: Surround the custards with poached dried fruit of your choosing. To make the poaching syrup: In a saucepan, heat 1 part honey or sugar to 4 parts water along with 1 cinnamon stick or 1 vanilla bean, split lengthwise. Once the syrup is warm, drop in pitted prunes; raisins; dried apricots, figs, cranberries, or cherries; or any combination of dried fruits. Simmer gently until the fruits are plump and soft.

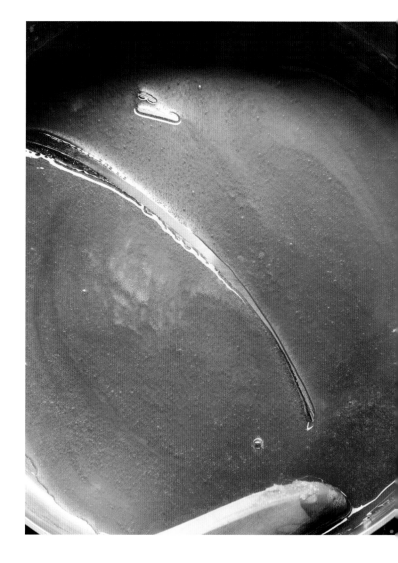

Butterscotch Flan

MAKES 8 SERVINGS

Some people might consider it overkill to mix caramelized sugar with the lush flavor of butterscotch. But since the beauty of being an adult is that we can do pretty much as we please, I don't feel the need to apologize for mixing the two in one cool custard. If you want to ramp up the flavor of the butterscotch custard with even more flavorful molasses notes than dark brown sugar can supply, try using one of the unrefined brown or cane sugars that can be found in natural food stores. Look for ones that are dark and ruddy, since they tend to have the most flavor.

CARAMEL

$^{1}/_{4}$ cup (60 ml) plus $^{1}/_{4}$ cup (60 ml) water

$^{3}/_{4}$ cup (150 g) granulated sugar

Pinch of cream of tartar or a few drops of lemon juice

CUSTARD

3 cups (750 ml) whole milk

4 large eggs

4 large egg yolks

$1^{1}/_{4}$ cups (275 g) packed dark brown sugar

$^{1}/_{4}$ teaspoon vanilla extract

Big pinch of salt

> Before preparing this recipe, see Caramelization Guidelines, page 265.

Set eight 4- to 6-ounce (125- to 180-ml) ramekins or custard cups in a roasting pan or deep baking dish.

To make the caramel, spread the $^{3}/_{4}$ cup (150 g) sugar in an even layer in a medium heavy-bottomed skillet or saucepan. Pour $^{1}/_{4}$ cup (60 ml) water evenly over the sugar to dampen it, but don't stir. Cook over medium heat until the sugar dissolves, then add the cream of tartar or lemon juice. Continue to cook without stirring, but swirl the pan if the sugar begins to brown unevenly. When the caramel turns dark amber in color and begins to foam a bit, remove from the heat and immediately add the remaining $^{1}/_{4}$ cup (60 ml) water. The caramel will bubble up vigorously, then the bubbling will subside. Stir with a heatproof utensil until any hardened bits of caramel completely dissolve. Divide the hot caramel evenly among the 8 ramekins, then carefully swirl each ramekin so that the caramel coats the sides halfway up. Let cool completely.

Preheat the oven to 325°F (160°C).

To make the custard, in a medium saucepan, heat the milk until warm. In a medium bowl, whisk together the eggs and egg yolks. Gradually whisk the warm milk into the eggs, whisking constantly as you pour to prevent the eggs from cooking. Add the brown sugar, vanilla, and salt and whisk until the sugar completely dissolves. Pour the mixture through a mesh strainer into a large measuring cup or pitcher.

Divide the custard mixture evenly among the caramel-lined ramekins. Fill the roasting pan or baking dish with warm water to reach halfway up the sides of the ramekins. Cover the pan tightly with aluminum foil and bake until the perimeters of the custards are just set and the centers are still slightly jiggly, 25 to 35 minutes.

Transfer the custards from the water bath to a wire rack and let cool completely. Cover with plastic wrap and refrigerate until chilled.

To unmold, run a sharp knife around the inside of each ramekin to loosen the custard, invert a serving plate or bowl over the ramekin, and turn them over together. Shake a few times to release the custard, then lift off the ramekin. (If the custard is stubborn, using a finger, gently pull it away from the side of the ramekin and invert again; it should slide out easily.) Pour any caramel remaining in the ramekin over the flan.

Serve the flans cold.

SERVING: I like these custards all by themselves, but I welcome Mexican Wedding Cookies (page 210) served alongside.

STORAGE: The baked flans will keep for up to 3 days in the refrigerator.

VARIATION: Experiment with different kinds of sugar in the custard, such as Mexican *piloncillo*, Asian palm sugar, and dark turbinado or *cassonade* (see Resources, page 270).

Lemon-Ginger Crème Brûlée

MAKES 6 SERVINGS

When I worked as a pastry chef, I became known as "the crème brûlée bully" because I decided one night that I had had enough of crème brûlée and stopped serving it altogether. The reason? It was all that was ever ordered, and everything else on my menu went ignored. I realize now that I should have been flattered that guests liked my crème brûlée so much, and I apologize to anyone who left the restaurant feeling denied their favorite dessert. As reparation, I offer this recipe for lemon-ginger crème brûlée, the most popular flavor of the many that I've made, and hope I'm forgiven.

3 ounces (85 g) fresh ginger, thinly sliced

3 cups (750 ml) heavy cream

$^1/_2$ cup (100 g) sugar, plus 12 teaspoons (60 g) for caramelizing

Grated zest of 2 lemons, preferably organic

6 large egg yolks

Pinch of salt

Put the ginger slices in a medium saucepan and add water to cover. Bring to a boil, then decrease the heat and simmer for 2 minutes. Pour off the water.

Add the cream, the $^1/_2$ cup (100 g) sugar, and the lemon zest to the ginger in the saucepan. Heat the mixture until warm, then remove from the heat, cover, and let steep for 1 hour.

Preheat the oven to 350°F (175°C). Set six 4- to 6-ounce (125- to 180-ml) ramekins or custard cups in a roasting pan or deep baking dish.

Using a slotted spoon, remove and discard the ginger slices from the cream mixture, add the salt, then reheat the cream until it's quite warm. In a medium bowl, whisk together the egg yolks, then gradually whisk in the warm cream, whisking constantly as you pour to prevent the eggs from cooking. Pour the mixture through a mesh strainer into a large measuring cup or pitcher.

Divide the custard mixture evenly among the ramekins. Fill the roasting pan or baking dish with warm water to reach halfway up the sides of the ramekins. Cover the pan tightly with aluminum foil and bake until the perimeters of the custards are just set and the centers are still slightly jiggly, about 30 minutes.

Transfer the custards from the water bath to a wire rack and let cool completely. Refrigerate until chilled.

Just before serving, evenly sprinkle each chilled custard with 2 teaspoons (10 g) sugar and caramelize with a kitchen torch: set the torch flame at medium and wave the tip of the flame over the sugar at close range until the sugar begins to melt. Rotate the ramekin for even caramelization, being careful not to burn yourself, until the sugar has darkened and caramelized. (If you like your crème brûlée served at room temperature, let the custards come to room temperature before caramelizing and serving.)

STORAGE: The baked custards will keep for up to 2 days in the refrigerator. Sprinkle them with sugar and caramelize the surfaces just before serving.

VARIATION: You can replace $1^1/_2$ cups (375 ml) of the heavy cream with half-and-half to lighten the custard, if you wish. If you don't have a kitchen torch, caramelize $^1/_2$ cup (100 g) sugar following the instructions for making dry caramel in Caramelization Guidelines (page 265). Pour the hot caramel over the top of each custard, swirling it very carefully to get as thin a layer of caramel as possible, then let it harden.

TIP: Fresh ginger contains an enzyme that can inhibit custards from setting. Parboiling it for a few minutes destroys the enzyme. If you want to maximize the lemon flavor, process the zest with the sugar in a food processor until very fine before adding it to the cream.

Black Currant Tea Crème Brûlée

MAKES 6 SERVINGS

A few years back, I attended a class at a French pastry school that was, of course, taught by a French chef. If you've not worked with French chefs before, you quickly realize that to them, there's one way to do things—and *only* one way. Our chef, for example, insisted on doing a cold infusion for tea, letting it steep in the refrigerator overnight. To prove his point, he steeped some tea in warm cream as well so we could later compare the results.

The next day, when we had the tasting, there were muted murmurs amongst the students that we much preferred the warm infusion, but no one dared say anything to the chef. We just all nodded in agreement that the cold infusion tasted better. I still infuse tea in warm cream for custards because to me, the proof is in the pudding. Or, in this case, the crème brûlée.

3 cups (750 ml) heavy cream

6 tablespoons (90 g) sugar, plus 12 teaspoons (60 g)
   for caramelizing

1/4 cup (15 g) loose black currant tea leaves

6 large egg yolks

In a medium saucepan, heat the cream, the 6 tablespoons (75 g) sugar, and the tea leaves until warm. Remove from the heat, cover, and let steep for 30 minutes.

Preheat the oven to 350°F (175°C). Set six 4- to 6-ounce (125- to 180-ml) ramekins or custard cups in a roasting pan or deep baking dish.

Reheat the cream until it's quite warm. In a medium bowl, whisk together the egg yolks, then gradually whisk in the warm cream, whisking constantly as you pour to prevent the eggs from cooking. Pour the mixture through a mesh strainer into a large measuring cup or pitcher.

Divide the custard mixture evenly among the ramekins. Fill the roasting pan or baking dish with warm water to reach halfway up the sides of the ramekins. Cover the pan tightly with aluminum foil and bake until the perimeters of the custards are just set and the centers are still slightly jiggly, about 30 minutes.

Transfer the custards from the water bath to a wire rack and let cool completely. Refrigerate until chilled.

Just before serving, evenly sprinkle each chilled custard with 2 teaspoons (10 g) sugar and caramelize with a kitchen torch: set the torch flame at medium and wave the tip of the flame over the sugar at close range until the sugar begins to melt. Rotate the ramekin for even caramelization, being careful not to burn yourself, until the sugar has darkened and caramelized. (If you like your crème brûlée served at room temperature, let the custards come to room temperature before caramelizing and serving.)

STORAGE: The baked custards will keep for up to 2 days in the refrigerator. Sprinkle them with sugar and caramelize the surfaces just before serving.

VARIATION: You can replace 1 1/2 cups (375 ml) of the heavy cream with half-and-half to lighten the custard, if you wish. If you don't have a kitchen torch, caramelize 1/2 cup (100 g) of sugar, following the instructions for making dry caramel in Caramelization Guidelines (page 265). Pour the hot caramel over the top of each custard, swirling it very carefully to get as thin a layer of caramel as possible, then let it harden.

Super-Lemony Soufflés

MAKES 6 SERVINGS

I think there are two types of people in this world: the lemon people and the chocolate people. This recipe is for the lemon people. But if you want to try to please both, you could add a scant $^1/_2$ cup white chocolate chips to the soufflé base when folding in the egg whites.

3 tablespoons (25 g) all-purpose flour

$^1/_3$ cup (65 g) plus $1^1/_2$ tablespoons sugar, plus more for sprinkling

Pinch of salt

$^2/_3$ cup (160 ml) whole milk

4 large eggs, separated

2 tablespoons (1 ounce/30 g) unsalted or salted butter

Grated zest of 1 lemon, preferably organic

$^1/_4$ cup (30 g) Soft-Candied Citrus Peel (page 253), made with lemons, chopped

$3^1/_2$ tablespoons (50 ml) plus $1^1/_2$ teaspoons freshly squeezed lemon juice

Position an oven rack in the upper third of the oven and preheat the oven to 400°F (200°C). Butter six 4-ounce (125-ml) ramekins or soufflé molds. Pour some sugar into each and tilt the ramekin to coat the sides; gently tap out any excess. Set the ramekins on a baking sheet.

To make the soufflé base, in a medium saucepan, whisk together the flour, the $^1/_3$ cup (65 g) sugar, and the salt. Whisk in about one-third of the milk to make a smooth paste, then whisk in the rest of the milk. Cook the mixture over medium heat, stirring frequently, until thickened to the consistency of thin yogurt, about 5 minutes. Remove from the heat and whisk in the egg yolks and butter. Return to the heat and cook until the mixture just begins to boil and a few bubbles pop on the surface. Transfer to a bowl that holds at least 4 quarts (4 liters). Stir in the fresh and candied lemon zest and let cool for 15 minutes. Stir in the $3^1/_2$ tablespoons (50 ml) lemon juice.

In a stand mixer fitted with the whip attachment (or in a bowl by hand), whisk the egg whites on low speed until frothy. Increase the speed to high, gradually add the remaining $1^1/_2$ tablespoons sugar, and continue whisking until the whites form shiny, stiff peaks.

Fold one-quarter of the whipped egg whites into the soufflé base, then gently fold in the remaining whites, taking care not to deflate them. A few streaks of egg whites are preferable to an overfolded and deflated soufflé mixture.

Divide the soufflé mixture evenly among the prepared ramekins. Sprinkle each with a light, even dusting of sugar and $^1/_4$ teaspoon lemon juice. Bake until the tops are light brown and the soufflés quiver when gently nudged, about 10 minutes.

Serve the soufflés right away.

SERVING: The soufflés are great served just as they are, but, if you like, pass a bowl of Raspberry Sauce (page 246) or Blackberry Sauce (page 248) at the table.

STORAGE: You can prepare and refrigerate the soufflé base up to 1 day in advance, then whip and fold in the egg whites when you are ready to bake. The soufflé mixture, once divided among the ramekins, can stand at room temperature for up to 1 hour before baking.

Apricot Soufflés

MAKES 4 SERVINGS

These light, lean soufflés get their lively flavor from the intensity of readily available dried apricots, so this dessert offers the added bonus that it can be made all year. It's imperative to use the highly flavorful dried apricots from California rather than imported varieties, which are bland and uninspiring. You won't be disappointed.

2^1/$_2$ ounces (70 g) California dried apricots halves (about 15), snipped in half

^{1}/$_2$ cup (125 ml) dry white wine

^{1}/$_2$ vanilla bean, split lengthwise

3 tablespoons (45 g) plus 3 tablespoons (45 g) sugar, plus more for sprinkling

1 large egg yolk

4 large egg whites, at room temperature

Pinch of salt

Add the apricot pieces and white wine to a small saucepan. Scrape the seeds from the vanilla bean and add them to the saucepan, then drop in the pod. Bring to a gentle simmer and cook until the apricots begin to soften, about 8 minutes. Remove from the heat, cover, and let stand until the apricots are tender, about 45 minutes.

Position an oven rack in the upper third of the oven and preheat the oven to 400°F (200°C). Butter four 4-ounce (125-ml) ramekins or soufflé molds. Pour some sugar into each and tilt the ramekin to coat the sides; gently tap out any excess. Set the ramekins on a baking sheet.

Remove the vanilla bean from the saucepan (it can be rinsed, dried, and used for another purpose; see page 14). In a food processor fitted with the metal blade or in a blender, process the apricots and their soaking liquid, along with 3 tablespoons (45 g) sugar and the egg yolk until smooth. Transfer the purée to a medium bowl.

In a stand mixer fitted with the whip attachment (or in a bowl by hand), whisk together the egg whites and salt on low speed until frothy. Increase the speed to high, gradually add the remaining 3 tablespoons (45 g) sugar, and continue whisking until the whites form shiny, stiff peaks.

Fold one-quarter of the whipped egg whites into the apricot purée, then gently fold in the remaining whites, taking care not to deflate them. A few streaks of egg whites are preferable to an overfolded and deflated soufflé mixture.

Divide the soufflé mixture evenly among the prepared ramekins (don't worry if the mixture rises a little above the rims), then sprinkle with a light, even dusting of sugar. Bake until the tops are browned and the soufflés quiver softly when gently nudged, about 9 minutes.

Serve the soufflés right away.

SERVING: Pass a pitcher of Raspberry Sauce (page 246), crème anglaise (page 237), or White Chocolate Sauce (page 244) at the table for pouring into the soufflés.

Chocolate-Caramel Soufflés

MAKES 4 SERVINGS

I don't think I have a bright future as a food stylist. For my first book, Michael, the photographer, insisted that I make and style all the food, even though I had no experience food styling. When it came time to shoot soufflés, I panicked and asked a real stylist for tips on how to keep them aloft while the camera clicked away. He suggested adding yeast to them, which sounded like it might work, so I gave it a try. But when I opened the oven door to pull out the first batch, they'd risen way high and arched over, looking like custardy Slinkys.

So I went back to making soufflés a few at a time the way I knew best—without yeast—and ran them from the oven to the set to be photographed. I breathed a sigh of relief each time the photographer was able to capture a few shots before the soufflés' inevitable descent. As soon as they started falling, we dove in and quickly polished them off before the next take.

Later, when we looked at the proofs, we noticed my face clearly reflected in the spoon resting alongside the soufflés, which was pretty amusing—and completely unprofessional. Although my future as a stylist was in question, no one in the studio doubted my ability to make fantastic, if not long-lasting, soufflés.

CARAMEL PASTRY CREAM

$1/2$ cup (100 g) granulated sugar

1 cup (250 ml) whole milk

3 tablespoons (25 g) all-purpose flour

3 large egg yolks

$1/2$ teaspoon vanilla extract

$1/4$ teaspoon salt

SOUFFLÉS

4 large egg whites, at room temperature

2 tablespoons (30 g) granulated sugar, plus more for sprinkling

2 ounces (60 g) bittersweet or semisweet chocolate, chopped into $1/2$-inch (1.5-cm) chunks or $1/2$ cup (80 g) chocolate chips

Powdered sugar, for dusting

Before preparing this recipe, see Caramelization Guidelines, page 265.

To make the pastry cream, spread the $1/2$ cup (100 g) granulated sugar in an even layer in a medium heavy-bottomed saucepan and cook over medium heat without stirring until the sugar begins to melt around the edges. Using a heatproof utensil, slowly drag the liquified sugar to the center and stir gently until all the sugar is melted. Continue to cook, stirring infrequently, until the caramel turns dark amber in color and begins to foam a bit. Remove from the heat and gradually stir in the milk. The caramel will bubble up vigorously, then the bubbling will subside. If the caramel seizes into a hardened mass, whisk the mixture over low heat until most of the caramel is dissolved. Don't worry about any small chunks; they'll dissolve later.

Sift the flour into the caramel mixture, then whisk to break up any lumps. Cook over medium heat, stirring frequently, until thickened. In a small bowl, whisk the egg yolks, then gradually whisk in a small amount of the hot thickened caramel mixture. Scrape the yolk mixture into the saucepan. Bring to a boil over medium heat, stirring constantly and scraping the bottom of the pan, and cook until thickened to the consistency of mayonnaise. Press the pastry cream through a mesh strainer set over a large bowl, then whisk in the vanilla and salt. Measure out $1/2$ cup (125 g) of the pastry cream and reserve it in a large bowl. Let cool completely. Cover remaining pastry cream, refrigerate, and reserve for another use.

To make the soufflés, preheat the oven to 400°F (200°C). Butter four 4-ounce (125-ml) ramekins or soufflé molds. Pour some granulated sugar into each and tilt the ramekin to coat the sides; gently tap out any excess. Set the ramekins on a baking sheet.

In a stand mixer fitted with the whip attachment (or in a bowl by hand), whisk the egg whites on low speed until frothy. Increase the speed to high, gradually add the 2 tablespoons (30 g) granulated sugar, and continue whisking until the whites form shiny, stiff peaks.

Fold one-quarter of the whipped egg whites into the reserved pastry cream, then gently fold in the chocolate chunks or chips. Fold in the remaining whites, taking care not to deflate them. A few streaks of egg whites are preferable to an overfolded and deflated soufflé mixture.

Divide the soufflé mixture evenly among the prepared ramekins, filling them just to the rims, then sprinkle with a generous dusting of granulated sugar. Run your thumb around inner edge of each ramekin, through the soufflé mixture, making a shallow, even channel as you go. This will allow the soufflés to bake up with nice crowns. Bake until the tops are browned and the soufflés quiver softly when gently nudged, about 9 minutes.

Serve the soufflés right away dusted with powdered sugar.

SERVING: Quickly split open at the table, the soufflés are great with very cold crème anglaise (page 237) poured into them, or with a scoop of Vanilla Ice Cream (page 143) or Chocolate Gelato (page 146) melting in the center.

STORAGE: The caramel pastry cream can be made up to 3 days in advance and refrigerated.

VARIATION: In lieu of topping each soufflé with powdered sugar before serving, scatter a few granules of good sea salt, such as *fleur de sel*, over the top of each soufflé before baking. The delicate flakes add a whisper of salty crunch to contrast against the warm caramel and melting chunks of chocolate.

Banana Soufflés

MAKES 4 SERVINGS

Sweet, creamy mashed banana pulp is an ideal soufflé base, but if you think bananas are just too humble to be turned into an elegant dessert worthy of serving to guests, try these simple soufflés spruced up with some warm chocolate sauce passed alongside. Be sure the bananas that you use are really ripe—the skins of yellow bananas (as opposed to red ones that are less common) should be covered with black speckles and their texture should be soft.

2 medium very ripe bananas, mashed

2 teaspoons rum

$1/2$ teaspoon freshly squeezed lemon juice

$1/2$ cup (125 ml) pastry cream (page 236)

4 large egg whites, at room temperature

Pinch of salt

2 tablespoons (30 g) sugar, plus more for sprinkling

Position an oven rack in the upper third of the oven and preheat the oven to 400°F (200°C). Butter four 4-ounce (125-ml) ramekins or soufflé molds. Pour some sugar into each and tilt the ramekin to coat the sides; gently tap out any excess. Set the ramekins on a baking sheet.

To make the soufflé base, in a large bowl, thoroughly mix together the mashed bananas, rum, lemon juice, and pastry cream.

In a stand mixer fitted with the whip attachment (or in a bowl by hand), whisk together the egg whites and salt on low speed until frothy. Increase the speed to high, gradually add the 2 tablespoons (30 g) sugar, and continue whisking until the whites form shiny, stiff peaks.

Fold one-quarter of the whipped egg whites into the soufflé base, then gently fold in the remaining whites, taking care not to deflate them. A few streaks of egg whites are preferable to an overfolded and deflated soufflé mixture.

Divide the soufflé mixture evenly among the prepared ramekins, filling each to just below the rim, then sprinkle with a light, even dusting of sugar. Bake until the tops are nicely browned and the soufflés quiver softly when gently nudged, about 10 minutes.

Serve the soufflés right away.

SERVING: Pass a pitcher of Bittersweet Chocolate Sauce (page 243) or Raspberry Sauce (page 246) at the table for pouring into the soufflés.

STORAGE: The soufflé mixture, once divided among the ramekins, can stand at room temperature for up to 1 hour before baking.

VARIATIONS: You can make a less rich version of these soufflés (that also happens to be gluten-free) by simply substituting 4 teaspoons of sugar for the pastry cream when making the soufflé base.

For CHOCOLATE CHIP BANANA SOUFFLÉS, add about 2 ounces (60 g) chopped dark or milk chocolate to the soufflé base when folding in the egg whites.

Buttermilk Panna Cotta with Blueberry Compote

MAKES 4 SERVINGS

Panna cotta quickly became a popular restaurant dessert for many of the same reasons that make it an ideal dessert to serve at home: it can be prepared well in advance and it tastes good. It's a win-win dessert if there ever was one.

I used to refer to this as "ranch panna cotta" because it was inspired by a tangy buttermilk-based drink that I had at a south-of-the-border spa. But because people said that moniker brought to mind ranch salad dressing, I decided to keep the name simple and straightforward—just like the dessert.

1¹/₃ cups (330 ml) half-and-half

¹/₂ cup (100 g) sugar

Grated zest of 2 lemons, preferably organic

2 cinnamon sticks

3 tablespoons (45 ml) cold water

1 envelope (7 g) unflavored gelatin

²/₃ cup (160 ml) buttermilk

Blueberry Compote (page 245)

Lightly grease four 4- to 6-ounce (125- to 180-ml) ramekins or custard cups with unflavored vegetable oil.

In a medium saucepan, heat the half-and-half, sugar, lemon zest, and cinnamon sticks, stirring to dissolve the sugar. Once warm, remove from the heat, cover, and let steep for 1 hour.

Pour the water into a medium bowl and sprinkle evenly with the gelatin. Allow the gelatin to soften and swell for 5 minutes. Set a mesh strainer across the bowl.

Reheat the half-and-half until it's quite warm, but not hot, and pour it through the strainer over the softened gelatin. Stir the mixture until the gelatin completely dissolves. Let the mixture cool slightly, then stir in the buttermilk. (If the half-and-half mixture is too hot, the buttermilk may separate when it's added. If it does, whisk vigorously and it will become smooth.)

Divide the mixture evenly among the ramekins. Cover with plastic wrap and refrigerate until chilled, at least 6 hours or preferably overnight.

To unmold, run a sharp knife around the inside of each ramekin to loosen the panna cotta, invert a serving plate over the ramekin, and turn them over together. Shake a few times to release the panna cotta, then lift off the ramekin.

Spoon the blueberry compote over and around the panna cotta.

STORAGE: The panna cotta will keep in the refrigerator for up to 5 days.

VARIATION: Instead of serving with blueberry compote, toss any mixture of fresh berries with some sugar and crème de cassis, let them sit for a while to soften, then spoon them over and around the panna cotta.

TIP: If you're in a hurry, after adding the buttermilk, set the bowl over an ice bath and stir to hasten the cooling, then pour the mixture into chilled ramekins so the panna cotta firms up faster. Or, you can pour the mixture into wine glasses, chill them, and serve the panna cotta in the glasses. Even if the panna cotta are not fully set by serving time, they'll be spoonable, and very elegant. This recipe can easily be doubled.

Orange-Almond Bread Pudding

MAKES 8 TO 10 SERVINGS

My grandmother used to throw a fit if I ordered something as simple as fruit salad or soup in a restaurant. "Why pay for that? You can make it at home," she'd say in a voice that made you feel like a fool if you had the temerity to disagree. "Order something else!" Anyone who met my grandmother knew it was best not to cross her. Otherwise, you'd hear about it, repeatedly, for the next three to five years. Minimum.

I feel that way about bread pudding. It's something I want at home, not in a restaurant. My version mingles orange and almond and is a much more refined and luxurious than the usual bread pudding. Enjoy it in the comfort of your own dining room, but pretend you're eating it in a restaurant, without anyone to harp on you about it. In case any of your guests decides to leave a tip, I'll gladly accept my 15 percent.

2 cups (500 ml) whole milk

2 cups (500 ml) heavy cream

Grated zest of 4 oranges, preferably organic

$^1/_2$ cup (100 g) sugar, plus more for sprinkling

6 large egg yolks

$^1/_2$ teaspoon vanilla extract

$^1/_4$ teaspoon almond extract

1 tablespoon orange-flavored liqueur, such as Grand Marnier, Cointreau, or Triple Sec

$^1/_2$ teaspoon ground cinnamon

1 large egg white, at room temperature

7 ounces (200 g) almond paste, crumbled

1 loaf (1 pound/450 g) firm-textured white bread (such as *pain de mie*), cut into $^1/_2$-inch (1.5-cm) slices

In a medium saucepan, warm the milk, cream, orange zest, and the $^1/_2$ cup (100 g) sugar, stirring to dissolve the sugar. Remove from the heat, cover, and let steep for 1 hour.

Reheat the milk-cream mixture until it's quite warm. In a medium bowl, whisk the egg yolks, then gradually whisk in the warm milk-cream mixture, whisking constantly as you pour to prevent the eggs from cooking. Whisk in the vanilla and almond extracts, orange liqueur, and cinnamon. Pour the mixture through a mesh strainer into a bowl or large pitcher. Set aside.

Butter a 2-quart (2-liter) shallow baking dish or soufflé mold.

In a small bowl, beat together the egg white and almond paste until smooth. Spread a spoonful of almond paste over one side of each bread slice. Layer the bread

slices in the prepared baking dish, almond paste side down. (If you are using a round or oval dish, halve each slice of bread diagonally to form triangles, then make layers of triangles arranged in a pinwheel pattern.) Pour the milk–egg yolk mixture over the bread and gently press the bread down, submerging the layers in the liquid. Cover with plastic wrap and refrigerate the pudding for at least 1 hour or up to overnight, pressing down the bread from time to time so that it becomes completely saturated.

Preheat the oven to 350°F (175°C).

Sprinkle the top of the pudding very liberally with sugar. Set the baking dish in a larger roasting pan and pour warm water into the pan to reach halfway up the sides of the baking dish. Bake until the bread pudding is puffed in the center and the top is rich golden brown, about 1 hour. Let cool until warm.

SERVING: Bread pudding is best served warm. It's good all by itself, but it's *great* with a ladleful of Rich Caramel Sauce (page 241) or Tangerine Butterscotch Sauce (page 242).

STORAGE: The unbaked pudding should be chilled for at least 1 hour or up to 1 day before baking. Once baked, it can be refrigerated overnight and rewarmed in a low oven, covered with aluminum foil.

VARIATION: To make a chocolate-studded bread pudding, add 10 ounces (280 g) coarsely chopped dark or milk chocolate, distributing some in the bottom of the baking dish and between the layers of bread as you arrange them in the dish.

Creamy Rice Pudding

MAKES 4 TO 6 SERVINGS

I definitely have obsessive-compulsive baking disorder. I'd hoped to recreate the classic *gâteau de riz*, a French cake made by baking rice pudding in a mold. I tried fourteen times. The first time I made it, it was perfect: custardy and topped with a deep-golden crust, the top and sides bathed with a slick of glossy, thick caramel. When I attempted to reproduce it, it came out completely different with each try. Flummoxed, I sent my recipe to a friend in California. She made it two or three times and each time she also had completely different results.

After a transcontinental tossing up of our hands, in her last anxiety-ridden response she told me, "but right out of the pot, it was the best rice pudding I've ever had." And when I made it again, for the fifteenth time, I realized she was right.

$1/4$ cup (30 g) raisins

2 tablespoons (30 ml) Armagnac or rum

5 cups (1.25 liters) whole milk

$3/4$ cup (150 g) Arborio rice

$1/2$ cup (100 g) sugar

$1/4$ teaspoon salt

1 vanilla bean, split lengthwise

In a small saucepan, heat the raisins and Armagnac or rum and simmer until most of the liquid is absorbed, about 1 minute. Remove from the heat, cover, and set aside.

In a large saucepan, combine the milk, rice, sugar, and salt. Scrape the seeds from the vanilla bean and add them to the saucepan, then drop in the pod. Cook over low heat at a gentle simmer, stirring frequently with a heatproof rubber spatula to make sure that the rice isn't sticking to the bottom. At first, the mixture will be rather liquidy, but as the mixture thickens, you'll need to be vigilant and stir almost constantly. When the milk has been absorbed by the rice and the pudding resembles a loose risotto, which will take about 45 minutes, remove the pan from the heat. Remove the vanilla pod (it can be rinsed, dried, and used for another purpose; see page 14), then stir in the raisins and any unabsorbed soaking liquid.

Serve warm or at room temperature.

SERVING: Drizzle individual servings with Cognac Caramel Sauce (page 240) or Orange Caramel Sauce (page 242).

STORAGE: The rice pudding can be stored in the refrigerator for up to 3 days. If it loses its creaminess, stir in some more milk or cream, until it reaches the desired consistency.

VARIATIONS: To make ORANGE–BAY LEAF RICE PUDDING, add 3 fresh or 2 dried bay leaves in place of the vanilla bean and four 1-inch (3-cm) wide strips of orange zest. Cook as directed, then remove the bay leaves and zest strips before serving.

If you like very rich rice pudding, substitute $2^{1}/2$ cups (625 ml) heavy cream or half-and-half for an equal amount of the milk.

> TIP: Arborio rice is used to make risotto and is sold in most supermarkets. Similar Italian short-grain rice, such as Carnaroli, can also be used. If you can't find either, substitute regular short-grain rice; the texture of the pudding will be a bit less creamy, but it will still taste delicious.

Coconut Tapioca Pudding

MAKES 8 SERVINGS

I feel sorry for people who tell me that their mother's cooking was terrible: I can't imagine eighteen years of eating bad food. Fortunately, my esteemed lineage included a mom who was a fantastic cook. Unfortunately, though, she was lacking the baking gene, so cookies and cakes were few and far between.

She did, however, make wonderful tapioca pudding, which she served warm in a bright-red '60s-style glass bowl. She always added an entire capful of aromatic vanilla extract to the pudding, stirred in at the last minute. Being hopelessly nostalgic (especially when it comes to desserts), I can still smell it to this day.

Of course, back then there wasn't much fusion cooking going on, but nowadays Thai coconut milk is readily available, and I use it in my version of tapioca pudding. In addition to vanilla extract, I include a vanilla bean for good measure. I don't have any children, but if I did, I would hope this pudding would be just as memorable for them as my mom's is for me.

$3^{1}/_{2}$ (875 ml) cups Thai coconut milk

$1^{3}/_{4}$ cups (430 ml) whole or low-fat milk

1 cup (200 g) sugar

1 cup (160 g) small pearl tapioca

Pinch of salt

1 vanilla bean, split lengthwise

3 large eggs, separated

$^{1}/_{2}$ teaspoon vanilla extract

Dried unsweetened shredded or flaked coconut or shards of fresh coconut, toasted

In a medium saucepan, combine the coconut milk, milk, sugar, tapioca, and salt. Scrape the seeds from the vanilla bean and add them to the saucepan, then drop in the pod. Cook over low heat, stirring constantly with a heatproof spatula to make sure the mixture isn't scorching on the bottom, until the pudding thickens and the tapioca pearls are completely cooked through and translucent, about 20 minutes. Remove from the heat.

Briskly stir the egg yolks into the pudding, incorporating them quickly. Let cool for about 10 minutes. Remove the vanilla pod (it can rinsed, dried, and used for another purpose; see page 14).

In a stand mixer fitted with the whip attachment (or in a bowl by hand), whisk the egg whites on medium speed until they form soft peaks. Fold the whipped egg whites into the pudding, then stir in the vanilla extract.

The pudding can be served warm or cold. Spoon it into individual serving dishes and top with toasted coconut.

SERVING: A simple compote of fresh tropical fruit, such as cubes of banana, mangoes, papayas, and pineapple, tossed in brown sugar, is a perfect accompaniment to the pudding.

STORAGE: Tapioca pudding will keep for 3 days in the refrigerator.

> TIP: Small pearl tapioca can be found in Asian markets along with Thai coconut milk, which is also available in well-stocked supermarkets.

Frozen Desserts

I've never met anyone who doesn't like ice cream, so I felt it was my duty to write a book, *The Perfect Scoop,* filled with recipes for frozen desserts of all kinds, as well as mix-ins, sauces, and accompaniments. Still, I wasn't prepared for the avalanche of feedback that I received from devout ice cream makers all over the world who churn up their own delights at home.

Working in professional kitchens for many years, I was fortunate to have access to top-quality equipment that made churning ice cream a breeze. Nowadays, ice cream machines for the home kitchen are affordably priced, so the only reason *not* to start churning out homemade ice cream is that once you start, you'll find it hard to stop!

Most ice creams are custard based, meaning the base mixture is made of eggs and dairy cooked gently on the stove top. It's quite easy to do, but be sure to prepare everything in advance before you start cooking. As the first step, read the recipe completely through and have all your equipment and ingredients ready. Once done, the custard should be cooled over an ice bath: fill a large bowl or your sink with ice and a small amount of water and set the bowl of hot custard in it to help cool it down quickly.

Sorbets and sherbets are ice cream's leaner cousins whose tastes rely on fresh fruits and flavorful liquids such as wine and coconut milk. Sorbets don't contain any dairy and eggs; most sherbets are made with a pour of milk that lends a touch of richness.

Some sorbets contain alcohol to keep them soft and scoopable when frozen, although sometimes the alcohol is there for flavor. If you're serving sorbets or ice creams to kids, or to people who are avoiding alcohol, in many cases you simply can omit the alcohol. The exceptions are those sorbets like the Sangria Sorbet (page 158) that uses wine as a base, and the No-Machine Chocolate-Banana Ice Cream (page 147) that relies on liquor for its texture since it isn't churned.

For those of you poor souls without ice cream makers, don't skip over this chapter: I've included a few desserts that don't require a machine, such as a frozen mousse (page 178) and a frozen wine-based sabayon (page 180). Both are so soft and creamy, and so utterly ethereal, that even if you have a machine, you should give them a spin.

LET IT CHILL: Ice cream, sorbet, gelato, and sherbet churn up much better—and faster—if the mixture is cold when it's poured into the ice cream machine. In ice cream recipes, I hold back part of the dairy and strain the custard into it, then chill the mixture over an ice bath to really speed things up.

A thoroughly chilled mixture spends a minimum amount of time churning in the machine. The shorter the churning time, the smaller the ice crystals, and the smoother the final texture will be. So, for best results, I recommend chilling all ice cream, sorbet, gelato, and sherbet mixtures for at least 8 hours, or, better yet, overnight before churning.

Vanilla Ice Cream

MAKES ABOUT 1 QUART (1 LITER)

This is the vanilla ice cream recipe that I've been using for over three decades, and I've not found one better. Some ask why I choose to use both vanilla extract and a bean. While I love the taste that the bean infuses into the custard, I find that a little extract boosts and brightens the vanilla flavor tremendously, so I use both.

You can use any kind of vanilla you prefer: Bourbon is the strongest, Tahitian is more floral, or real Mexican (not the cheap stuff), which is a revelation if you haven't had it.

1 cup (250 ml) whole milk

Pinch of salt

$^3/_4$ cups (150 g) sugar

1 vanilla bean, split lengthwise

2 cups (500 ml) heavy cream

5 large egg yolks

$^3/_4$ teaspoon vanilla extract

In a medium saucepan, warm the milk, salt, and sugar, stirring to dissolve the sugar. Scrape the seeds from the vanilla bean and add them to the saucepan, then drop in the pod. Cover, remove from the heat, and let steep for 30 minutes.

Pour the cream into a medium bowl and set a mesh strainer across the top.

Reheat the milk mixture until it's warm. In a separate bowl, whisk the egg yolks, then gradually add some of the warm milk mixture, whisking constantly as you pour. Pour the warmed yolks back into the saucepan. Cook over low heat, stirring constantly and scraping the bottom of the pan with a heatproof spatula, until the custard is thick enough to coat the spatula. Pour the custard through the mesh strainer into the heavy cream. Rinse the vanilla pod and return it to the custard to continue steeping; stir in the vanilla extract.

Set the bowl containing the custard over a larger bowl of ice water. Stir the custard until cool, then cover and refrigerate until thoroughly chilled.

Remove the vanilla bean (it can be rinsed, dried, and used for another purpose; see page 14) and freeze the chilled custard in an ice cream machine according to the manufacturer's instructions.

Caramel Ice Cream

MAKES ABOUT 1 QUART (1 LITER)

If there's anything better than a big, melty scoop of caramel ice cream, I don't know what it could be.

On second thought, I take that back. How about a big scoop of caramel ice doused with lots of warm chocolate sauce and sprinkled with toasted pecans?

To make this ice cream the most perfect caramel ice cream you'll ever eat, it's crucial to cook the sugar until it's dark amber in color and as close to—but just shy of—burnt as possible. I call it "taking it right to the edge."

I like the flavor of the ice cream made with the larger amount of salt, but because some people are salt sensitive, the recipe says to start with less, then taste the custard and add more if desired. No matter how long it's frozen, this caramel ice cream stays scoopably soft, a big relief to those of us who are irked by homemade ice cream that freezes rock-solid and delays immediate gratification.

1 cup (200 g) sugar

2 cups (500 ml) whole milk

1/4 to 1/2 teaspoon sea salt

1 cup (250 ml) heavy cream

5 large egg yolks

1/2 teaspoon vanilla extract

> Before preparing this recipe, see Caramelization Guidelines, page 265.

Spread the sugar in an even layer in a large, heavy-bottomed saucepan and cook over medium heat, without stirring, until the sugar begins to melt around the edges. Using a heatproof utensil, slowly drag the liquified sugar to the center and stir gently until all the sugar is melted. Continue to cook, stirring infrequently, until the caramel turns dark amber in color and begins to foam a bit. Remove from the heat and immediately add the milk. The caramel will bubble up vigorously, then the bubbling will subside.

Set the saucepan over low heat, add 1/4 teaspoon salt, and stir until almost all of the hardened caramel has dissolved into the milk. A few bits may remain, but don't worry; they'll melt later on.

Pour the cream into a medium bowl and set a mesh strainer across the top.

In a separate bowl, whisk the egg yolks, then gradually add some of the warm caramel mixture, whisking constantly as you pour. Pour the warmed yolks back into the saucepan. Cook over low heat, stirring constantly and scraping the bottom of the pan with a heatproof spatula, until the custard is thick enough to coat the spatula. Pour the custard through the mesh strainer into the heavy cream. Stir in the vanilla, then taste, and add up to 1/4 teaspoon more salt, if desired.

Set the bowl containing the custard over a larger bowl of ice water. Stir the custard until cool, then cover and refrigerate until thoroughly chilled.

Freeze in an ice cream machine according to the manufacturer's instructions.

VARIATIONS: Although wonderful by itself, caramel ice cream is also a perfect base for mix-ins such as chopped chocolate or candy bars, bits of broken caramel, crumbled brownies, or toasted nuts. Stir in 1 to 2 cups (100 to 200 g) just after churning.

I often substitute 1 cup (240 g) of sour cream or crème fraîche for the cream in this recipe. If you use crème fraîche, be sure to cool and freeze the ice cream mixture within a few hours. If you leave it overnight, the crème fraîche's culture may make the mixture too tangy.

Chocolate Gelato

MAKES ABOUT 3 CUPS (750 ML)

When you live in San Francisco, it's likely that at least 50 percent of your friends are real estate agents. One of my realtor friends is whippet-thin because he's always watching what he eats. But he met his match with this frozen dessert. When he isn't trying to talk me into buying or selling something, he talks about this gelato.

People often ask about the difference between ice cream and gelato. As with most things Italian, it depends on whom you ask. But most people agree that gelato has a lower-fat base, which allows the flavors to shine through. This chocolate gelato has no cream and is proof of that theory. As is the waistline of a certain San Francisco realtor.

This gelato is inspired by a recipe from Marcella Hazan.

5 ounces (140 g) bittersweet or semisweet chocolate, chopped

1/2 cup (50 g) unsweetened cocoa powder, preferably Dutch-process

1 cup (250 ml) plus 1 cup (250 ml) whole milk

Pinch of salt

3/4 cup (150 g) sugar

4 large egg yolks

Put the chocolate in a large bowl.

In a medium saucepan, whisk together the cocoa, 1 cup (250 ml) milk, and the salt. Bring to a full boil, then pour the mixture over the chocolate, scraping the pan clean. Stir until the chocolate is melted and the mixture is smooth. Set a mesh strainer across the top of the bowl.

In the same saucepan, warm the remaining 1 cup (250 ml) milk with the sugar, stirring to dissolve the sugar.

In a separate bowl, whisk the egg yolks, then gradually add some of the warm milk-sugar mixture, whisking constantly as you pour. Pour the warmed yolks back into the saucepan. Cook over low heat, stirring constantly and scraping the bottom of the pan with a heatproof spatula, until the custard is thick enough to coat the spatula. Pour the custard through the mesh strainer into the chocolate mixture and stir until smooth.

Set the bowl containing the custard over a larger bowl of ice water. Stir the custard until cool, then cover and refrigerate until thoroughly chilled.

Freeze in an ice cream machine according to the manufacturer's instructions.

No-Machine Chocolate-Banana Ice Cream

MAKES ABOUT 3 CUPS (750 ML)

This is the world's easiest ice cream. It takes literally a minute to put together, and doesn't require an ice cream maker. You just toss everything in a blender, then pour the mixture into a container and freeze it, so there's no excuse for even the machineless not to enjoy homemade ice cream. The one caveat is that the generous amount of alcohol is necessary to prevent the ice cream from freezing too hard. The good news is that all that booze means you don't have to share your ice cream with the kids.

6 ounces (170 g) bittersweet or semisweet chocolate, chopped

1 cup plus 2 tablespoons (280 ml) whole or low-fat milk

1 cup plus 2 tablespoons (280 ml) Irish cream liqueur, such as Bailey's Irish Cream

3 very ripe medium bananas, peeled and cut into chunks

3 tablespoons (45 ml) dark rum

In a small heatproof bowl, combine the chocolate and milk. Set the bowl over a saucepan of simmering water and stir occasionally until the chocolate is melted and smooth. Remove the bowl from the heat.

Pour the liqueur into a blender or food processor fitted with the metal blade. Add the bananas, rum, and the melted chocolate mixture and purée until smooth.

Pour the mixture into a shallow plastic container, cover, and freeze until solid enough to scoop, at least 8 hours, preferably overnight.

Mexican Chocolate Ice Cream

MAKES ABOUT 1 QUART (1 LITER)

The first time I went to Mexico, I had no idea that ice cream was such a popular treat there. I had always associated ice cream with Italy, France, and the United States. Who knew?

During that first trip, and more than a few subsequent ones, I made it a point to try the more unusual flavors, like ice cream flavored with cheese, smoked milk, and kernels of corn, and even fried ice cream (which was delicious!). But as much as I enjoyed trying new ice creams, I always found myself going back to chocolate.

Here's a recipe inspired by those coarse chunks of chocolate for sale in Mexico. They taste nothing like the disks of Mexican "drinking chocolate" sold in America, which are mostly sugar and rather skimpy on the chocolate. For this ice cream, use real chocolate and add freshly ground cinnamon for the best flavor.

3 ounces (85 g) bittersweet or semisweet chocolate, chopped

2 1/2 ounces (70 g) unsweetened chocolate, chopped

2 cups (500 ml) heavy cream

3 tablespoons (45 ml) brandy

1 cup (250 ml) whole milk

3/4 cup (150 g) sugar

3/4 teaspoon ground cinnamon

4 large egg yolks

1 cup (135 g) almonds, toasted and coarsely chopped

In a large heatproof bowl, combine the chocolates, cream, and brandy. Set the bowl over a saucepan of simmering water and stir occasionally until the chocolate is melted and smooth. Remove the bowl from the heat and set a mesh strainer across the top.

In a medium saucepan, warm the milk, sugar, and cinnamon, stirring to dissolve the sugar.

In a separate bowl, whisk the egg yolks, then gradually add some of the warm milk-sugar mixture, whisking constantly as you pour. Pour the warmed yolks back into the saucepan. Cook over low heat, stirring constantly and scraping the bottom of the pan with a heatproof spatula, until the custard is thick enough to coat the spatula. Pour the custard through the mesh strainer into the chocolate mixture and stir until smooth.

Set the bowl containing the custard over a larger bowl of ice water. Stir the custard until cool, then cover and refrigerate until thoroughly chilled.

Freeze in an ice cream machine according to the manufacturer's instructions. Stir the almonds into the just-churned ice cream when you remove it from the ice cream machine.

White Chocolate–Ginger Ice Cream with Chocolate Covered Peanuts

MAKES ABOUT 1 QUART (1 LITER)

Some folks tell me they don't like white chocolate. "It's not chocolate!" they'll say with a bit of smug certitude. True, but that's like saying "I don't like Champagne because it's not white wine." Both have merits and to say you don't like one because it isn't the other isn't very logical.

I fall into the camp of white chocolate lovers. To convince people of how good white chocolate can be, I often make ice cream with it and add fresh ginger for spicy contrast. And if that's not enough, I stir in shiny, dark chocolate–covered roasted peanuts to give it nice crunch. If anyone still has any resistance to white chocolate, I call it their loss and am happy to eat the ice cream all by myself.

WHITE CHOCOLATE–GINGER ICE CREAM

3-inch (8-cm) piece fresh ginger, thinly sliced

1/2 cup (100 g) sugar

1 cup (250 ml) whole milk

1 cup (250 ml) plus 1 cup (250 ml) heavy cream

7 ounces (200 g) white chocolate, chopped

4 large egg yolks

CHOCOLATE COVERED PEANUTS

5 ounces (140 g) bittersweet or semisweet chocolate, chopped

1 cup (150 g) unsalted roasted peanuts

To make the ice cream, put the ginger slices in a medium saucepan and add water to cover. Bring to a boil, then decrease the heat and simmer for 2 minutes. Pour off the water. Add the sugar, milk, and 1 cup (250 ml) cream. Heat the mixture until warm, remove from the heat, cover, and let steep for 1 hour.

Using a slotted spoon, remove and discard the ginger slices, then reheat the cream mixture until it's warm.

Put the white chocolate in a large bowl and set a mesh strainer across the top.

In a separate bowl, whisk the egg yolks, then gradually add some of the warmed milk mixture, whisking constantly as you pour. Pour the warmed yolks back into the saucepan.

Cook over low heat, stirring constantly and scraping the bottom of the pan with a heatproof spatula, until the custard is thick enough to coat the spatula. Pour the custard through the mesh strainer into the chocolate and stir until the chocolate is melted and smooth. Add the remaining 1 cup (250 ml) cream.

Set the bowl containing the custard over a larger bowl of ice water. Stir the custard until cool, then cover and refrigerate until thoroughly chilled.

To make the chocolate covered peanuts, add the chocolate to a medium heatproof bowl, set the bowl over a saucepan of simmering water, and stir occasionally until the chocolate is melted and smooth.

Line a dinner plate with plastic wrap or parchment paper. Remove the chocolate from the heat, add the peanuts, and stir until coated, then spread the mixture on the plate. Refrigerate until firm, then chop into small pieces.

Freeze the custard in an ice cream machine according to the manufacturer's instructions. Stir the chopped chocolate covered peanuts into the just-churned ice cream when you remove it from the ice cream machine.

VARIATIONS: White chocolate–ginger ice cream made without the chocolate covered peanuts is terrific served with summer fruit desserts, such as Nectarine-Berry Cobbler (page 104). Or, for an extra dose of spiciness, you can replace the chocolate-covered peanuts with 1/2 cup (50 g) finely chopped Candied Ginger (page 252).

> TIP: Make sure to use real white chocolate. Bars labeled "white bar" and "baking white" often aren't white chocolate but imitations that lack the cocoa butter–rich flavor of true white chocolate. Real white chocolate (which is ivory in color) is labeled as such.

Butterscotch-Pecan Ice Cream

MAKES ABOUT 1 QUART (1 LITER)

My parents were pretty strict with desserts. I wasn't completely deprived, but sweets were few and far between. (I've since made up for lost time.) One treat they did keep on hand was a bag of store-bought pecan shortbreads, which were quite thick, had a sandy texture, and seemed a bit more sophisticated and "adult" than most other supermarket snacks. Whenever these cookies were in the house, I ate as many as I could and left a seriously plundered bag for my parents to discover.

Times have changed and I'm sure the quantity of pecans in those cookies has dwindled since the good ol' days. Now that I'm all grown up, I can enjoy pecans in any way I choose, and that doesn't mean just pecan shortbread, but also this rich pecan-studded ice cream.

6 tablespoons (75 g) granulated sugar

$3/4$ cup (170 g) packed dark brown sugar

4 tablespoons (2 ounces/60g) unsalted or salted butter, cut into pieces

$1/2$ cup (125 ml) plus $1 1/2$ cups (375 ml) heavy cream

$3/4$ cup (180 ml) half-and-half or whole milk

$1/2$ teaspoon salt

6 large egg yolks

$1 1/2$ cups (150 g) pecans, toasted and coarsely chopped

> Before preparing this recipe, see Caramelization Guidelines, page 265.

To make the butterscotch mixture, spread the granulated sugar in an even layer in a medium heavy-bottomed saucepan and cook over medium heat without stirring until the sugar begins to melt around the edges. Using a heatproof utensil, slowly drag the liquified sugar to the center and stir gently until all the sugar is melted. Continue to cook, stirring infrequently, until the caramel turns dark amber in color and begins to foam a bit. Remove from the heat and immediately stir in the brown sugar, butter, the $1/2$ cup (125 ml) cream, the half-and-half or milk, and salt. The mixture will steam and bubble up vigorously, then the bubling will subside.

Pour the remaining $1 1/2$ cups (375 ml) cream into a large bowl and set a mesh strainer across the top.

In a separate bowl, whisk the egg yolks, then gradually add some of the warm butterscotch mixture, whisking constantly as you pour. Pour the warmed yolks back into the saucepan. Cook over low heat, stirring constantly and scraping the bottom of the pan with a heatproof spatula, until the custard is thick enough to coat the spatula. Pour the custard through the mesh strainer into the cream.

Set the bowl containing the custard over a larger bowl of ice water. Stir the custard until cool, then cover and refrigerate until thoroughly chilled.

Freeze in an ice cream machine according to the manufacturer's instructions. Stir the pecans into the just-churned ice cream when you remove it from the ice cream machine.

VARIATION: Use $1 1/2$ cups (150 g) of Spiced Candied Pecans (page 224) in place of the plain pecans.

> TIP: Because brown sugar is acidic, the mixture can look curdled during the custard-making process. Not to worry; it'll smooth out during cooking.

Toasted Coconut Sherbet

MAKES ABOUT 1 QUART (1 LITER)

There are some very strange people out there who claim not to like coconut. I don't know how on earth a person couldn't love something that's naturally sweet, creamy, and the ideal companion to any and all tropical fruits—and a perfect mate to chocolate, too. This sherbet drizzled with Bittersweet Chocolate Sauce (page 243) will make a coconut convert of any nonbeliever.

4 cups (1 liter) whole milk

1 cup (200 g) sugar

1¼ cups (90 g) dried unsweetened shredded coconut, toasted

¼ vanilla bean, split lengthwise

3 large egg whites

Pinch of salt

In a medium saucepan, combine the milk, sugar, and toasted coconut. Scrape the seeds from the vanilla bean and add them to the saucepan, then drop in the pod. Heat the mixture until it's warm, then remove from the heat, cover, and let steep for 1 hour.

Pour the mixture through a mesh strainer set over a bowl and squeeze the coconut with your hand to fully extract the flavor; discard the coconut. (The vanilla pod can be rinsed, dried, and used for another purpose; see page 14.) Cover and refrigerate until thoroughly chilled.

Just before churning, in a stand mixer fitted with the whip attachment (or in a bowl by hand), whisk together the egg whites and salt on high speed until they form soft peaks. Fold the whipped egg whites into the chilled coconut-infused milk.

Freeze in an ice cream machine according to the manufacturer's instructions.

SERVING: A scoop of this sherbet is perfect nestled in a dish with Passion Fruit–Tangerine Sorbet (page 159) or Strawberry-Mango Sorbet (page 166). And I've been known to blend it with an imprudent amount of dark rum and fresh pineapple for an extraordinary piña colada.

TIPS: If you have concerns about using uncooked egg whites, use pasteurized egg whites designated "suitable for whipping," available in the refrigerated section of the supermarket. Or, you can make the sherbet without them.

I prefer to use unsweetened coconut, but if you can only find the sweetened type, reduce the sugar in the recipe by 2 tablespoons (30 g).

Chocolate-Coconut Sherbet

MAKES ABOUT 1 QUART (1 LITER)

In case anyone thinks that the Internet is a cold, impersonal place, I've got evidence to prove them wrong. One day, completely out of the blue, I received an e-mail from a server who worked at a restaurant where I'd been the pastry chef, saying that not only did I have the sweetest smile, but that she loved the sherbets and sorbets that I made there. I don't know which compliment was more touching, but I take any and all whenever I can, and via whatever medium they are sent.

This was one of the sherbets I made at that restaurant, where I remember a different server taking a bite and her face lighting right up. "This tastes like a Mounds bar!" she exclaimed with a mix of surprise and delight. For me, that was another compliment, since that's one of my favorite candy bars.

1 cup (250 ml) water

1 cup (200 g) sugar

5 ounces (140 g) bittersweet or semisweet chocolate, chopped

2 cups (500 ml) canned Thai coconut milk

1 to 2 tablespoons dark rum

In a medium saucepan, bring the water and sugar to a boil, stirring to dissolve the sugar. Remove from the heat, add the chocolate, and whisk until the chocolate is completely melted. Stir in the coconut milk and 1 tablespoon of the rum.

Pour the mixture into a blender and process until completely smooth. Taste and add 1 tablespoon more rum, if desired. Cover and refrigerate until thoroughly chilled.

Freeze in an ice cream machine according to the manufacturer's instructions.

Fresh Mint Sherbet
with Figs Roasted in Chartreuse and Honey

MAKES ABOUT 5 CUPS (1.25 L) SHERBET; 6 TO 8 SERVINGS

Somewhere along the way, mint sherbet got a bad rap. Perhaps too many catered wedding receptions began with a pallid artificially green scoop melting away in the middle of a melon half, the sherbet chosen because it matched the bridesmaids' dresses rather than for its taste. Thankfully, any color you'll find in this mint sherbet comes naturally from a big handful of fragrant, zesty fresh mint.

Unlike ice cream, sherbet is usually made with milk, and no cream or eggs, so I never feel guilty about indulging in a couple of scoops. Nor do I feel deprived if I'm craving something a tad creamy. Light yet creamy—it's a recipe for a perfect marriage.

MINT SHERBET

4 cups (1 liter) whole milk

1 cup (200 g) sugar

2 cups (80 g) lightly packed fresh mint leaves, crushed, plus a few leaves for mixing in

3 large egg whites, at room temperature

Pinch of salt

FIGS ROASTED WITH CHARTREUSE AND HONEY

1 pound (450 g) fresh figs

3 tablespoons (45 ml) Chartreuse

2 tablespoons (30 ml) honey

2 or 3 sprigs fresh thyme

To make the sherbet, in a medium saucepan, warm the milk, sugar, and crushed mint leaves, stirring to dissolve the sugar. Remove from the heat, cover, and let steep for 1 hour.

Pour the milk through a mesh strainer into a medium bowl, squeezing the mint leaves firmly to fully extract the flavor; discard the leaves. Cover the mint-infused milk and refrigerate until thoroughly chilled.

Just before churning, in a stand mixer fitted with the whip attachment (or in a bowl by hand), whisk the egg whites and salt on high speed until they form soft peaks. Fold the whipped egg whites into the chilled milk.

Freeze in an ice cream machine according to the manufacturer's instructions. Finely chop the mint leaves and fold them into the just-churned sherbet when you remove it from the ice cream machine.

To make the roasted figs, preheat the oven to 400°F (200°C). Remove the tough stem ends from the figs, then halve each one. Toss the figs in a shallow baking dish that holds them in a single layer with Chartreuse, honey, and thyme sprigs; turn the figs so they're cut side down. Cover with aluminum foil and bake until the figs are soft and tender, about 25 minutes.

Serve the figs warm or at room temperature with scoops of the mint sherbet.

STORAGE: The figs benefit from being cooked in advance—the liquid that they exude during baking becomes syrupy as they sit and is perfect for drizzling over the sherbet. If possible, bake the figs a few hours or up to 2 days before you plan to serve them, then reheat them in a low oven if you want to serve them warm.

> TIP: If you have concerns about using uncooked egg whites, use pasteurized egg whites designated "suitable for whipping," available in the refrigerated section of the supermarket. Or, you can make the sherbet without them.

Wine Grape Sorbet

MAKES ABOUT 1 QUART (1 LITER)

Lots of people eat grapes out of hand, but they don't quite know what else to do with them. Well, I do. I use them to make sorbet. Though seedless grapes are great for snacking, they're the least flavorful varieties. If you're lucky enough to live near a farmers' market, or if you can get your hands on grapes that are good for wine making, like Chardonnay, Merlot, or Zinfandel, you'll find they make the most amazing sorbets.

I have a few older Jewish aunts who swear that Concord grapes make good wine (that comes in a square bottle). I'm not so convinced about the wine, but Concord grapes do, indeed, make one of my favorite sorbets.

2¼ pounds (1 kg) wine grapes or Concord grapes, stemmed (see Tip)

¼ cup (60 ml) water

1 tablespoon sugar if using wine grapes or ¼ cup sugar (50 g) if using Concord grapes

2 tablespoons (30 ml) light corn syrup or agave nectar

Put the stemmed grapes in a large saucepan with the water. Cover and cook over medium heat, stirring occasionally, until the grapes are juicy and softened.

Remove the seeds and skins by passing the grapes through a food mill fitted with a fine disk or by pressing them through a mesh strainer set over a large bowl. Whisk the sugar and corn syrup or agave nectar into the still-warm grape juice until dissolved. (If the grape juice has cooled, rewarm it gently in a saucepan over low heat.) Cover and refrigerate until thoroughly chilled.

Freeze in an ice cream machine according to the manufacturer's instructions.

TIP: Grapes can be stemmed quickly in a stand mixer fitted with the dough hook: Put the grapes in the bowl and run the mixer on the lowest speed. The hook will pull the grapes off the stems and crush them so they cook quicker; the stems will rise to the top and can be easily removed and discarded.

SERVING: Because grapes have a lot of water, sorbet made from them tends to freeze very firmly. The sorbet is best eaten shortly after it's made; otherwise, be sure to remove it from the freezer before serving to allow it to soften.

A pour of Champagne or other sparkling wine over each serving of sorbet is a nice touch. If you used Concord grapes, a spoonful of whipped cream (page 239) provides creamy contrast.

VARIATIONS: If you don't have an ice cream machine, you can make GRAPE GRANITA. Pour the mixture into a shallow plastic container and place it in the freezer. Check periodically, and as the mixture freezes over the course of a few hours, stir and rake the mixture with a fork several times to create grainy crystals.

Instead of using fresh grapes, you can use 3 cups (750 ml) good-quality unsweetened grape juice. Warm 1 cup (250 ml) of it with the sugar and corn syrup or agave nectar until the sugar dissolves, then mix in the remaining grape juice.

Blood Orange Sorbet Surprise

MAKES ABOUT 3 CUPS (750 ML) SORBET; 8 SERVINGS

I read an article in a magazine about the difference between being "frugal" and "cheap" and was relieved to find myself in the frugal category. I'm certainly not cheap when it comes to buying ingredients, but it does go against my frugal nature to throw anything away.

Here, oranges do double duty: the insides supply the juice and the rinds become the serving dishes for the sorbet. Those who are extra thrifty can candy some of the leftover peels to go alongside (see Candied Orange Peel, page 254). Egg whites left over from another project can be used to make the fluffy meringue that hides the sorbet surprise underneath.

BLOOD ORANGE SORBET

$2^{1}/_{2}$ cups (625 ml) freshly squeezed blood orange juice (from about 4 pounds/2 kg oranges), juiced halves reserved

$^{2}/_{3}$ cup (130 g) sugar

2 teaspoons orange-flavored liqueur, such as Grand Marnier, Cointreau, or Triple Sec

MERINGUE

3 large egg whites, at room temperature

$^{1}/_{2}$ cup (100 g) sugar

$^{1}/_{2}$ teaspoon vanilla extract

To make the sorbet, in a small saucepan, warm $^{1}/_{2}$ cup (125 ml) of the orange juice and the $^{2}/_{3}$ cup (130 g) sugar, stirring until the sugar completely dissolves. Pour the mixture into a medium bowl and add the remaining orange juice and the orange-flavored liqueur. Cover and refrigerate until thoroughly chilled.

Using a spoon, scrape out the membranes and any remnants of pulp from 8 of the most attractive juiced orange halves. Slice a small disk off the bottom of each half so it sits upright without wobbling.

Freeze the sorbet mixture in an ice cream machine according to the manufacturer's instructions.

To serve, spoon the just-churned sorbet into the orange halves, filling each to about $^{1}/_{2}$ inch (1.5 cm) from the top. Place the filled orange halves on a baking sheet and freeze until firm.

Preheat the oven to 450°F (230°C).

To make the meringue, in a stand mixer fitted with the whip attachment (or in a bowl by hand), whisk the egg whites on low speed until frothy. Increase the speed to high and continue whisking until the whites just begin to hold their shape. Gradually sprinkle in the $^{1}/_{2}$ cup (100 g) sugar and whisk until the whites are stiff and shiny. Whisk in the vanilla.

Spoon the meringue onto the sorbet-filled orange halves, dividing it evenly, and bake until the meringue is nicely browned, about 5 minutes. Serve right away.

STORAGE: Before baking, the meringue-topped oranges can be kept in the freezer for up to 8 hours.

VARIATION: You can make this dessert using tangerines or regular oranges instead.

Sangria Sorbet

MAKES ABOUT 3 CUPS (750 ML)

In the '80s, sangria's reputation took a nosedive when it came to be known as a syrupy-sweet wine sold in green bottles with a toreador deftly skirting a charging bull on the label. But if you go to Spain, you'll quickly realize that real sangria isn't a sugary liquid confection, but a fruity, icy cold drink that goes down easily, especially when the temperature outside is soaring. This simple-to-make sorbet turns sangria into a frozen dessert that's even more refreshing than it is as a beverage. And that's no bull.

$^3/_4$ cup (150 g) sugar

6 tablespoons (90 ml) water

1 cup (250 ml) fruity red wine, such as Zinfandel or Merlot

$1^1/_2$ cups (375 ml) freshly squeezed orange or tangerine juice

1 tablespoon orange-flavored liqueur, such as Grand Marnier, Cointreau, or Triple Sec

Grated zest of 1 orange, preferably organic

In a medium saucepan, warm the sugar and water, stirring until the sugar completely dissolves. Pour the mixture into a medium bowl, add the red wine, orange or tangerine juice, orange-flavored liqueur, and orange zest. Cover and refrigerate until thoroughly chilled.

Freeze in an ice cream machine according to the manufacturer's instructions.

SERVING: The ideal summertime accompaniment is lightly sweetened slices of peaches or nectarines with a few berries tossed in the mix. In the winter, use orange and grapefruit segments.

Chocolate-Tangerine Sorbet

MAKES ABOUT 1 QUART (1 LITER)

If you can't decide whether to serve something chocolatey or fruity for dessert, this sorbet is for you (and your guests). It's incredibly easy to make, and even people like me, who aren't especially fond of chocolate and fruit combinations, will be won over.

$1^1/_2$ cups (375 ml) water

$^2/_3$ cup (130 g) sugar

6 ounces (170 g) bittersweet or semisweet chocolate, chopped

$1^1/_2$ cups (375 ml) freshly squeezed tangerine juice

In a medium saucepan, bring the water and sugar to a boil, stirring to dissolve the sugar. Remove from the heat, add the chopped chocolate, and whisk until the chocolate is melted and smooth. Stir in the tangerine juice.

Pour the mixture into a medium bowl, cover, and refrigerate until thoroughly chilled.

Freeze in an ice cream machine according to the manufacturer's instructions.

VARIATION: You can replace the tangerine juice with freshly squeezed orange juice, but make sure that it's flavorful so that it stands up to the taste of the chocolate.

Passion Fruit–Tangerine Sorbet

MAKES ABOUT 1 QUART (1 LITER)

The first time I split open a passion fruit and slurped down the dripping juices, the intense flavor knocked me for such a loop that I felt as if a tropical bomb had gone off in my head. From then on, I was hooked.

Depending on where you live, fresh passion fruit may be hard to find, but they're well worth tracking down. Don't shy away from ones that are a tad wrinkled, as the creases indicate ripeness (they're often marked down in price, too!). You can also buy frozen passion fruit purée (see Resources, page 270), which is inexpensive and convenient. It's great to have on hand in the freezer: I'll often lop off a chunk and add it to a pitcher of orange juice for a morning tropical blast.

3 cups (750 ml) freshly squeezed tangerine juice

1 cup (200 g) sugar

1 cup (250 ml) strained fresh passion fruit pulp (from about 12 passion fruits; see Tip) or thawed frozen purée

$^1/_4$ cup (60 ml) Champagne or other sparkling wine, or 2 tablespoons (30 ml) vodka

TIP: To strain fresh passion fruit pulp, halve the fruits, scoop the pulp into a strainer set over a bowl, and press the pulp to separate the seeds from the juice. Save a few of the seeds and mix them into the sorbet just after churning.

In a medium saucepan, warm 1 cup of the tangerine juice with the sugar, stirring until the sugar completely dissolves. Pour the mixture into a medium bowl and add the remaining tangerine juice, the passion fruit pulp or purée, and the Champagne, other sparkling wine, or vodka. Cover and refrigerate until thoroughly chilled.

Freeze in an ice cream machine according to the manufacturer's instructions.

VARIATION: To make TANGERINE SORBET, omit the passion fruit juice and use a total of 4 cups (1 liter) freshly squeezed tangerine juice.

Meyer Lemon Sorbet

MAKES ABOUT 1 QUART (1 LITER)

There were quite a few things I missed about the Bay Area when I packed up my bags and moved to France. Burritos, bean-to-bar chocolates, and "centered" people were some of them. Okay, I didn't miss the centered people. But I was surprised at how much I missed Meyer lemons, which are sweeter and more perfumed than regular Eureka lemons. Their vibrant, deep yellow color makes other lemons pale in comparison.

If you're lucky enough to know someone with a Meyer lemon tree, you're likely to be handed a large sack of them when the fruits are in season. Some greengrocers and specialty markets now carry them, too. Otherwise, you can use regular Eureka lemons in this recipe, but increase the sugar to 1 cup (200 g).

$2^1/_2$ cups (625 ml) water

$^3/_4$ cup (150 g) sugar

Grated zest of 1 Meyer lemon, preferably organic

1 cup (250 ml) freshly squeezed Meyer lemon juice

$^1/_4$ cup (60 ml) Champagne or other sparkling wine, or 2 tablespoons (30 ml) vodka

TIP: This sorbet will freeze quite hard because it contains an especially large amount of water, so it's best eaten shortly after it's frozen. Or, remove it from the freezer ahead of serving so that it's soft enough to scoop. You can omit the alcohol, but the sorbet will freeze up even harder.

In a medium saucepan, bring the water, sugar, and lemon zest to a boil, stirring to dissolve the sugar. Pour into a medium bowl and let cool to room temperature.

Stir in the lemon juice and Champagne, other sparkling wine, or vodka. Cover and refrigerate until thoroughly chilled.

Freeze in an ice cream machine according to the manufacturer's instructions.

Margarita Sorbet with Salted Peanut Crisps

MAKES 1 QUART (1 LITER) SORBET AND ABOUT 40 COOKIES; 6 TO 8 SERVINGS

Sitting in the sun, overlooking the beach, I could drink margaritas all day. Unfortunately, or maybe I should say, fortunately, I don't live in a warm climate or anywhere near a beach. If I did, I'd never get anything done.

Whenever I'm looking for a taste of the tropics at home in Paris, I'll start squeezing limes in my kitchen and I'm immediately transported to paradise (albeit with bills piled up on the counter and the dishes in the sink).

Practically obligatory to serve alongside margarita sorbet are salted peanut cookies. They were inspired by the disks of solid peanut paste sold in Mexican markets called *mazapan* or *dulce de cacahuate*, which I've been known to nibble on with a margarita, or two, south of the border. And above it, as well.

SORBET

3 cups (750 ml) water

1 cup (200 g) granulated sugar

Grated zest of 4 limes, preferably organic

1 cup (250 ml) freshly squeezed lime juice

$^1/_2$ cup (125 ml) tequila

2 tablespoons (30 ml) plus 2 teaspoons orange-flavored liqueur, such as Grand Marnier, Cointreau, or Triple Sec

COOKIES

$^3/_4$ cup (115 g) unsalted roasted peanuts

$^3/_4$ cup (110 g) all-purpose flour

$^1/_2$ cup (4 ounces/115 g) unsalted butter, at room temperature

$^1/_2$ cup (100 g) granulated sugar

$^1/_4$ cup (60 g) packed light brown sugar

1 large egg

1 tablespoon boiling water

$^1/_2$ teaspoon baking soda

Flaky sea salt, for sprinkling

To make the sorbet, in a medium saucepan, bring the water, 1 cup (200 g) granulated sugar, and lime zest to a boil, stirring to dissolve the sugar. Pour the mixture into a medium bowl and let cool completely. Stir in the lime juice, tequila, and orange-flavored liqueur. Cover and refrigerate until thoroughly chilled.

Freeze in an ice cream machine according to the manufacturer's instructions.

To make the cookies, position the racks in the upper and lower thirds of the oven; preheat the oven to 325°F

(160°C). Line 2 baking sheets with parchment paper or silicone baking mats.

In a food processor fitted with the metal blade, grind the peanuts with the flour until the peanuts are in small but discernable pieces—not too fine.

In a stand mixer fitted with the paddle attachment (or in a bowl by hand), beat together the butter, $^1/_2$ cup (100 g) granulated sugar, and the brown sugar on medium speed until just combined, about 30 seconds. Beat in the egg.

In a small bowl, mix together the boiling water and baking soda and then mix it into the butter mixture. Add the peanut-flour mixture and stir just until combined.

Place heaping teaspoons of the batter in mounds at least 2$^1/_2$ inches (6 cm) apart on the prepared baking sheets. (You should be able to fit 8 per sheet.) Rap the pan a few times on the counter to flatten the mounds slightly, then sprinkle each with a very generous pinch of sea salt.

Bake, rotating the baking sheets midway during baking, until the cookies are evenly deep golden brown, about 10 minutes. Let cool completely, then use a thin metal spatula to transfer the cookies to a wire rack. Repeat to bake the remaining batter.

To serve, offer a few scoops of margarita sorbet with a few peanut crisps alongside.

STORAGE: The cookie batter can be refrigerated for up to 5 days or frozen for up to 1 month. The crisps can be made up to 2 days in advance and stored in an airtight container.

> TIP: Make sure the lime zest is grated very finely so that its texture is barely noticeable in the sorbet. A rasp-style grater does the trick nicely, but if you don't own one, mince the zest with a chef's knife.

Pink Grapefruit–Champagne Sorbet Cocktail

MAKES ABOUT 1 QUART (1 LITER) SORBET; 8 SERVINGS

There's nothing I like better than very, *very* cold Champagne. So cold that I usually drop a small ice cube into my glass to make sure it's as chilled as possible. I always feared that it was offensive and crass to ice down Champagne until I went to a tasting of Krug Champagne, considered by many to be the finest of them all. I didn't dare drop an ice cube into any of the glasses that were presented to me, but I did confide that I often did so to one of their experts, who surprised me by saying that it's perfectly acceptable to put a bit of ice in Champagne for the very reason I do it.

For this sorbet, you don't need to use the finest French Champagne. In fact, I've made it successfully with Italian prosecco and Spanish cava—without offending anyone.

2 cups (500 ml) freshly squeezed pink grapefruit juice

3/4 cup (150 g) sugar

1 cup (250 ml) Champagne or other sparkling wine

Champagne or other sparkling wine, for serving

> TIP: You can scoop the sorbet onto a chilled baking sheet and store the balls in the freezer so that they are quickly and easily dropped into the serving glasses just before serving.

In a small saucepan, warm 1/2 cup (125 ml) of the grapefruit juice and the sugar, stirring until the sugar completely dissolves.

Pour the mixture into a medium bowl and add the remaining grapefruit juice and the Champagne or other sparkling wine. Cover and refrigerate until thoroughly chilled.

Freeze in an ice cream machine according to the manufacturer's instructions.

To serve, scoop the sorbet into chilled serving glasses or Champagne flutes and pour Champagne or other sparkling wine over. Serve right away.

Watermelon-Sake Sorbet

MAKES ABOUT 1 QUART (1 LITER)

I know you're going to be tempted to use seedless watermelon here, but don't. I've never tasted one that I particularly liked. And because I have a penchant for making things harder than they should be, I don't mind plucking out the seeds. For some reason, the harder something is to make, the better it tastes. (And I wonder why I spend a majority of my life in the kitchen.)

Don't worry about using a fancy sake—inexpensive brands work really well in this recipe. And unless you read Japanese, you're not likely to be able to ascertain the difference trying to read the labels at the store.

4 cups (1¼ pounds/600 g) small watermelon chunks, seeded

⅔ cup (130 g) sugar

⅔ cup (160 ml) sake

Freshly squeezed lime juice

In a food processor fitted with the metal blade or in a blender, purée the watermelon chunks with the sugar and sake until smooth. Pour into a medium bowl, taste, and add a few drops of lime juice to adjust the sweetness to your liking. Cover and refrigerate until thoroughly chilled.

Freeze in an ice cream machine according to the manufacturer's instructions.

VARIATION: This sorbet makes excellent popsicles that are very refreshing in the summertime. Rather than churning the mixture in an ice cream machine, simply pour it into popsicle molds and freeze.

Simple Cherry Sorbet

MAKES ABOUT 3 CUPS (750 ML)

I was asked to do a frozen dessert demonstration on the *Today* show and figured it was going to be my big break-through. In my imagination, I would dazzle the media and viewers with my ability to make sorbet without an ice cream machine, catapulting my career into the culinary stratosphere. However, as soon as I pitted the first cherry, the host, Katie Couric, became fixated on my spring-loaded cherry pitter and challenged me to a cherry-pitting duel (I should have realized those who get to the top have a competitive streak). She insisted on using a paperclip, which I knew would put her at a disadvantage. Her method was slower than mine, but being a good guest, I let her win (which explains why I'm not at the top). And because of the nature of live morning television, we barely had time to get to the sorbet. In the end, she went on to make millions of dollars as a celebrity and I went home with my cherry pitter in my suitcase.

I'll leave it up to you to decide whether to use a cherry pitter or a paperclip to pit your cherries for this sorbet. But you definitely won't need an ice cream machine—the food processor is the machine for this frozen dessert.

4 cups (1¹/₂ pounds/675 g) sweet cherries, stemmed and pitted

¹/₂ cup (100 g) sugar

1 cup (250 ml) water

1 tablespoon lemon juice

A few drops almond extract

1 tablespoon kirsch (optional)

In a large skillet or saucepan, combine the cherries, sugar, water, and lemon juice and cook, stirring occasionally, until the cherries have softened and released their juices, about 10 minutes. Remove from the heat and add the almond extract and kirsch, if using. Let cool completely.

Transfer the cherries and their syrup to a shallow container, cover, and freeze until firm, at least 2 hours.

Once the cherry mixture has frozen completely, remove it from the freezer, break it up, and process it in a food processor fitted with the metal blade until completely smooth.

Serve right away.

SERVING: Serve Amaretti (page 215) as an accompaniment. Their almond flavor is a perfect complement to the cherry flavor.

STORAGE: Once the sorbet is processed, you can return it to the freezer until ready to serve.

Strawberry-Mango Sorbet

MAKES ABOUT 1 QUART (1 LITER)

Many consider the area behind the Gare du Nord in Paris rather dubious. Yes, it's home to the Paris headquarters for the Hell's Angels. But lots of amazing ethnic foods can also be found there, for which I'm happy to brave the bikers and travel a bit out of the way.

Of the various cultures that have opened restaurants and grocers in that part of Paris, Indian is the most prominent. At night, the blue neon–illuminated stands of the Indian *épiceries* feature all sorts of odd-looking produce that remain a mystery to me.

But I do know mangoes. During their season in late spring, I head to that neighborhood and buy them by the case. I use them in everything, from tropical fruit salads to mango daiquiris (which I'm sure aren't as popular with the Hell's Angels as they are with my crowd). But a few invariably get churned up into a batch of this sorbet, along with a basket of strawberries from my local market and a dash of rum, which even the gruffest biker couldn't resist.

2^1/$_2$ cups (1 pound/450 g) strawberries, hulled and sliced

2 medium mangoes (1 pound/450 g), peeled, pitted, and diced

^{2}/$_3$ cup (130 g) sugar

1^1/$_2$ tablespoons rum

Freshly squeezed lime juice

In a food processor fitted with a metal blade or in a blender, purée the strawberries and mangoes with the sugar and rum. Pour into a medium bowl and add lime juice to taste. Cover and refrigerate until thoroughly chilled.

Freeze in an ice cream machine according to the manufacturer's instructions.

SERVING: This sorbet is particularly good served with berries and tropical fruit tossed with some sugar and a generous amount of dark rum.

Blackberry Sorbet

MAKES ABOUT 1 QUART (1 LITER)

One late summer weekend, I was visiting a friend who lives in the wilds of Northern California, and I noticed lots of wild blackberry bushes with berries that were so plump and ripe that they were practically falling off the branches. I can never resist free food, so I set out for an afternoon of heavy picking. When I came back, my basket loaded down with fresh berries, my friend casually asked, "Did you see the rattlesnakes?" "Um . . . no, I . . . I didn't," I replied. Actually, I was really glad to have missed them. That incident didn't quite scare me away from picking other types of fruits and berries, but I'll let others risk their lives for blackberries, which I've been happy to plunk down money for ever since that day.

8 cups (3 pounds/1.4 kg) blackberries

1 cup (250 ml) water

1 cup (200 g) sugar

2 teaspoons freshly squeezed lemon juice,
    or more to taste

2 teaspoons kirsch or vodka, or more to taste

> TIP: You can use frozen blackberries, thawed, in this recipe.

Purée the berries and remove the seeds by passing them through a food mill fitted with a fine disk into a medium bowl. Or, process the berries in a food processor fitted with the metal blade, then, using a rubber spatula, press the purée through a mesh strainer set over a medium bowl.

In a small saucepan, warm the water and sugar, stirring until the sugar dissolves. Stir the sugar syrup into the blackberry purée, then mix in the lemon juice and kirsch or vodka. Taste and adjust the flavoring, adding more lemon juice and kirsch or vodka, if desired. Cover and refrigerate until thoroughly chilled.

Freeze in an ice cream machine according to the manufacturer's instructions.

Red Wine–Raspberry Sorbet

MAKES ABOUT 1 QUART (1 LITER)

If you don't believe the saying that the whole is greater than the sum of its parts, this simple yet incredibly good sorbet is proof positive that it can be true. This is my all-time favorite sorbet.

1 cup (200 g) sugar

3/4 cup (180 ml) water

1 bottle (750 ml) fruity red wine, such as Merlot, Zinfandel, or Beaujolais

3 cups (15 ounces/400 g) raspberries

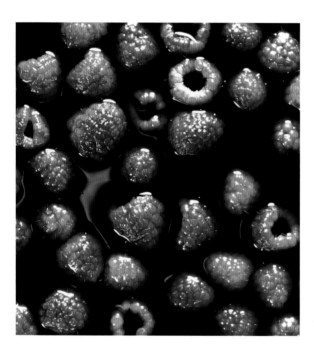

In a medium saucepan, bring the sugar, water, and red wine to a boil and let boil for 1 minute, stirring to dissolve the sugar. Remove from the heat and add the raspberries. Cover and let steep for 1 hour.

To purée the berries and remove the seeds, using a rubber spatula, press the mixture through a mesh strainer set over a medium bowl or pass it through a food mill fitted with a fine disk into a medium bowl. Cover and refrigerate until thoroughly chilled.

Freeze in an ice cream machine according to the manufacturer's instructions.

VARIATION: For a lighter-tasting sorbet, use rosé in place of the red wine.

> TIP: You can use frozen raspberries in this recipe. There's no need to thaw the berries before adding them to the warm wine.

White Nectarine Sorbet with Blackberries in Five-Spice Cookie Cups

MAKES ABOUT 1 QUART (1 LITER) SORBET; 6 SERVINGS

Up until a few years ago, white peaches and nectarines were an oddity in America and finding them was nearly impossible. Happily, they've now become fairly common, and you can spot them in grocery stores and farmers' markets across the land. Their flavor is not as intense as their yellow counterparts, but their delicacy is part of their appeal. Also appealing is how when white nectarines are cooked with their skins and then puréed, the finished mixture is an ivory hue with a faint touch of rosy pink.

I came up with this dessert when I was the pastry chef at Monsoon, an Asian restaurant run by Bruce Cost, one of the best cooks I've ever met in my life. Unlike American dinners, most Asian meals don't end with a full-on dessert. So my challenge was to create desserts that customers would find appealing enough to order after sharing spicy, authentic, and sometimes challenging fare—like the turtle soup served with raw turtle eggs floating on the surface, or the sea slugs that tasted (slightly) better than they looked. I had to make sure the desserts would bring people back from whatever culinary precipice we took them to. This fruit sorbet, resting in a five-spice cookie cup and served with berries steeped in sweet plum wine, was the perfect landing pad.

SORBET

6 medium white nectarines (1$^1/_2$ pounds/675 g), pitted and sliced

$^2/_3$ cup (160 ml) water

$^3/_4$ cup (150 g) sugar

Freshly squeezed lemon juice or kirsch

COOKIE CUPS

$^1/_3$ cup (45 g) all-purpose flour

1 teaspoon ground cinnamon

1 teaspoon ground ginger

$^1/_2$ teaspoon ground cloves

$^1/_8$ teaspoon ground star anise

$^1/_2$ teaspoon ground Szechuan pepper

4 tablespoons (2 ounces/60 g) butter, at room temperature

$^1/_3$ cup (65 g) sugar

2 large egg whites, at room temperature

BLACKBERRIES

1$^1/_2$ cups (375 ml) plum wine

2$^1/_2$ cups (12 ounces/340 g) blackberries

2 tablespoons (30 g) sugar

Sliced almonds or sesame seeds, toasted, for garnish

To make the sorbet, in a medium saucepan, combine the nectarine slices and water and cook, stirring occasionally, until the nectarines are soft and tender, about 10 minutes. Add the $^3/_4$ cup (150 g) sugar and stir until the sugar dissolves. Remove from the heat and let cool completely.

Purée the nectarines with their cooking liquid in a food processor fitted with the metal blade or in a blender. Pour the purée into a medium bowl, taste, and add lemon juice or kirsch to your liking. Cover and refrigerate until thoroughly chilled.

Freeze in an ice cream machine according to the manufacturer's instructions.

To make the cookie cups, preheat the oven to 350°F (175°C). Butter 2 baking sheets, dust the baking sheets with flour, and tap off any excess. (You can line the baking sheets with parchment paper instead, but the cookies won't come off as easily.)

In a small bowl, whisk together the flour, cinnamon, ginger, cloves, star anise, and Szechuan pepper. In a stand mixer fitted with the paddle attachment (or in a bowl by hand), beat together the butter and $^1/_3$ cup (65 g) sugar on medium speed until thoroughly combined. Beat in the egg whites one at a time, then stir in the flour mixture.

Spoon $1^1/_2$ tablespoons of batter in a mound for each cookie; allow only 3 per baking sheet and space them evenly apart. Using an offset metal spatula or the back of a spoon, spread the mounds into 6-inch (15-cm) circles as evenly as possible. Have ready 3 overturned custard cups or tea cups.

Bake one baking sheet at a time until the cookies are lightly browned, about 6 minutes. Remove from the oven and, using a thin metal spatula, quickly lift each cookie off the baking sheet and drape it over an overturned cup. Immediately mold the cookie around the cup using your hands. (If the cookies cool and harden before you can shape them all, resoften them by warming in the oven for 30 to 45 seconds.) Let the cookies cool on the cups. Once firm enough to handle, lift the cookies off the cups and set on a wire rack to crisp. Repeat with the second baking sheet.

To prepare the blackberries, in a medium skillet, boil the plum wine until reduced by about one-third. Add the blackberries and 2 tablespoons (30 g) sugar, decrease the heat to low, and cook until the berries soften and the juices become thick and syrupy. Remove from the heat and let cool for at least 15 minutes.

To serve, center a cookie cup on each of 6 individual plates. Fill with 2 or 3 scoops of sorbet, then spoon some of the berries and their syrup over and around the sorbet. Sprinkle with toasted sliced almonds or sesame seeds.

STORAGE: The batter for the cookie cups can be prepared up to 1 week in advance and refrigerated. The cookie cups can be baked 1 day ahead and stored in an airtight container.

The blackberries can be prepared up to 3 days ahead and refrigerated; they actually benefit from being made in advance.

VARIATION: Yellow nectarines can be used in place of white nectarines.

TIPS: You can substitute 1 tablespoon premixed store-bought five-spice powder in place of the spice mixture I've suggested.

Asian grocery stores and well-stocked supermarkets carry plum wine. If unavailable, you can substitute white or rosé wine.

Anise-Orange Ice Cream Profiteroles with Chocolate Sauce

MAKES ABOUT 1 QUART (1 LITER) ICE CREAM; 8 TO 10 SERVINGS

Anise is used liberally in Mediterranean and Middle Eastern desserts, but it is an underused spice in the American pastry repertoire. I find it adds an exotic touch, at once familiar yet a tad elusive. It seems especially intriguing to people who aren't used to it paired with orange or chocolate, or both, as it is in this twist on classic ice cream puffs.

ANISE-ORANGE ICE CREAM

1$^{1}/_{2}$ teaspoons aniseed

1$^{1}/_{2}$ cups (375 ml) whole milk

$^{1}/_{2}$ cup (125 ml) plus 1 cup (250 ml) heavy cream

$^{3}/_{4}$ cup (150 g) sugar

Grated zest of 2 oranges, preferably organic

Pinch of salt

5 large egg yolks

Pâte à Choux Puffs (page 232)

Bittersweet Chocolate Sauce (page 243) or Rich Chocolate Sauce (page 244), warmed

To make the ice cream, crush the aniseed in a mortar and pestle or seal them inside a sturdy plastic bag and crush them with a rolling pin.

In a medium saucepan, warm the milk, the $^{1}/_{2}$ cup (125 ml) cream, the crushed aniseed, sugar, orange zest, and salt, stirring to dissolve the sugar. Remove from the heat, cover, and let steep for 1 hour.

Pour the remaining 1 cup (250 ml) cream into a large bowl and set a mesh strainer across the top. Reheat the milk mixture until it's warm.

In a separate bowl, whisk the egg yolks, then gradually add some of the warm milk mixture, whisking constantly as you pour. Pour the warmed yolks back into the saucepan. Cook over low heat, stirring constantly and scraping the bottom of the pan with a heatproof spatula, until the custard is thick enough to coat the spatula. Pour the custard through the mesh strainer into the cream; discard the bits of aniseed and orange zest.

Set the bowl containing the custard over a larger bowl of ice water. Stir the custard until cool, then cover and refrigerate until thoroughly chilled.

Freeze in an ice cream machine according to the manufacturer's instructions.

To serve, split each pâte à choux puff in half and place a scoop of ice cream on each bottom. Replace the tops and spoon warm chocolate sauce over the profiteroles.

Berries Romanoff with Frozen Sour Cream

MAKES 4 SERVINGS

Although this dessert sounds old-fashioned, the frozen sour cream is a modern-day update. And the fact remains that it's a wonderful way to use a bounty of ripe summer berries. Such an elegant dessert couldn't be easier to make—the frozen sour cream, which doesn't require any cooking, is churned like ice cream while the berries marinate in orange-flavored liqueur, and the two come together in wine glasses for serving.

BERRIES

$^3/_4$ cup (180 ml) Triple Sec or clear curaçao

$^1/_2$ cup (100 g) sugar

Grated zest of 1 orange, preferably organic

$1^1/_2$ to 2 pounds (5 to 6 cups/675 g to 1 kg) mixed berries (a combination of blackberries, blueberries, raspberries, and hulled and quartered strawberries)

FROZEN SOUR CREAM

$^2/_3$ cup (160 ml) whole milk

$^1/_3$ cup (80 g) regular or low-fat sour cream

$^1/_4$ cup (50 g) sugar

2 teaspoons kirsch or vodka

To prepare the berries, in a medium bowl, whisk together the Triple Sec or curaçao with the $^1/_2$ cup (100 g) sugar and orange zest until the sugar dissolves. Stir in the berries and let marinate at room temperature for about 1 hour, stirring gently once or twice.

To make the frozen sour cream, in a blender, mix together the milk, sour cream, $^1/_4$ cup (50 g) sugar, and kirsch or vodka until combined. Freeze the mixture in an ice cream machine according to the manufacturer's instructions.

To assemble, spoon the berries into 4 stemmed wine glasses, dividing them evenly, and top with a scoop of the frozen sour cream. Pour some of the berry syrup over each and serve right away.

STORAGE: The frozen sour cream can be made up to 1 month in advance.

VARIATION: Sliced peaches, nectarines, or plums are nice additions to the berry mix.

Tangy Lemon Frozen Yogurt

MAKES 1 QUART (1 LITER)

Recipes aren't written in stone, which is a good thing (literally speaking), because lifting a cookbook would be a Herculean chore, and because (figuratively speaking), I love to tinker with recipes and am always thinking of ways to improve them.

Lemon has always been one of my favorite flavors of frozen yogurt, as I like things that are tart and tangy. But I often wondered how some commercial lemon ice creams and frozen yogurts got that extra zing that homemade batches lacked. The answer came to me when I was in an ethnic spice market and saw little bags of citric acid crystals. I brought some home and did a test, adding just a few granules to the frozen yogurt mix before churning. When I dug my spoon in, I realized with the first taste that I'd found exactly the flavor I was looking for.

3 cups (720 g) plain whole-milk yogurt,
    preferably Greek-style

Grated zest from 1 lemon, preferably organic

1/4 cup (60 ml) freshly squeezed lemon juice

2/3 cup (130 g) sugar

1 tablespoon agave nectar or mild-flavored honey

1/4 teaspoon citric acid (see Tip), or more to taste

Pinch of salt

In a blender, process the yogurt, lemon zest and juice, sugar, agave nectar or honey, citric acid, and the salt until smooth.

Pour the mixture in a medium bowl. Taste and add a little more citric acid to adjust the tanginess to your liking. Cover and refrigerate until thoroughly chilled.

Freeze in an ice cream machine according to the manufacturer's instructions.

> TIP: Citric acid crystals, sometimes called "sour salt," are available in Middle Eastern markets, some pharmacies, and online (see Resources, page 270). Fruit Fresh, sold in supermarkets for use in canning and preserving, is mostly citric acid—in powder form—and can be used in place of citric acid crystals.

Blanco y Negro

MAKES 1 QUART (1 LITER); 8 SERVINGS

It seems during the last decade or so, America has gone completely crazy for coffee drinks. All sorts of overpriced caffeinated concoctions are foisted on the public under the guise of coffee. But there's nothing you can buy that can beat this simple coffee dessert.

Blanco y negro is the Spanish variation of *affogato*, an Italian creation consisting of an innocent bowl of ice cream drowned in hot espresso; *affogato* comes from the Italian verb *affogare*, meaning "to drown." I'm not fond of dessert names that reference morbid things like drowning and death (as in "death by chocolate"), so I opt for the kinder, gentler Spanish interpretation that refers to snowy, white (*blanco*) sherbet mingling agreeably with the black (*negro*) espresso that's poured over the top. They come together in an unexpected, but very winning, way.

4 cups (1 liter) whole milk

3/4 cup (150 g) sugar

Grated zest of 2 lemons, preferably organic

2 cinnamon sticks, coarsely crushed

2 tablespoons (30 g) sugar

1 cup (250 ml) freshly brewed espresso, warm

Soft-Candied Citrus Peel (page 253), made with lemons, for garnish (optional)

> TIP: You might want to have extra espresso on hand, in case anyone wants seconds. They likely will.

To make the sherbet, in a medium saucepan, warm the milk, 3/4 cup (150 g) sugar, lemon zest, and cinnamon sticks, stirring to dissolve the sugar. Remove from the heat, cover, and let steep for 1 hour.

Pour the mixture through a mesh strainer set over a medium bowl; discard the zest and cinnamon. Cover and refrigerate until thoroughly chilled.

Freeze in an ice cream machine according to the manufacturer's instructions.

In a small bowl, dissolve the 2 tablespoons sugar in the warm espresso.

To serve, place 2 scoops sherbet in each stemmed glass or small, deep bowl. Pour 2 tablespoons (30 ml) of the sweetened espresso over the sherbet. Garnish with a few wisps of candied lemon peel, if using.

Frozen Nougat

MAKES ABOUT 1 QUART (1 LITER)

From the roadside stands in the French countryside to the village shops of Greece to the markets of Italy, wherever I spot a market vendor selling jars of thick, sticky, locally produced honey, I feel obligated to buy some. If you think all honey is the same, you haven't tasted ruggedly bitter Italian chestnut honey or the syrupy, aromatic lavender honey from sunny Provence. This recipe is a good way to use any type of interesting honey that you may have in your pantry. Be sure to use the freshest, crispest, best-quality pistachios you can find. And never toast them, which subdues their vibrant green color.

PRALINE

$^1/_3$ cup (65 g) sugar

$^1/_2$ cup (40 g) sliced almonds, lightly toasted

FROZEN NOUGAT

6 tablespoons (90 ml) honey

2 tablespoons (30 g) sugar

4 large egg whites, at room temperature

Pinch of salt

1 cup (250 ml) heavy cream

$^1/_3$ cup (45 g) shelled unsalted pistachio nuts, very coarsely chopped

$^1/_2$ teaspoon orange-flower water

Grated zest of $^1/_2$ orange, preferably organic

2 tablespoons (30 g) chopped Candied Orange Peel (page 254)

> Before preparing this recipe, see Caramelization Guidelines, page 265.

To make the praline, lightly grease a baking sheet or line it with a silicone baking mat. Spread the $^1/_3$ cup (65 g) sugar in an even layer in a medium heavy-bottomed skillet and cook over medium heat without stirring until the sugar begins to melt around the edges. Using a heatproof utensil, slowly drag the liquified sugar to the center and stir gently until all the sugar is melted. Continue to cook, stirring infrequently, until the caramel is dark amber in color and begins to foam a bit. Immediately stir in the almonds until evenly coated. Pour the mixture onto the prepared baking sheet and spread it in an even layer. Let cool completely. The praline will harden with cooling.

Once cool, break up the praline with your hands. In a food processor fitted with a metal blade or with a chef's knife, chop the praline into small pieces.

To make the frozen nougat, in a small saucepan fitted with a candy thermometer, heat the honey and the 2 tablespoons (30 g) sugar over medium heat. When the syrup reaches about 200°F (100°C), in a stand mixer fitted with the whip attachment, start whisking the egg whites and salt at medium-high speed. When the whites form soft peaks and the syrup has climbed to 250°F (121°C), with the mixer running, slowly dribble the syrup into the whites, being careful to avoid pouring syrup on the beater (the beater will fling the syrup onto the sides of the bowl, where it will stick). Continue whisking until the meringue has completely cooled.

In the stand mixer fitted with the whip attachment (or in a bowl by hand), whisk the cream on medium-high speed until it holds soft peaks. Fold the whipped cream into the meringue, then fold in the pistachios, orange-flower water, orange zest, crushed praline, and candied orange peel. Transfer to a shallow container and freeze until firm, at least 8 hours, preferably overnight.

SERVING: Serve scoops of frozen nougat unadorned or sprinkled with additional toasted sliced almonds and drizzled with Bittersweet Chocolate Sauce (page 243). Other options for accompaniments are sliced ripe pears or Figs Roasted with Chartreuse and Honey (page 154).

> TIPS: A quantity of syrup this small is easy to overheat. If you do, add a few tablespoons of water to cool it down and cook until the temperature again reads 250°F (121ºC).
>
> Orange-flower water is sold in Middle Eastern markets and well-stocked supermarkets.

Frozen Caramel Mousse with Sherry-Glazed Pears, Chocolate, and Salted Almonds

MAKES ABOUT 1 QUART (1 LITER) FROZEN MOUSSE; 8 SERVINGS

When I was going over the recipes to include in this book, next to this one my editor wrote in big letters "BY ALL MEANS." So I took that as a "yes."

Because of the caramel, the mousse is slightly soft even when frozen, so it's best stored in the coldest part of your freezer. But don't forget about it back there. Once you taste it, I doubt that you will.

FROZEN MOUSSE

$^3/_4$ cup (150 g) granulated sugar

$^1/_4$ cup (60 ml) plus $^1/_4$ cup (60 ml) water

5 large egg yolks

2 tablespoons (30 g) packed dark brown sugar

1 teaspoon vanilla extract

$^1/_4$ teaspoon salt

$^3/_4$ cup (180 ml) heavy cream

SALTED ALMONDS

1 tablespoon water

1 tablespoon granulated sugar

1 cup (80 g) slivered or sliced almonds

$^1/_2$ teaspoon flaky sea salt

GLAZED PEARS AND SAUCE

4 firm, ripe medium pears (1$^1/_2$ pounds/675 g), such as Bosc, Winter Nellis, or d'Anjou, peeled, quartered, and cored

$^2/_3$ cup (160 ml) sherry

$^1/_4$ cup (60 g) packed dark brown sugar

6 ounces (170 g) bittersweet or semisweet chocolate, chopped

> Before preparing this recipe, see Caramelization Guidelines, page 265.

To make the frozen mousse, spread the $^3/_4$ cup (150 g) granulated sugar in an even layer in a medium heavy-bottomed skillet or saucepan. Pour $^1/_4$ cup (60 ml) water evenly over the sugar to dampen it, but don't stir. Cook over medium heat, without stirring, until the sugar dissolves, swirling the pan if the sugar clumps or begins to brown unevenly. When the caramel turns dark amber in color and begins to foam a bit, remove the pan from the heat and immediately add the remaining $^1/_4$ cup (60 ml) water. The caramel will bubble up vigorously, then the bubbling will subside. Stir with a heatproof utensil until any hardened bits of caramel have completely dissolved.

In a stand mixer fitted with the paddle attachment, beat together the egg yolks and the 2 tablespoons (30 g) brown sugar on high speed until light and fluffy, about 5 minutes.

With the mixer running on high speed, slowly drizzle the warm caramel in a thin stream into the yolks, being careful to avoid pouring it on the beater (the beater will fling the caramel onto the sides of the bowl, where it will stick). Add the vanilla and $^1/_4$ teaspoon salt and continue to beat until the mixture has completely cooled.

In the stand mixer fitted with the whip attachment (or in a bowl by hand), whisk the cream on medium-high speed until it forms soft peaks. Fold the whipped cream into the caramel–egg yolk mixture. Transfer the mousse to a shallow container, cover, and freeze until firm, at least 8 hours, preferably overnight.

To make the salted almonds, preheat the oven to 350°F (175°C). Line a baking sheet with parchment paper or a silicone baking mat.

In a medium skillet, heat the 1 tablespoon water and 1 tablespoon granulated sugar over medium heat, stirring to dissolve the sugar. Remove from the heat and mix in the almonds, stirring until well coated. Gently stir in the $1/2$ teaspoon flaky salt. Spread the almonds on the prepared baking sheet and bake, stirring occasionally, until golden brown, 15 to 20 minutes. Let cool completely.

For the pears and chocolate sauce, increase the oven temperature to 400°F (200°C).

In a shallow baking dish, toss the pears with the sherry and $1/4$ cup (60 g) brown sugar. Cover with aluminum foil and bake until the pears are tender (a sharp paring knife inserted into the center meets no resistance), 30 to 45 minutes.

Pour the hot juices from the pears into a small bowl. Immediately add the chocolate and stir until completely melted and the sauce is smooth.

To serve, cut the pear quarters lengthwise into $1/2$-inch (1.5-cm) slices. Divide the slices among 8 individual serving bowls. Spoon a mound of the frozen caramel mousse over or next to the pears, drizzle with chocolate sauce, and sprinkle with salted almonds.

STORAGE: The mousse can be frozen for up to 1 month, if well covered. The almonds will keep for 1 week, stored in airtight container at room temperature. Leftover chocolate sauce can be covered and kept in the refrigerator for up to 5 days.

Frozen Sabayon with Blood Orange Soup

MAKES ABOUT 1 QUART (1 LITER) FROZEN SABAYON; 8 SERVINGS

Sabayon is the French term for *zabaglione*, the frothy Italian dessert made of egg yolks and wine. It was a great day when I discovered that it could be frozen and scooped like ice cream without being churned in an ice cream maker. Because of the less-than-shy wine flavor, it holds its place in a bowl of fruit soup, especially one made with intensely flavored blood oranges.

FROZEN SABAYON

4 large egg yolks

$^3/_4$ cup (180 ml) sweet white dessert wine, such as Muscat, Sauternes, or late-harvest Riesling

$^1/_2$ cup (100 g) sugar

1 cup (250 ml) heavy cream

A few drops of lemon juice

BLOOD ORANGE SOUP

2 cups (500 ml) freshly squeezed orange juice

$^1/_4$ cup (50 g) sugar

4 teaspoons light rum or orange-flavored liqueur, such as Grand Marnier, Cointreau, or Triple Sec

6 blood oranges, peeled and sliced

2 navel oranges, peeled and sliced

12 to 16 fresh mint leaves

To make the frozen sabayon, in a large heatproof bowl, whisk together the egg yolks, wine, and the $^1/_2$ cup (100 g) sugar. Set the bowl over a saucepan of simmering water and whisk vigorously and constantly. The mixture will first become frothy, then as you continue to whisk, it will turn thick and creamy. When the mixture holds its shape when you lift the whisk, remove the bowl from the heat. Set the bowl over a larger bowl of ice water and whisk gently for 1 minute. Leave the bowl over the ice water bath.

In a stand mixer fitted with the whip attachment (or in a bowl by hand), whisk the cream on medium speed until it holds soft peaks. Fold the whipped cream into the sabayon along with the lemon juice. Transfer the mixture to a shallow container, cover, and freeze until firm, at least 8 hours, preferably overnight.

To make the soup, in a small saucepan, warm $^1/_2$ cup (125 ml) of the orange juice with the $^1/_4$ cup (50 g) sugar, stirring until the sugar completely dissolves. Pour into a bowl and add the remaining orange juice and the rum or orange-flavored liqueur. Cover and refrigerate until thoroughly chilled.

To serve, divide the blood orange segments among 8 shallow chilled serving bowls and ladle the chilled soup over the orange segments. Chop the mint leaves, scatter them over the bowls, and place a scoop of the frozen sabayon in the center of each.

VARIATION: Sliced fresh pineapple, sliced kumquats, or any flavorful berries are nice additions to the soup.

TIP: Be sure to chill the soup bowls well in advance of serving.

Kiwifruit, Pineapple, and Toasted Coconut Baked Alaska

MAKES 12 TO 16 SERVINGS

If you're having a party, this dessert is the most dramatic way I can think of to dazzle the crowd, no matter the setting. I made this towering version of the classic baked Alaska for the birthday of my friend Susan Loomis, who lives in the rural French countryside, and I don't think the locals ever saw anything like it. Nor have they stopped talking about it, as I learned from subsequent visits. It left quite an impression!

In spite of the fanciful name, baked Alaska is simply made of layers of ice cream or sorbet, a cakelike bed for them to rest on, and billows of meringue to cover it all. The recipes for the sorbets make 1 pint (500 ml) each. The recipe for the toasted coconut ice cream makes about 1 quart (1 liter), so there will be more than enough to fill up the bowl that the baked Alaska is built in.

KIWIFRUIT SORBET

10 ripe kiwifruit (about 2 pounds/1 kg), peeled

$^1/_2$ cup (100 g) sugar

PINEAPPLE SORBET

$^1/_2$ fresh pineapple, peeled, eyes removed, cored, and cubed

$^1/_4$ cup (50 g) sugar

2 teaspoons freshly squeezed lime juice

1 teaspoon rum

TOASTED COCONUT ICE CREAM

2 cups (500 ml) plus 1 cup (250 ml) half-and-half

$^3/_4$ cup (150 g) sugar

1 cup (70 g) dried unsweetened shredded coconut, toasted

$^1/_8$ teaspoon salt

6 large egg yolks

$^1/_2$ teaspoon vanilla extract

MACAROON LAYER

$^1/_4$ cup (20 g) sliced or slivered almonds

$^1/_4$ cup (35 g) all-purpose flour

$^1/_2$ cup (100 g) sugar

$^1/_8$ teaspoon salt

2 large egg whites, at room temperature

$^1/_2$ cup (35 g) dried sweetened or unsweetened shredded coconut

3 tablespoons (45 ml) rum

MERINGUE

6 large egg whites, at room temperature

$^3/_4$ cup (150 g) sugar

1 teaspoon vanilla extract

To make the kiwifruit sorbet, in a food processor fitted with the metal blade or in a blender, purée the kiwifruit with the $^1/_2$ cup (100 g) sugar until smooth and the sugar has dissolved. Pour into a bowl, cover, and refrigerate until thoroughly chilled.

To make the pineapple sorbet, in the food processor fitted with the metal blade or in the blender, purée the pineapple pieces with the $^1/_4$ cup (50 g) sugar, the lime juice, and 1 teaspoon rum until smooth and the sugar has dissolved. Pour into a separate bowl, cover, and refrigerate until thoroughly chilled.

To make the coconut ice cream, in a medium saucepan, warm the 2 cups (500 ml) half-and-half, the $^3/_4$ cup (150 g) sugar, 1 cup (70 g) toasted coconut, and $^1/_8$ teaspoon salt, stirring to dissolve the sugar. Remove from the heat, cover, and let stand for 1 hour.

Pour the mixture through a mesh strainer set over a bowl and squeeze the coconut with your hand to fully extract the flavor. Discard the coconut and return the coconut-infused mixture to the saucepan. Pour the remaining 1 cup (250 ml) half-and-half into a large bowl and set a mesh strainer across the top.

Reheat the coconut-infused mixture until it's warm. In a separate bowl, whisk the egg yolks, then gradually add some of the warm coconut-infused mixture, whisking constantly as you pour. Pour the warmed yolks back into the saucepan. Cook over low heat, stirring constantly and scraping the bottom of the pan with a heatproof spatula, until the custard is thick enough to coat the spatula. Pour the custard through the mesh strainer into the half-and-half, then stir in the $1/2$ teaspoon vanilla.

Set the bowl containing the custard over a larger bowl of ice water. Stir the custard until cool, then cover and refrigerate until thoroughly chilled.

Begin assembling the baked Alaska: Line a deep bowl with a 2-quart (2-liter) capacity with plastic wrap and place it in the freezer. Freeze the chilled kiwifruit purée in an ice cream machine according to the manufacturer's instructions. Spread the just-churned sorbet evenly into the bottom of the plastic-lined bowl and return it to the freezer.

Freeze the coconut custard in the ice cream machine. Spread 2 cups (500ml) of the just-churned ice cream over the kiwifruit sorbet; freeze the remaining ice cream in a separate container. Return the bowl to the freezer.

Freeze the chilled pineapple purée in the ice cream machine. Spread the just-churned sorbet evenly over the ice cream. Return the bowl to the freezer.

To make the macaroon layer, preheat the oven to 350°F (175°C). Butter a 9-inch (23-cm) pie plate, dust it lightly with flour, and tap out any excess.

In the food processor fitted with the metal blade, grind the almonds with the flour, the $1/2$ cup (100 g) sugar, and $1/8$ teaspoon salt until very fine. Add the 2 egg whites and $1/2$ cup (35 g) coconut and process until combined.

Spread the mixture in the prepared pie plate and bake until golden brown, about 20 minutes. Let cool completely.

Run a knife around the inside of the pie plate to loosen the macaroon, then lift it out. Place it over the last layer of sorbet in the bowl, trimming it to fit. Brush the macaroon evenly with the 3 tablespoons (45 ml) rum. Freeze until firm, at least 8 hours, preferably overnight.

To make the meringue, position an oven rack so that the oven will accommodate the height of the baked Alaska; preheat the oven to 500°F (260°C). Line a baking sheet with a silicone baking mat or parchment paper.

In a stand mixer fitted with the whip attachment (or in a bowl by hand), whisk the egg whites on low speed until frothy. Increase the speed to high and continue whisking until the whites just begin to hold their shape. Gradually sprinkle in the $3/4$ cup (150 g) sugar, add the vanilla, and continue whisking until the meringue is stiff and shiny.

Invert the bowl onto the prepared baking sheet and peel off the plastic wrap. Use a spatula to spread the meringue over the entire surface of the baked Alaska and create peaks and swirls. Bake until the meringue is nicely browned all over and slightly darkened in places, 3 to 5 minutes. Watch carefully!

To serve, using a long serrated knife, slice the baked Alaska into wedges, dipping the knife blade into a pitcher of hot water and shaking off the water before each cut.

VARIATION: I like the color and flavor of the kiwifruit sorbet, but if you're not a fan of kiwifruit, feel free to substitute your favorite fruit-based sorbet, such as Chocolate-Tangerine Sorbet (page 158), Passion Fruit–Tangerine Sorbet (page 159), or Strawberry-Mango Sorbet (page 166).

TIPS: I prefer to use unsweetened coconut, but if you can only find sweetened coconut, reduce the sugar in the ice cream by 1 tablespoon.

For assembly, the sorbets and ice cream must be spreadable. Although I give instructions to freeze them in succession, your ice cream machine canister will likely need to be refrozen between batches, so you may have to churn them over the course of a day or two. This means that the first two batches will be hard from being stored in the freezer; if they are, let them stand at room temperature until soft enough to spread.

If your freezer has enough space, you can unmold the baked Alaska and apply the meringue, then store the dessert in the freezer for up to 1 day until you're ready to bake and serve.

Cookies and Candies

If I had to name the one baked item I couldn't live without, it would be, unequivocally, the chocolate chip cookie. Is there anything that doesn't encapsulate all there is to love about baking in a neat 3-inch (8-cm) disk? Bittersweet chocolate? Check. Butter? Check. Toasted nuts? Check. Brown sugar? Check. I don't think anything can top chocolate chip cookies as the source of the greatest number of baking obsessions. And it all started by accident back in the 1930s when a baker ran out of baking chocolate and substituted broken semisweet chocolate pieces from a bar, hoping they'd melt into the dough. Like millions of other fans out there, I'm glad that they didn't.

I treat each cookie that I bake like a precious gem, which is especially important if you're one of those people who are able to eat just one at a sitting. (If you are, you have more restraint than I do.) To me, each cookie is just as important as the one baking next to it. I spend an inordinate amount of time making sure all my cookies come out of the oven baked just right.

The question people ask most frequently about cookies is "Why do my cookies spread?" The main culprit is overbeating the butter and sugar, which incorporates air into the batter. The air expands during baking, causing the cookies to spread. So when the first step in a recipe instructs you to beat or mix the butter and sugar, blend the ingredients for about 1 minute only, just enough to incorporate the two into a smooth paste without fluffing them up.

More than anything that goes in and out of the oven, cookies need to be watched carefully as they bake—just 1 minute can mean the difference between a texture that's chewy and one that's crisp. Always check cookies a few minutes before the baking time indicates. If you think they're done, trust your instincts and take them out. Ovens vary, and even if they are set to the same temperature and our thermometers read the same, our ovens probably bake differently—9 minutes in mine might be 8 minutes in yours. Also, I've found that cookies baked on a silicone baking mat require slightly longer cooking times than those baked on parchment paper because the mat's thickness shields the cookies a bit from the heat of the pan.

Be sure to rotate baking sheets midway during cooking to ensure that the cookies bake at the same rate. And follow the specifics of the recipe, which is especially important with delicate cookies like Sesame-Orange Almond Tuiles (page 212), where parchment is used purposefully so that the cookies are easier to remove without breaking. Because no one wants broken cookies. But I will gladly take any off your hands.

BATCH BAKING: Because people who like cookies like a lot of cookies, many of the recipes in this chapter make more than just a dozen or so. It's often recommended that you bake two sheets of cookies at a time, but even so, in many instances you'll still have more dough that's begging to be baked off. If you do, let the baking sheets cool completely (if buttered and floured, wash and dry them between uses), then bake the remaining dough on the cooled baking sheets. Or, you can refrigerate or freeze the dough for baking at a later date.

Chocolate Chocolate-Chip Cookies

MAKES ABOUT 40 COOKIES

These are the darkest, most chocolatey cookies you'll ever sink your teeth into. A whopping full pound of chocolate and two cups of chocolate chips ensure an express route to chocolate heaven.

While the cookies bake, watch them carefully and remove them from the oven while they still feel molten in the center and just barely cooked around the outer edges because you want them to remain soft and chewy once they're cool. But I suspect a few will go missing before they have a chance to cool completely.

1 pound (450 g) bittersweet or semisweet chocolate, chopped

4 tablespoons (2 ounces/60 g) unsalted butter, cut into pieces

$1/2$ cup (70 g) all-purpose flour

$1/2$ teaspoon baking powder

$1/4$ teaspoon salt

4 large eggs, at room temperature

$1^3/4$ cups (350 g) sugar

$1/2$ teaspoon vanilla extract

2 cups (320 g) bittersweet or semisweet chocolate chips

1 cup (100 g) walnuts or pecans, toasted and coarsely chopped

Add the chocolate and butter to a large heatproof bowl. Set the bowl over a saucepan of simmering water, stirring occasionally until melted and smooth. Remove the bowl from the heat.

In a small bowl, whisk together the flour, baking powder, and salt.

In a stand mixer fitted with the whip attachment, whisk together the eggs, sugar, and vanilla on high speed until the mixture forms a well-defined ribbon when the beater is lifted, about 5 minutes. With the mixer running on low speed, mix in the melted chocolate-butter mixture until thoroughly incorporated, then stir in the flour mixture followed by the chocolate chips and nuts.

Cover and refrigerate the dough until it is firm enough to handle, at least 30 minutes.

Position racks in the upper and lower thirds of the oven; preheat the oven to 350°F (175°C). Line 2 baking sheets with parchment paper or silicone baking mats.

On a lightly floured work surface, divide the dough in half. Shape each half into a log 10 inches (25 cm) long and $1^1/2$ inches (4 cm) in diameter. (If the dough is too cold and firm to shape, let it stand at room temperature until it becomes malleable.)

Slice the logs into disks $1/2$ inch (1.5 cm) thick and place the disks on the baking sheets, spaced about 1 inch (3 cm) apart. If they crumble a bit, simply push them back together on the baking sheet.

Bake, rotating the baking sheets midway through baking, until the cookies feel just slightly firm at the edges, about 9 minutes.

Let the cookies cool on the baking sheets until firm enough to handle, then use a spatula to transfer them to a wire rack.

STORAGE: The dough can be refrigerated for 1 week or frozen for up to 1 month. The baked cookies will keep well in an airtight container for up to 4 days.

> TIP: These cookies can be baked immediately, without first chilling the dough and rolling it into logs. Drop the dough in generous tablespoonfuls onto the baking sheets, spacing them evenly.

Chocolate Chip Cookies

MAKES ABOUT 48 COOKIES

A while back, a recipe for chocolate chip cookies appeared in a newspaper food section—the cookies were supposed to be the best thing since sliced bread (or sliced cookies). Word spread quickly and it seemed folks couldn't pull out their flour bins fast enough to give them a try. Indeed, the recipe and accompanying story had a great pedigree: it was well written and well researched, with input from some of the best bakers in the land.

Not to be outdone, I went into the kitchen and whipped up a batch of my chocolate chip cookies, which, admittedly, I hadn't made in a while, just to see if they still held up. When I bit into one bursting with gooey chocolate chips and crisp toasted nuts, with all due respect to the author of that recipe, I couldn't imagine chocolate chip cookies tasting any better.

One thing I did take from that article was that chocolate chip cookie dough improves with resting for at least 24 hours before baking. I'm a big fan of keeping logs of dough in my refrigerator or freezer, so my dough was usually rested, even if inadvertently, but now I recommend making it a point to give the dough time to chill out.

$2^1/_2$ cups (350 g) all-purpose flour

$^3/_4$ teaspoon baking soda

$^1/_8$ teaspoon salt

1 cup (8 ounces/225 g) unsalted butter, at room temperature

1 cup (215 g) packed light brown sugar

$^3/_4$ cup (150 g) granulated sugar

1 teaspoon vanilla extract

2 large eggs, at room temperature

2 cups (about 225 g) nuts, such as walnuts, pecans, almonds, or macadamia nuts, toasted and coarsely chopped

14 ounces (400 g) bittersweet or semisweet chocolate, coarsely chopped into $^1/_2$- to 1-inch (1.5- to 3-cm) chunks or 3 cups (340 g) chocolate drops (see Tip)

In a small bowl, whisk together the flour, baking soda, and salt.

In a stand mixer fitted with the paddle attachment (or in a bowl by hand), beat together the butter, brown sugar, granulated sugar, and vanilla on medium speed just until smooth. Beat in the eggs one at a time until thoroughly incorporated, then stir in the flour mixture followed by the nuts and chocolate chunks.

On a lightly floured work surface, divide the dough into quarters. Shape each quarter into a log about 9 inches (23 cm) long. Wrap the logs in plastic wrap and refrigerate until firm, preferably for 24 hours.

Position racks in the upper and lower thirds of the oven; preheat the oven to 350°F (175°C). Line 2 baking sheets with parchment paper or silicone baking mats.

Slice the logs into disks $^3/_4$ inch (2 cm) thick and place the disks 3 inches (8 cm) apart on the prepared baking sheets. If the nuts or chips crumble out, simply push them back in.

Bake, rotating the baking sheets midway through baking, until the cookies are very lightly browned in the centers, about 10 minutes. If you like soft chocolate chip cookies, as I do, err on the side of underbaking.

Let the cookies cool on the baking sheets until firm enough to handle, then use a spatula to transfer them to a wire rack.

STORAGE: The dough logs can be refrigerated for 1 week or frozen for up to 1 month. The baked cookies will keep well in an airtight container for up to 4 days.

> TIP: Many chocolate makers now produce chocolate "drops" or "chunks" that are suitable for use in this recipe. Regular chocolate chips are designed to resist melting, so I don't use them in my chocolate chip cookies.

Chocolate Crack Cookies

MAKES ABOUT 40 COOKIES

In the kitchen at Chez Panisse, we called these "chocolate crack cookies" because of the craggy fissures that formed on the surface of the cookies as they baked. But because the restaurant was (and still is) located in Berkeley, California, we were conscious of what that name suggested, so we came up with all sorts of less objectionable aliases: baked chocolate truffles and chocolate quake cookies, to name just a couple.

Nowadays, "crack" is a term freely used to describe anything addictive. And I feel comfortable using it to describe these cookies, which are a perfectly legit way to get a chocolate fix.

8 ounces (225 g) bittersweet or semisweet chocolate, chopped

3 tablespoons (1½ ounces/45 g) unsalted or salted butter

1½ tablespoons liquor (see Tip)

1 cup (125 g) almonds, toasted

½ cup (70 g) all-purpose flour

½ teaspoon baking powder

¼ teaspoon salt

2 large eggs, at room temperature

⅓ cup (65 g) granulated sugar, plus more for coating the cookies

Powdered sugar, for coating the cookies

Add the chocolate, butter, and liquor to a medium heat-proof bowl. Set the bowl over a saucepan of simmering water, stirring occasionally until melted and smooth. Remove the bowl from the heat.

In a food processor fitted with the metal blade, pulverize the almonds with the flour, baking powder, and salt until as finely ground as possible.

In a stand mixer fitted with the whip attachment, whisk together the eggs and granulated sugar on high speed until the mixture forms a well-defined ribbon when the beater is lifted, about 5 minutes. Using a rubber spatula, mix in the melted chocolate-butter mixture, then stir in the almond mixture. Cover and refrigerate the dough until chilled and firm, 1 to 2 hours.

Position racks in the upper and lower thirds of the oven; preheat the oven to 325°F (160°C). Line 2 baking sheets with parchment paper or silicone baking mats.

Pour some granulated sugar into a small bowl and sift some powdered sugar into another. Shape the cookie dough into 1-inch (3-cm) balls. Working a few at a time, rolls the balls of dough in the granulated sugar until coated, then roll them in the powdered sugar, coating them completely. Set the sugared cookies on the baking sheets, spacing them about 1 inch (3 cm) apart.

Bake, rotating the baking sheets midway through baking, until the cookies are just slightly firm at the edges but still quite soft at the centers, 12 to 14 minutes. The cookies should slide on the baking sheet when you nudge them with your finger. Don't overbake them.

Let the cookies cool on the baking sheets until firm enough to handle, then use a spatula to transfer them to a wire rack.

STORAGE: The dough can be refrigerated for up to 5 days or frozen for up to 1 month. The cookies are best eaten the day they're baked.

> TIP: You can use any kind of liquor in these cookies to vary the flavor, from dark rum to Grand Marnier. If you're avoiding alcohol, use coffee or water.

Flo's Chocolate Snaps

MAKES ABOUT 80 COOKIES

The day we start cloning people, we must begin with Flo Braker. Not only is she a lovely woman, but she's one of the best bakers in America. And I'm all for propagating our species with as many great bakers as we can. I've been making her chocolate snaps for years—they're just right when I'm craving a crispy cookie that tastes of pure and unadulterated deep, dark chocolate. Luckily, these cookies are easy to make and a snap to reproduce in any home kitchen.

3 cups (420 g) all-purpose flour

$3/4$ cup (75 g) unsweetened Dutch-process cocoa powder

$2^1/_2$ teaspoons baking powder

$1/4$ teaspoon salt

1 cup (8 ounces/225 g) unsalted butter, at room temperature

$1^1/_4$ cups (250 g) sugar, plus more for sprinkling

$1/2$ teaspoon vanilla extract

1 large egg, at room temperature

1 large egg yolk, at room temperature

Into a small bowl, sift together the flour, cocoa, baking powder, and salt.

In a stand mixer fitter with the paddle attachment (or in a bowl by hand), beat together the butter and the sugar on medium speed just until smooth. Add the vanilla, then beat in the egg and egg yolk.

Gradually add the cocoa mixture to the butter mixture, mixing until completely incorporated and no streaks of butter remain.

On a lightly floured work surface, divide the dough into quarters, and shape each quarter into a log about 7 inches (18 cm) long and $1^1/_2$ inches (4 cm) in diameter. Wrap the logs in plastic wrap and refrigerate until they're firm enough to slice, about 1 hour.

Position racks in the upper and lower thirds of the oven; preheat the oven to 350°F (175°C). Line 2 baking sheets with parchment paper or silicone baking mats.

Slice the logs into disks $1/2$ inch (1.5 cm) thick and place the disks on the prepared baking sheets, spaced about $1/2$ inch (1.5 cm) apart.

Bake, rotating the baking sheets midway through baking, until the cookies are puffed and slightly firm, 10 to 12 minutes. Remove from the oven and immediately sprinkle the cookies with a bit of sugar.

Let the cookies cool on the baking sheets until firm enough to handle, then use a spatula to transfer them to a wire rack. They will continue to firm up and get "snappy" as they cool.

STORAGE: The dough can be refrigerated for up to 5 days or frozen for up to 1 month. The baked cookies can be kept in an airtight container for 2 days.

VARIATIONS: Instead of forming the dough into logs and slicing them, the dough can be rolled out and cut into shapes with cookie cutters.

If you have coarse-crystal sugar, the sliced unbaked cookies can be dredged in them on one side, then baked sugar side up.

Black and White Cookies

MAKES ABOUT 22 COOKIES

I almost started an international incident when I put some pictures of my black and white cookies on my blog. People went ballistic because I didn't include a recipe. The problem was that I didn't know who to credit since my recipe is culled from a variety of sources.

Like New York City, the spiritual home to these cookies, my sources and inspiration for them are the ultimate melting pot: a *Seinfeld* episode, an email from food maven Arthur Schwartz, a recipe from the legendary Zabar's, and George Greenstein's comprehensive tome, *Secrets of a Jewish Baker*.

COOKIES

1 cup (140 g) all-purpose flour

1 cup (130 g) cake flour

1 teaspoon baking powder

$^1/_4$ teaspoon salt

6 tablespoons (90 ml) whole or low-fat milk

1 teaspoon vanilla extract

Grated zest of $^1/_2$ lemon, preferably organic

$^1/_2$ cup (4 ounces/115 g) unsalted butter, at room temperature

$^2/_3$ cup (130 g) granulated sugar

2 large eggs, at room temperature

ICINGS

2 cups plus 2 tablespoons (250 g) powdered sugar, or more if needed

2 teaspoons plus 2 teaspoons light corn syrup

$^1/_2$ teaspoon freshly squeezed lemon juice

1 teaspoon vanilla extract

3 tablespoons (45 ml) water, or more if needed

3 tablespoons (20 g) unsweetened Dutch-process cocoa powder

To make the cookies, position racks in the upper and lower thirds of the oven; preheat the oven to 375°F (190°C). Line 2 baking sheets with parchment paper or silicone baking mats.

In a small bowl, whisk together the all-purpose and cake flours, baking powder, and salt. In another small bowl, mix together the milk, 1 teaspoon vanilla, and lemon zest.

In a stand mixer fitted with the paddle attachment (or in a bowl by hand), beat together the butter and granulated sugar on medium speed until completely smooth. Beat in the eggs one at a time. Stir in half of the flour mixture, followed by the milk mixture, then stir in the remaining flour mixture and beat until the batter is smooth.

Drop 2 tablespoons (30 ml) batter in mounds spaced 2 inches (5 cm) apart on the prepared baking sheets. Bake, rotating the baking sheets midway through baking, until the cookies feel just set in the centers, about 15 minutes. Let cool completely on the baking sheets.

To make the icings, in a medium bowl, whisk together the 2 cups (225 g) powdered sugar with 2 teaspoons corn syrup, the lemon juice, the 1 teaspoon vanilla, and water until smooth.

Transfer half of the mixture to a small bowl and whisk in the cocoa and remaining 2 teaspoons corn syrup to make the "black" icing. Add up to 2 teaspoons more water, if necessary, to make the icing spreadable; it should not be too thin, so begin by adding 1 teaspoon and add another teaspoon only if needed. Whisk the remaining 2 tablespoons powdered sugar into the white icing. The two icings should have the same consistency: thick, but spreadable. (If the white icing is too thin, add a bit more powdered sugar.)

With a small icing spatula or a butter knife, spread white icing over one half of the flat (bottom) side of each cookie. Spread black icing over the other half. Let the icing set for a few minutes before serving.

STORAGE: The finished cookies can be stored for up to 2 days in an airtight container, preferably in a single layer so that the icing won't be marred.

Peanut Butter Cookies

MAKES 30 COOKIES

Shortly after my first book came out, my phone rang one night a little after 10:30 P.M. A reader had tracked me down to let me know, with urgency, that she loved these cookies, but that they took 10 minutes to bake in her oven instead of the 9 minutes indicated in the recipe.

When in doubt, err on the side of underbaking so your peanut butter cookies remain moist. Take them out when they're still a bit soft, as they'll continue to firm up a bit after cooling. This time around, I've given a bit more latitude with the timing so as to avoid any late-night baking-related emergency phone calls.

1¼ cups (175 g) all-purpose flour

1 tablespoon baking powder (see Tips)

¼ teaspoon salt

½ cup (4 ounces/115 g) unsalted butter, melted

½ cup (100 g) granulated sugar, plus more for coating the cookies

½ cup (120 g) packed light brown sugar

1 cup (260 g) creamy peanut butter (not natural-style, see Tip)

1 large egg, at room temperature

In a small bowl, whisk together the flour, baking powder, and salt.

In a stand mixer fitted with the paddle attachment (or in a bowl by hand), beat together the butter, granulated and brown sugars, and the peanut butter on medium speed just until smooth. Beat in the egg. Add the flour mixture and mix just until the dough comes together. If necessary, knead the dough with your hands until smooth.

Cover and refrigerate the dough for at least 2 hours or up to overnight. (The rest gives the ingredients time to meld so the cookies bake up especially softy and chewy.)

Remove the dough from the refrigerator and let it come to room temperature.

Position racks in the upper and lower thirds of the oven; preheat the oven to 350°F (175°C). Line 2 baking sheets with parchment paper or silicone baking mats. Pour some granulated sugar into a small bowl.

Pinch off pieces of dough and roll them into 1-inch (3-cm) balls. Roll the balls in the granulated sugar and place them 3 inches (8 cm) apart on the prepared baking sheets. When you've filled the baking sheets, flatten and make a crosshatch pattern on each cookie by pressing down on the ball with the back of the tines of a fork.

Bake, rotating the baking sheets midway through baking, until the cookies begin to brown around the edges but the centers still look somewhat uncooked, 9 to 10 minutes. (Remove them from the oven before they look done so they'll stay chewy once cooled.)

Let the cookies cool on the baking sheets until firm enough to handle, then use a spatula to transfer them to a wire rack.

STORAGE: These cookies will keep well, stored in an airtight container, for up to 3 days.

TIPS: Although I do prefer natural-style peanut butter for eating, I don't use it for these cookies. It makes the dough crumbly and hard to roll, and the cookies bake up somewhat drier.

The dough requires a good dose of baking powder for leavening, so make sure to use aluminum free baking powder, which won't leave the cookies with an unpleasant aftertaste.

Cheesecake Brownies

MAKES 9 TO 12 BROWNIES

It's a misconception that the French don't like American food. Step into any bakery in Paris and you're likely to see one of two things: *le gâteau au fromage or les brownies.* Usually the cheesecake is pretty good, but the brownies are too often pale facsimiles. For some reason that I don't understand, the French never put enough chocolate in their brownies.

In my efforts to promote international understanding, I hand out brownies freely to my Parisian friends in hopes that pretty soon, someone will get the message and ramp up the fudginess of French brownies. (Perhaps it's because the word "fud-*gee*" isn't part of the French vocabulary?)

And because I sometimes can't help showing off my American audaciousness, I'll whip up this recipe that combines the best of both the cheesecake and brownie worlds and pass the squares around. They tend to take people by surprise—I think the French need a little more time to get used to such a cra-*zee* combination.

BROWNIES

6 tablespoons (3 ounces/85 g) unsalted butter, cut into pieces

4 ounces (115 g) bittersweet or semisweet chocolate, chopped

$2/3$ cup (130 g) sugar

2 large eggs, at room temperature

$1/2$ cup (70 g) all-purpose flour

1 tablespoon (8 g) unsweetened natural or Dutch-process cocoa powder

$1/8$ teaspoon salt

1 teaspoon vanilla extract

$1/2$ cup (80 g) bittersweet or semisweet chocolate chips

CHEESECAKE TOPPING

8 ounces (225 g) cream cheese, at room temperature

1 large egg yolk

5 tablespoons (75 g) sugar

$1/8$ teaspoon vanilla extract

Preheat the oven to 350°F (175°C). Line the inside of a 9-inch (23-cm) square pan with 2 lengths of foil, positioning the sheets perpendicular to each other and allowing the excess to extend beyond the edges of the pan. Or, use one large sheet of extrawide foil. Lightly grease the foil with butter or nonstick cooking spray.

To make the brownies, in a medium saucepan, melt the butter, then add the chopped bittersweet or semisweet chocolate and stir over low heat until the chocolate is melted and smooth. Remove from the heat and stir in the $2/3$ cup (130 g) sugar followed by the 2 eggs. Mix in the flour, cocoa powder, and salt, then stir in the 1 teaspoon vanilla and the chocolate chips. Scrape the batter into the prepared pan and spread evenly.

To make the cheesecake topping, in a medium bowl, beat together the cream cheese, egg yolk, the 5 tablespoons (75 g) sugar, and $1/8$ teaspoon vanilla until smooth.

Distribute the cream cheese mixture in 8 dollops across the top of the brownie batter, then, with a butter knife or spatula, swirl the cream cheese mixture very slightly into the batter. Resist the urge to mix and swirl too much, as you'll just make the brownies muddy—you want big pockets of cheesecake.

Bake until the brownies feel just set in the center, about 35 minutes. Let cool completely in the pan before lifting out the foil to remove the brownies.

STORAGE: The brownies will keep in an airtight container for 2 days. They can also be frozen, wrapped well, for 1 month. (And in fact, if you cut them and store them individually wrapped, they're terrific—and convenient—to eat while frozen. See Tip, page 196, for brownie-cutting techniques.)

Robert's Absolute Best Brownies

MAKES 9 TO 12 BROWNIES

I have a blanket mistrust of any recipe with a superlative in the title. "The ultimate" or "the world's finest" always makes me raise an eyebrow. But how else can I describe these brownines? I've made a lot of brownies in my life, and these really are the best. I learned to make them from the late Robert Steinberg, who changed the world of American chocolate when he cofounded Scharffen Berger chocolate. Part of Robert's unique charm was that he was quick to argue, but I learned that like most people who hold strong opinions (at least food-wise), they're invariably right when you taste the results. He adapted his recipe from one by cookbook author Maida Heatter.

The first time I made these brownies, they were a dry, crumbly disaster. Still unconvinced that they were worthy of their accolades, I listened carefully as he walked me through the steps. When he asked if I had stirred the batter vigorously for 1 full minute, I stammered and then finally admitted that I cut that step short. "Aha!" he said. So I made them again, and discovered that was one life-changing minute.

6 tablespoons (3 ounces/85 g) unsalted or salted butter, cut into pieces

8 ounces (225 g) bittersweet or semisweet chocolate, chopped

3/4 cup (150 g) sugar

1 teaspoon vanilla extract

2 large eggs, at room temperature

1/4 cup (35 g) all-purpose flour

1 cup (about 135 g) walnuts, almonds, hazelnuts, or pecans, toasted and coarsely chopped

Preheat the oven to 350°F (175°C). Line the inside of a 9-inch (23-cm) square pan with 2 lengths of foil, positioning the sheets perpendicular to each other and allowing the excess to extend beyond the edges of the pan. Or, use one large sheet of extrawide foil or parchment paper. Lightly grease the foil or parchment with butter or nonstick cooking spray.

In a medium saucepan, melt the butter, then add the chocolate and stir over low heat until the chocolate is melted and smooth. Remove from the heat and stir in the sugar and vanilla until combined. Beat in the eggs one at a time. Add the flour and stir energetically for 1 full minute, until the batter loses its graininess, becomes smooth and glossy, and pulls away a bit from the sides of the saucepan. Stir in the chopped nuts.

Scrape the batter into the prepared pan and bake until the center feels almost set, about 30 minutes. Don't overbake.

Let cool completely in the pan before lifting out the foil or parchment to remove the brownies.

STORAGE: These brownies will keep well for up to 4 days and can be frozen for 1 month.

VARIATION: This recipe takes well to mix-ins. I'll sometimes add 1/3 cup (45 g) chopped dried cherries or 1/3 cup (45 g) cocoa nibs to the batter.

To make MINTY BROWNIES, crush the contents of one 50-g tin of peppermint Altoids in a sturdy plastic bag. Add the crushed mints to the brownies along with the nuts (or omit the nuts). If you like *very* minty brownies, add 1/2 teaspoon mint extract along with the crushed mints.

TIP: To cut brownies perfectly, remove them from the pan, peel away the foil or parchment, and set them on a cutting board. Use a long serrated bread knife, dipping the blade in very hot water and wiping it on a paper towel between each slice. Trim off the edges of the brownies with long, slicing strokes, then, use the same motion to cut the brownies into squares or rectangles.

For positively picture-perfect brownies with neat, clean edges, freeze the brownies in the pan before cutting.

Brown Sugar–Pecan Shortbread

MAKES ABOUT 48 COOKIES

The Scottish have shortbread and the French have their *sablés* (sandy-textured butter cookies), but both cultures and cookies are so hidebound in tradition that you'll rarely find variations.

To them I say kick off those highlanders, get your heads out of the *sablé,* and think again. These pecan shortbread cookies are delightfully crisp, with a delicately caramelized flavor thanks to the addition of brown sugar. If you've seen a fancy European-style butter or a locally made cultured one and you've been wondering what's a good use for it, these buttery rectangles are just the things.

2 cups (280 g) all-purpose flour

$^1/_4$ teaspoon salt

1 cup (8 ounces/225 g) unsalted or salted butter, at room temperature

$^2/_3$ cup (140 g) packed light brown sugar

$^1/_2$ teaspoon vanilla extract

1 cup (100 g) pecans, toasted and coarsely chopped

In a small bowl, whisk together the flour and salt.

In a stand mixer fitted with the paddle attachment (or in a bowl by hand), beat together the butter and brown sugar on medium speed just until completely smooth and no streaks of butter remain. Mix in the vanilla. Add the flour mixture and beat until completely incorporated. Stir in the pecans.

Turn out the dough onto a sheet of plastic wrap and form it into a 4$^1/_2$ by 6-inch (11 by 15-cm) rectangle about 1 inch (3 cm) thick. Wrap the dough tightly and refrigerate until chilled and firm, at least 1 hour.

Position racks in the upper and lower thirds of the oven; preheat the oven to 350°F (175°C). Line 2 baking sheets with parchment paper or silicone baking mats.

Cut the rectangle of dough lengthwise into 2 equal pieces. Cut each half crosswise into rectangles $^1/_4$ inch (6 mm) wide. Place the cookies 1 inch (3 cm) apart on the prepared baking sheets.

Bake, rotating the baking sheets midway through baking, until the cookies are deep golden brown, about 15 minutes.

Let the cookies cool on the baking sheets until firm enough to handle, then use a spatula to transfer them to a wire rack.

STORAGE: The dough can be refrigerated for 4 days, or frozen for up to 1 month. Shortbread is always best the day it's baked, but these can be kept in an airtight container for up to 4 days.

VARIATIONS: It's become au courant to use delicate sea salt, such as *fleur de sel*, on cookies to accentuate the butter flavor. Flick a few grains onto each cookie before baking and gently press them in.

I often dip these shortbreads in chocolate. Once the cookies are cool, chop and melt 4 ounces (115 g) of bittersweet or semisweet chocolate in a bowl set over a saucepan of simmering water. Dip one half of each cookie in the chocolate then sweep off some of the excess. Let the chocolate-dipped cookies rest on a baking sheet lined with parchment paper or plastic wrap until the chocolate sets.

Gingersnaps

MAKES 60 COOKIES

This is the classic gingersnap: thin, crisp, with a spicy bite. For the best flavor, use very fresh spices. I grind my own cinnamon and cloves for these, and never, ever use preground black pepper. If you don't have a pepper mill, shame on you. Go get one.

Although not a pantry staple, coarse-crystal sugar—such as Demerara or turbinado—is wonderful embedded in the surface of each snappy cookie. I find it pretty indispensable for these cookies and use it for sprinkling onto many different baked goods before they go into the oven, so I always keep a tub of it in my kitchen cabinet.

3 cups (420 g) all-purpose flour

2¹/₂ teaspoons baking soda

¹/₂ teaspoon salt

2¹/₂ teaspoons ground cinnamon

2 teaspoons ground ginger

1¹/₂ teaspoons freshly ground black pepper

¹/₂ teaspoon ground cloves

1 cup (8 ounces/225 g) unsalted butter, at room temperature

1¹/₄ cups (250 g) granulated sugar

¹/₄ cup (60 ml) mild molasses

1 teaspoon vanilla extract

2 large eggs, at room temperature

Coarse-crystal or granulated sugar, for coating the cookies

In a medium bowl, whisk together the flour, baking soda, salt, cinnamon, ginger, pepper, and cloves.

In a stand mixer fitted with the paddle attachment (or in a bowl by hand), beat together the butter and granulated sugar on medium speed just until smooth. Mix in the molasses and vanilla, then beat in the eggs, one at a time, until thoroughly incorporated. Add the flour mixture and mix until well combined and no streaks of butter remain.

On a lightly floured work surface, divide the dough into quarters. Shape each quarter into a log about 8 inches (20 cm) long and 1¹/₂ inches (4 cm) in diameter. Wrap the logs in plastic wrap and refrigerate until they're firm enough to slice, about 1 hour.

Position racks in the upper and lower thirds of the oven; preheat the oven to 350°F (175°C). Line 2 baking sheets with parchment paper or silicone baking mats. Pour some coarse-crystal or granulated sugar into a small bowl.

Slice the chilled dough into disks ¹/₂ inch (1.5 cm) thick. Press one flat side of each disk firmly in the coarse-crystal sugar. Place the cookies, sugared side up, 3 inches (8 cm) apart on the prepared baking s

Bake, rotating the baking sheet baking, until the cookies are uni brown, about 10 minutes.

Let the cookies cool on enough to handle, then u   m to a wire rack.

STORAGE: The do   y s in the refrigerator or 1   aked ginger-snaps will kee   ntainer, for up to 3 days

Nonfat Gingersnaps

MAKES ABOUT 20 COOKIES

The name may lead you to think these are crisp cookies, but they're not. They are snappy in another way—there are plenty of spices in the batter, plus a generous helping of candied ginger, making them deserving of the *snap* moniker. They're good on their own, but with such a soft, chewy texture, I had a hunch that they would make dynamite ice cream sandwiches, so I filled a few with Tangy Lemon Frozen Yogurt (page 174) and popped them in the freezer. The next day, when I pulled a sandwich out of the freezer and took a bite, I stopped dead in my tracks because I was so stunned: it was the best ice cream sandwich I've ever had.

2^1/$_4$ cups (315 g) all-purpose flour

1 teaspoon baking soda

^{1}/$_4$ teaspoon salt

2^1/$_2$ teaspoons plus a big pinch ground cinnamon

1^1/$_2$ teaspoons ground ginger

^{1}/$_4$ teaspoon ground cloves

^{1}/$_2$ teaspoon freshly ground black pepper

1 cup (215 g) packed dark brown sugar

^{1}/$_4$ cup (75 g) unsweetened applesauce

^{1}/$_3$ cup (80 ml) mild molasses

2 large egg whites, at room temperature

^{1}/$_2$ cup (50 g) finely chopped Candied Ginger (page 252)

^{1}/$_2$ cup (100 g) granulated sugar

Into a medium bowl, sift together the flour, baking soda, salt, 2^1/$_2$ teaspoons cinnamon, the ginger, cloves, and pepper.

In a stand mixer fitted with the paddle attachment, beat together the brown sugar, applesauce, and molasses on medium speed for 5 minutes. Stop the mixer and scrape the bottom and sides of the bowl. Add the egg whites and beat 1 minute. With the mixer running on the lowest speed, add the dry ingredients and mix until completely incorporated, then increase the speed to medium and continue mixing for 1 minute more. Stir in the candied ginger. Cover and refrigerate the dough until firm, at least 1 hour.

Position racks in the upper and lower thirds of the oven; preheat the oven to 350°F (175°C). Line 2 baking sheets with parchment paper or silicone baking mats. In a small bowl, stir together the granulated sugar and big pinch of cinnamon.

Using two spoons or a small spring-loaded ice cream scoop, drop heaping tablespoons of dough (about the size of an unshelled walnut) a few at a time into the sugar-cinnamon mixture. Use your hands to form the dough into balls and coat them heavily with the cinnamon sugar. They'll be sticky, which is normal, and don't worry if they're not perfectly round. Place the balls at least 3 inches (8 cm) apart on the prepared baking sheets.

Bake, rotating the baking sheets midway during baking, until the cookies feel just barely set in the centers, about 13 minutes. If they puff a lot during baking, flatten the tops very gently with a spatula, just enough so they're no longer rounded.

Let the cookies cool on the baking sheets until firm enough to handle, then use a spatula to transfer them to a wire rack.

STORAGE: The dough can be stored in the refrigerator for up to 1 week or frozen for 2 months. The cookies can be kept in an airtight container for up to 3 days.

VARIATION: If you like extrachewy cookies, midway during baking, press each cookie firmly with a flat spatula so they are about ^{1}/$_2$ inch (1.5 cm) high, then continue baking.

Zimtsterne

MAKES ABOUT 25 COOKIES

My first experience making Swiss cookies was less than optimal. A friend had given me his mother's recipe for Basler *leckerle*, a spiced almond cookie swathed with a kirsch glaze. They're meant to be kept in a tin for 6 months before eating, during which time they supposedly soften up and become toothsome delights. To make a six-month story short, I was skeptical when I plucked one of the cookies out of the tin. Then I bit down and almost lost a tooth they were so hard. Since then, I've avoided Swiss cookies.

But, some time later, at Stohrer bakery on the rue Montorgueil in Paris, I tasted the lovely *zimtsterne*, star-shaped cinnamon-almond cookies of Swiss origin that are made only around the holidays, and fell in love. I was prompted to come up with a recipe that I could have year-round—as well as one that wouldn't require a trip to the dentist. I couldn't find a cookie cutter in the traditional *zimtsterne* shape of a six-point star in France where I live, so a friend brought me one from New York, which I guess makes this Swiss cookie a star of international proportions.

COOKIES

3 cups (240 g) sliced almonds, preferably unblanched

1 cup (140 g) powdered sugar, plus more for rolling the cookies

1 tablespoon plus 1 teaspoon ground cinnamon

$1/8$ teaspoon salt

1 tablespoon honey

1 large egg white

GLAZE

$1^1/_3$ cups (175 g) powdered sugar, or more if needed

1 large egg white

1 teaspoon kirsch or other clear brandy or eau-de-vie, or freshly squeezed lemon juice

Preheat the oven to 300°F (150°C). Line a baking sheet with parchment paper or a silicone baking mat.

To make the cookies, in a food processor fitted with a metal blade or in a blender, pulverize the almonds, 1 cup (140 g) powdered sugar, the cinnamon, and salt until the almonds are very finely ground. If using a food processor, add the honey and egg white and process until the mixture is smooth. If it's dry and cracking, add a tiny bit

> TIP: The 6-point star shape is traditional to *zimtsterne*, but you can use any similar-size cookie cutter.

of water and process until the dough comes together. If using a blender, transfer the mixture to a large bowl. Add the honey and egg white and stir until the dough begins to come together, then knead by hand until smooth.

Dust a work surface with powdered sugar and roll out the dough $1/_3$ inch (8 mm) thick (no thinner), dusting the work surface with just enough powdered sugar to keep the dough from sticking. With a 6-point star cookie cutter about 2 inches (5 cm) in diameter (see Tip), cut out stars, and arrange them, evenly spaced, on the prepared baking sheet. Reroll the dough scraps, cut out as many cookies as you can, and place them on the baking sheet. Repeat until all the dough is used.

Bake, rotating the baking sheet midway during baking, until the cookies are very lightly browned, about 12 minutes. They should be soft; don't overbake them. Let cool completely on the baking sheet.

To make the glaze, in a small bowl, mix together the $1^1/_3$ cups (175 g) powdered sugar and the egg white until smooth, then mix in the kirsch. The glaze should be quite thick, opaque, and almost hard to stir. If necessary, stir in additional powdered sugar.

Spread glaze on the surface of each cookie. Sweep off some of the excess, but leave a layer just thick enough so that you can't see the cookie through it. Let the cookies rest until the glaze is completely dry.

STORAGE: These cookies will keep for at least 3 months in an airtight container.

Cranzac Cookies

MAKES ABOUT 26 COOKIES

I was doing a cooking demonstration in health-conscious Los Angeles, and when I melted the half-stick of butter that this recipe calls for—a modest amount by my standards—a woman near the front row panicked and exclaimed, "Oh my God! Look at all that butter he's using!"

I'm not sure these cookies fall into the "healthy" category, but with just a half-stick of butter for nearly 2 dozen cookies, I'd say you shouldn't feel all that guilty about indulging in one—or maybe two, for those of you who really want to live on the edge.

These cookies are a riff on Anzac biscuits that were created as sustenance for the Australian and New Zealand Army Corps (Anzac). I adapted a recipe from *Cooking Light* magazine, adding dried cranberries and naming them "cranzac cookies," but I've left them lean enough to keep those who eat them in fighting weight.

1 cup (95 g) rolled oats

1 cup (215 g) packed light brown sugar

1¼ cups (175 g) all-purpose flour

1 cup (90 g) dried sweetened or unsweetened shredded coconut

½ cup (60 g) dried cranberries

½ teaspoon baking soda

¼ teaspoon salt

3 tablespoons (45 ml) water

4 tablespoons (2 ounces/60 g) unsalted butter, melted

¼ cup (60 ml) golden syrup (see Tip)

Position racks in the upper and lower thirds of the oven; preheat the oven to 350°F (175°C). Line 2 baking sheets with parchment paper or silicone baking mats.

In a large bowl, toss together the oats, brown sugar, flour, coconut, dried cranberries, baking soda, and salt. Stir in the water, melted butter, and golden syrup until the dough is evenly moistened.

Using your hands, shape the cookie dough into 1¼-inch (3-cm) balls. Place the balls on the prepared baking sheets and flatten them into 2-inch (5-cm) disks spaced 1 inch (3 cm) apart.

Bake, rotating the baking sheets midway through baking, until the cookies are light golden brown, about 12 minutes.

Let the cookies cool on the baking sheets until firm enough to handle, then use a spatula to transfer them to a wire rack.

STORAGE: The dough can be kept in the refrigerator for up to 5 days, or frozen for up to 1 month. The baked cookies will keep well, stored in an airtight container, for up to 4 days.

VARIATION: Substitute raisins or dried cherries for the dried cranberries.

TIP: Lyle's Golden Syrup, available in well-stocked supermarkets, gives these cookies their special flavor, so it's worth seeking out. If you can't find golden syrup, substitute cane syrup or a mild-flavored honey.

Orange–Poppy Seed Sandwich Cookies

MAKES ABOUT 18 COOKIES

After years of carefully studying dessert habits, I've begun to refine my theory that there are two types of people—those who like lemon desserts and those who like chocolate. I've observed that there's a subspecies that likes desserts with a crunch, a group that includes me. I'm a big fan of seeds, and I like to add them to these jam-filled cookies to put them squarely in the crunchy camp. Or should I say "roundly," since they are, indeed, round. But feel free to use any cookie cutters you have—round, square, oval, or even heart-shaped.

2 cups (280 g) all-purpose flour

6 tablespoons (70 g) poppy seeds

$^1/_2$ teaspoon salt

1 cup (8 ounces/225 g) unsalted butter, at room temperature

$^1/_2$ cup (100 g) sugar

1 large egg yolk

Grated zest of 2 oranges, preferably organic

$^1/_2$ teaspoon vanilla extract

2 teaspoons orange-flavored liqueur, such as Grand Marnier, Cointreau, or Triple Sec

About $^1/_2$ cup (160 g) strained apricot or raspberry jam

In a small bowl, stir together the flour, poppy seeds, and salt.

In a stand mixer fitted with the paddle attachment (or in a bowl by hand), beat together the butter and the sugar on medium speed just until smooth. Stir in the egg yolk, orange zest, vanilla, and orange-flavored liqueur until completely incorporated. Add the flour mixture and beat just until the dough comes together and no streaks of butter remain.

Turn out the dough onto a sheet of plastic wrap and form it into a rectangle about 1 inch (3 cm) thick. Wrap the dough tightly and refrigerate for 1 hour.

Position racks in the upper and lower thirds of the oven; preheat the oven to 350°F (175°C). Line 2 baking sheets with parchment paper or silicone baking mats.

Divide the dough into 2 pieces. On a lightly floured work surface, roll out 1 piece of dough about $^1/_2$ inch (1.5 cm) thick, sprinkling the work surface with only as much flour as needed to prevent the dough from sticking (too much flour can make the cookies tough).

Using a 2-inch (5-cm) round cookie cutter, cut out circles of dough. Place them on one of the prepared baking sheets, spacing them 1 inch (3 cm) apart. Repeat with the second piece of dough, then reroll the dough scraps. Using a $^1/_2$-inch (1.5-cm) round cookie cutter (the wide end of a metal pastry tip works well, too), cut out the centers of half of the circles, making sure you have the same number of solid cookies as you do those with cut-outs.

Bake, rotating the baking sheets midway through baking, until the cookies are lightly browned, about 12 minutes. Let cool completely on the baking sheets.

Spread a rounded teaspoon of jam on all of the solid cookies, then top with the cut-out cookies, making sandwiches.

STORAGE: The dough can be chilled for up to 4 days, or frozen for up to 1 month. The filled cookies will keep well, stored in an airtight container, for up to 4 days.

VARIATIONS: For a slightly exotic taste, substitute $^1/_2$ teaspoon of orange-flower water for the orange liqueur. Or, for lemon-flavored cookies, use the grated zest of 2 lemons.

You can fill the orange-flavored cookies with chocolate instead of jam: Heat 2 ounces (60 g) of chopped bittersweet or semisweet chocolate with 3 tablespoons (45 ml) heavy cream in a bowl set over a saucepan of simmering water. Use 1 teaspoon of the chocolate mixture for each cookie sandwich. Another option is to fill them with Nutella or a similar spreadable chocolate-hazelnut paste.

Rosemary Cookies with Tomato Jam

MAKES ABOUT 24 COOKIES

At dinner at an Italian *vinoteca*, on the dessert menu was something I'd never seen before: ricotta-stuffed eggplant with candied orange and chocolate sauce. My curiosity piqued, I placed my order with the waiter, only to have him come back with "You won't like it. Order something else." Not one to be easily swayed from ordering an intriguing dessert, I ordered it in spite of his admonition, and you know what? I liked it—quite a bit, in fact.

With that experience in mind, when I saw a fresh fennel cake on a dessert menu at a fancy three-star Michelin restaurant, I didn't hesitate to order it. I had high hopes and was ready for anything. But so was the waiter, who informed me as soon as he set it down that if I didn't like it, he'd replace it with something else. He saw my expression after I took my first bite, and he briskly returned to the table to make good on his offer.

Still, I do believe in giving a chance to things that are out of the ordinary, otherwise, how would we discover new flavors and tastes? I haven't gotten around to trying to come up with my own version of an eggplant dessert (and I'm not exactly chomping at the bit to come up with a fresh fennel one, either), but I've made these tomato jam–filled cookies many times and not once have I had to rush over to offer guests anything in their place.

2 cups (280 g) all-purpose flour

$^1/_4$ cup (40 g) stone-ground yellow cornmeal or polenta

$^1/_2$ teaspoon salt

1 cup (8 ounces/225 g) unsalted butter, at room temperature

10 tablespoons (135 g) sugar

2 large egg yolks

$1^1/_2$ tablespoons finely chopped fresh rosemary leaves

Tomato Jam (page 261)

In a small bowl, whisk together the flour, cornmeal, and salt.

In a stand mixer fitted with the paddle attachment (or in a bowl by hand), beat together the butter and sugar on medium speed just until smooth. Mix in the egg yolks, then the rosemary. Add the flour mixture and mix until the dough is smooth and holds together.

On a lightly floured work surface, divide the dough in half. Shape each half into a log about 6 inches (15 cm) long and $1^3/_4$ inches (4 cm) in diameter. Wrap the logs in plastic wrap and refrigerate until chilled and firm, at least 1 hour.

Position racks in the upper and lower thirds of the oven; preheat the oven to 350°F (175°C). Line 2 baking sheets with parchment paper or silicone baking mats.

Slice the logs into disks $^1/_4$ inch (6 mm) inch thick and place the disks about $^1/_2$ inch (1.5 cm) apart on the prepared baking sheets.

Bake, rotating the baking sheets midway through baking, until the edges of the cookies are lightly browned, about 12 minutes. Let cool completely.

Spread a scant $1^1/_2$ teaspoons of the jam on the underside of half of the cookies. Top the jam with a second cookie, bottom side down, to make sandwiches.

STORAGE: The dough can be frozen for up to 1 month. Once filled, the cookies can be stored in an airtight container for up to 3 days.

Chocolate-Dipped Coconut Macaroons

MAKES ABOUT 60 COOKIES

Writing an ice cream book means two things: (1) you'll need to buy a separate freezer, and (2) you're going to have buckets of egg whites left over. Because this recipe uses quite of bit of egg whites, it was a staple in my repertoire for a while. I was certain all my friends (and neighbors, and delivery men, and local merchants, and the people who work in my doctor's office) would tire of eating these coconut macaroons, but never once did I hear a complaint. Dipping the bottoms in dark chocolate isn't required, but it really lifts the macaroons to a whole different level. I very highly recommend it.

8 large egg whites (1 cup/250 ml)

2^1/$_2$ cups (500 g) sugar

^{1}/$_2$ teaspoon salt

2 tablespoons (30 ml) honey

5 cups (350 g) dried unsweetened shredded coconut

^{1}/$_2$ cup (70 g) all-purpose flour

1 teaspoon vanilla extract

4 ounces (115 g) bittersweet or semisweet chocolate, chopped

In a Dutch oven or very large saucepan, mix together the egg whites, sugar, salt, honey, coconut, flour, and vanilla. Set over medium-low heat and gently cooking the mixture, stirring frequently to dry it out a bit. When the bottom just begins to sizzle, transfer the mixture to a medium bowl and let cool slightly.

Position racks in the upper and lower thirds of the oven; preheat the oven to 350°F (175°C). Line 2 baking sheets with parchment paper or silicone baking mats.

When the mixture is cool enough to handle, use your fingers to form it into tight 1^1/$_4$-inch (3-cm) pyramids and place them on the prepared baking sheets (they won't spread during baking so you can place them fairly close together).

Bake, rotating the baking sheets midway during baking, until the macaroons are uniformly deep golden brown, about 20 minutes. Let cool completely on the baking sheets.

To dip the macaroons in chocolate, remove the cookies from the baking sheets. Turn over the parchment paper sheets so the clean sides are facing up or line the baking sheets with plastic wrap.

Add the chocolate to a medium heatproof bowl. Set the bowl over a saucepan of simmering water, stirring occasionally until melted and smooth.

Dip the bottom of each macaroon into the melted chocolate, scraping any excess chocolate against the inside rim of the bowl. After dipping, place the cookie, dipped side down, on the prepared baking sheet. Refrigerate until the chocolate hardens.

STORAGE: The batter can be refrigerated for up to 1 week or frozen for up to 1 month. The macaroons, dipped or undipped, can be kept in an airtight container for up to 3 days.

VARIATIONS: Milk chocolate can be used in place of the dark chocolate. To make these cookies for Passover, substitute ground almonds or matzoh meal for the flour.

Green Tea Financiers

MAKES 24 BITE-SIZE CAKES

It was as if someone hit the switch one day and all of a sudden, a flash of electric-green took Paris by storm. You couldn't walk past a pâtisserie without seeing something sweet and shockingly green standing out among the more traditional-looking pastries in the lavish window displays. Although the deluge of green tea desserts spread far and wide throughout the city, the best can be found at the shop of Sadaharu Aoki, a Japanese *pâtissier* who wows normally blasé Parisians with his classic French desserts made with a twist. He incorporates ingredients like black sesame seeds and sweet red beans into his pastries, creating a marriage of flavors that would've stunned Escoffier.

I came up with my own recipe for these flavor-packed almond teacakes flecked with a bit of salt and sesame seeds because I was certain that the staff at his shop was tired of wiping my nose prints off the windows.

SESAME-SALT MIXTURE

2 teaspoons sesame seeds (white, or a mix of black and white)

1/8 teaspoon flaky sea salt

FINANCIERS

2/3 cup (55 g) sliced almonds

1/2 cup (100 g) sugar

1 tablespoon white sesame seeds

5 tablespoons (45 g) all-purpose flour

2 1/2 teaspoons green tea powder (*matcha*)

1/4 teaspoon baking powder

Big pinch of salt

Grated zest of 1/2 orange, preferably organic

1/2 cup (125 ml) egg whites (about 4 large egg whites)

6 tablespoons (3 ounces/85 g) unsalted or salted butter, melted and cooled slightly

Preheat the oven to 375°F (190°C). Butter a 24-cup mini muffin tin or similar-size molds (see Tips).

In a small bowl, mix together the 2 teaspoons sesame seeds and sea salt and sprinkle the muffin cups with two-thirds of the mixture.

To make the *financiers*, in a food processor fitted with the metal blade or in a blender, pulverize the almonds, sugar, the 1 tablespoon white sesame seeds, the flour, green tea, baking powder, salt, and orange zest until the nuts are finely ground. Add the egg whites and butter and pulse until the mixture is smooth, stopping to scrape down the bowl or blender jar as needed to ensure the ingredients are thoroughly combined.

Divide the batter evenly among the prepared muffin cups or molds, then sprinkle the tops with the remaining sesame-salt mixture. Rap the muffin tin or molds on the counter once or twice to release any air pockets and level the batter. Bake just until the *financiers* feel firm when gently pressed with a finger, about 12 minutes.

Let cool completely, then remove the *financiers* from the muffin cups or molds.

STORAGE: The batter can be stored in the refrigerator for up to 3 days before baking. Although *financiers* will keep for up to 1 week stored in a cookie tin, their crusts will soften, so I prefer to bake them on the day they'll be served.

VARIATION: For GREEN TEA MADELEINES, use 2 madeleine plaques (each with 12 shell-shaped molds) in place of the mini muffin tin and reduce the baking time to 11 minutes.

TIPS: Green tea powder, or *matcha*, can usually be found in Asian markets, especially those that specialize in Japanese products. Freshly purchased *matcha* will yield the most vibrant-green *financiers*.

I like the color contrast of the black and white sesame seeds. Black sesame seeds are available in Asian markets. If you can't get them, use just white sesame seeds.

Financiers are traditionally baked in small rectangular molds, but they're highly adaptable to other baking pans. For this recipe, I use a mini muffin tin with cups that hold $1^1/_2$ tablespoons each. You can use any tiny pans or molds of a similar size made of metal or silicone; simply fill each mold three-quarters full and adjust the baking time accordingly.

Mexican Wedding Cookies

MAKES ABOUT 45 COOKIES

When I think of cookie cultures, Mexico doesn't immediately spring to mind. However, there are Mexican wedding cookies, or *polvorones*, the nation's answer to Scottish shortbread. Their delicate texture and mild sweetness make them *muy simpático* next to a bowl of Sangria Sorbet (page 158) or Mexican Chocolate Ice Cream (page 148).

1 cup (8 ounces/225 g) unsalted butter, at room temperature

$^1/_2$ cup (100 g) granulated sugar

1 teaspoon vanilla extract

$2^1/_4$ cups (315 g) all-purpose flour

Big pinch of salt

1 teaspoon water

1 cup (100 g) pecans, toasted and finely chopped

Powdered sugar, for coating the cookies

Position racks in the upper and lower thirds of the oven; preheat the oven to 350°F (175°C). Line 2 baking sheets with parchment paper or silicone baking mats.

In a stand mixer fitted with the paddle attachment (or in a bowl by hand), beat together the butter, granulated sugar, and vanilla on medium speed just until smooth. Stir in half of the flour and the salt, then add the water. Mix in the remaining flour and the chopped pecans.

Using your hands, form the dough into 1-inch (3-cm) balls and place them about 1 inch (3 cm) apart on the prepared baking sheets.

Bake, rotating the baking sheets midway through baking, until the cookies feel almost, but not quite, firm, about 15 minutes. Let cool completely on the baking sheets.

Sift some powdered sugar into a bowl. Toss the cooled cookies a few at a time in the sugar until completely coated with a thick layer (there is relatively little sugar in the cookie dough, so be generous when coating them).

STORAGE: The dough can be frozen for up to 1 month. Store the baked and sugar-coated cookies in an airtight container for up to 5 days.

Croquants

MAKES 60 COOKIES

This recipe is the result of a 12-year obsession. I first fell for these wispy cookies when I bought a startlingly pricey pack of them at an upscale gourmet store in America. When I moved to France, I was surprised how common these crackly cookies are. I was so excited—they were everywhere!

Have I mentioned that I'm obsessive? It shouldn't come as a surprise, then, that I just had to come up with a recipe for the cookies myself. I checked the ingredients list on as many packages as I could get my hands on, and they certainly seemed simple enough. What followed was years of duds as I searched for ways to combine the mere handful of ingredients into the lightly caramelized *croquants* of my dreams.

Then, suddenly, one day, after a lot of trial and just as much error, I got it right. I wasn't the only one pleased with the results: I left a sack for the highly opinionated French woman who cleans my apartment, and arrived home later to find a little note that read *"EXTRA DELICIEUX. Merci,* David!"

1 cup (200 g) sugar

5 1/2 tablespoons (50 g) all-purpose flour

1/4 cup (60 ml) egg whites (about 2 large egg whites)

Pinch of salt

3/4 cup (90 g) almonds or hazelnuts, toasted and very coarsely chopped (see Tip)

TIP: For this recipe, the almonds or hazelnuts should be very coarsely chopped—basically cut into rough halves or thirds.

Position racks in the upper and lower thirds of the oven; preheat the oven to 400°F (200°C). Line 2 baking sheets with parchment paper. (I don't recommend using silicone baking mats for this recipe as the *croquants* won't be as crisp.)

In a medium bowl, mix together the sugar and flour, then stir in the egg whites and salt until smooth. Stir in the almonds or hazelnuts.

Drop level teaspoons of batter at least 2 inches (5 cm) apart on the prepared baking sheets.

Bake, rotating the baking sheets midway during baking, until the cookies are toasty brown in color, 10 to 12 minutes. Let cool completely on the baking sheets.

STORAGE: The batter can be kept in the refrigerator for up to 1 week or frozen for up to 1 month. Let it come to room temperature before spooning and baking. Store the baked *croquants* in an airtight container for up to 5 days.

Sesame-Orange Almond Tuiles

MAKES 20 COOKIES

These lacy cookies have an exotic appeal thanks to the tiny sesame seeds inlaid in the surface, as well as the spoonful of sesame oil in the batter that adds a toasty sesame scent. Black sesame seeds make the *tuiles* especially striking. They're great paired with tropical fruit desserts such as Passion Fruit–Tangerine Sorbet (page 159) or Tropical Fruit Soup with Coconut Sherbet and Meringue (page 112). Like the Pecan-Butterscotch Tuiles (page 214), they can be shaped into tubes or cookie cups.

3 tablespoons ($1^1/_2$ ounces/45 g) unsalted or salted butter

1 tablespoon toasted sesame oil

3 tablespoons (45 ml) freshly squeezed orange juice

Grated zest of 1 orange, preferably organic

10 tablespoons (135 g) sugar

$^1/_4$ cup (35 g) all-purpose flour

$^3/_4$ cup (60 g) unblanched or blanched sliced almonds

2 tablespoons (40 g) white sesame seeds

$1^1/_2$ teaspoons black sesame seeds (see Tip)

In a small saucepan, warm the butter, sesame oil, orange juice, orange zest, and sugar over low heat until melted and smooth. Remove from the heat and stir in the flour, almonds, and white and black sesame seeds. Let the batter rest for 1 hour at room temperature.

Preheat the oven to 375°F (190°C). Line 2 baking sheets with parchment paper. (Don't use silicone baking mats because the cookies may be difficult to remove.) Set a rolling pin for shaping the *tuiles* on a folded dish towel to steady it and have ready a wire rack.

Drop level tablespoons of batter on the prepared baking sheets, placing only 4 on each sheet and spacing them evenly apart. Slightly flatten the batter with dampened fingers.

Bake one sheet at a time, rotating the baking sheet midway during baking, until the cookies are evenly browned, 8 to 9 minutes.

Let cool briefly, about 1 minute. Using a metal spatula, lift each cookie off the baking sheet and drape it over the rolling pin. (If the cookies cool and harden before you have time to shape them, they can be softened by putting them back in the oven for 30 to 45 seconds.) Let cool on the rolling pin, then transfer the *tuiles* to a wire rack. Repeat with the remaining batter.

Serve the *tuiles* within a few hours of baking.

STORAGE: The batter can be made up to 1 week in advance and stored in the refrigerator. You can store the baked *tuiles* in an airtight container until ready to serve later the same day.

TIP: Like toasted sesame oil, black sesame seeds are available in Asian markets. If you can't get them, use white sesame seeds in their place.

Pecan-Butterscotch Tuiles

MAKES ABOUT 12 COOKIES

This recipe is much easier to make than conventional *tuiles* because the batter isn't as fussy and it doesn't need to be painstakingly spread out on a baking sheet with a spatula. The heat of the oven takes care of the spreading, making sure that the cookies expand to the right dimensions as they bake. No, unfortunately, the oven can't mix up the batter for you, but maybe in a few years kitchen technology will make that an option.

The cookies can be coaxed into an endless variety of shapes warm out of the oven—they can be curled over a rolling pin for traditional *tuiles*, wrapped around the handle of a wooden spoon into cigar-like tubes, or molded over the bottom of an overturned teacup into nifty cookie cups for holding ice cream. You'll have to do that part yourself, too, but then again, why let your oven have all the fun?

4 tablespoons (2 ounces/60 g) unsalted or salted butter

1/4 cup (60 g) packed light brown sugar

1/4 cup (60 ml) light corn syrup

1/4 cup (30 g) pecans, toasted and very finely chopped

6 tablespoons (60 g) all-purpose flour

Preheat the oven to 400°F (200°C). Line 2 baking sheets with parchment paper. (Don't use silicone baking mats because the cookies may be difficult to remove.) Set a rolling pin for shaping the *tuiles* on a folded dish towel to steady it and have ready a wire rack.

In a small saucepan, warm the butter, brown sugar, and corn syrup over low heat until melted and smooth. Stir in the pecans and flour.

Drop level tablespoons of batter on the prepared baking sheets, placing only 4 on each sheet and spacing them evenly apart. Slightly flatten the batter with dampened fingers.

Bake one sheet at a time, rotating the baking sheet midway during baking, until the cookies are deep golden brown, about 7 minutes.

Let cool briefly, about 1 minute. Using a metal spatula, lift each cookie off the baking sheet and drape it over the rolling pin. (If the cookies cool and harden before you have time to shape them, they can be softened by putting them back in the oven for 30 to 45 seconds.) Let cool on the rolling pin, then transfer the *tuiles* to a wire rack. Repeat with the remaining batter.

Serve the *tuiles* within a few hours of baking.

STORAGE: The batter can be made up to 1 week in advance and stored in the refrigerator. You can store the baked *tuiles* in an airtight container until ready to serve later the same day.

VARIATION: You can substitute toasted almonds or walnuts for the pecans.

Amaretti

MAKES ABOUT 35 COOKIES

These barely sweet crisp little cookies are the definitive Italian nibble. Not only do I serve them as perfect bites alongside a *ristretto* (a "tight" espresso), but I also crumble them up and use the bitter almond-scented crumbs in desserts. They make a perfect topping for Lemon Semifreddo (page 65) and give a decidedly Italian touch to Peach-Amaretti Crisp (page 102).

True amaretti are made with sweet apricot kernels rather than almonds, but since apricot kernels can be difficult to find and not everyone's keen on eating them (they contain cyanide), I call for almonds in this recipe.

1 cup (125 g) almonds, toasted

1 teaspoon all-purpose flour

$^1/_2$ cup (70 g) powdered sugar

2 large egg whites, at room temperature

Pinch of salt

6 tablespoons (75 g) granulated sugar

1 teaspoon almond extract

Position racks in the upper and lower thirds of the oven; preheat the oven to 300°F (150°C). Line 2 baking sheets with parchment paper or silicone baking mats.

In a food processor fitted with the metal blade, pulverize the almonds with the flour and powdered sugar until the almonds are very finely ground.

In a stand mixer fitted with the whip attachment (or in a bowl by hand), whisk the egg whites on low speed until frothy. Add the salt, increase the speed to high, and continue whisking until the egg whites begin to hold their shape. Add the granulated sugar 1 tablespoon at a time and continue whisking until the whites form shiny, stiff peaks.

Sprinkle one-third of the almond mixture over the whipped egg whites and fold using a rubber spatula. Fold in the remaining almond mixture in two additions, adding the almond extract with the last addition.

Using a pastry bag fitted with a plain $^1/_2$-inch (1.5-cm) tip, pipe mounds of batter that are $1^1/_2$ inches (4 cm) in diameter on the prepared baking sheets, spacing them about $^3/_4$ inch (2 cm) apart.

Bake, rotating the baking sheets midway through baking, until the cookies are lightly browned, about 20 minutes. Turn off the oven and let the cookies dry in the oven for 20 minutes.

Let the cookies cool on the baking sheets until firm enough to handle, then use a spatula to transfer them to a wire rack. Let cool completely.

STORAGE: Amaretti can be stored in an airtight container for at least 2 weeks.

TIP: If you don't have a pastry bag, fill a plastic freezer bag with the batter and snip off a corner to form a $^1/_2$-inch (2-cm) opening for piping. You can also use 2 teaspoons to form mounds of batter that bake up into rustic-looking amaretti.

Almond and Chocolate Chunk Biscotti

MAKES ABOUT 60 COOKIES

I got a perplexing message from someone who made these biscotti: "They were good, but full of big chunks of chocolate." I'm not sure if that was meant as a compliment or a criticism, but I do know for sure that it wasn't a mistake—that's exactly what I had in mind when I came up with these superchunky chocolate biscotti. They're perfect for dipping in a large cup of dark coffee or alongside a glass of Cognac after dinner. They're also great travel cookies—I'm always happy when I pull out a bag midway through a flight or train trip. I make sure to bring extras because when I see the longing looks of passengers around me, I feel pressured to share—and I do, reluctantly.

2$^{1}/_{2}$ cups (350 g) all-purpose flour

1 teaspoon baking powder

3 large eggs, at room temperature

1 cup (200 g) sugar

$^{1}/_{2}$ teaspoon vanilla extract

1$^{1}/_{4}$ cups (155 g) almonds, toasted and coarsely chopped

7 ounces (200 g) bittersweet or semisweet chocolate, chopped into $^{1}/_{2}$-inch (1.5-cm) chunks

Preheat the oven to 350°F (175°C). Line a baking sheet with parchment paper or a silicone baking mat.

In a small bowl, whisk together the flour and the baking powder.

In a stand mixer fitted with the whip attachment, whisk the eggs, sugar, and vanilla on medium speed until the mixture thickens and holds its shape, about 5 minutes. Using a rubber spatula, stir the flour mixture into the egg mixture, then mix in the almonds and chocolate.

On a lightly floured work surface, divide the dough in half. Using dampened hands, shape each half into a log 3 inches (8 cm) in diameter. Set the logs lengthwise on the prepared baking sheet, evenly spacing them apart. Dampen your hands and smooth the surface of the logs.

Bake, rotating the baking sheet midway through baking, until the logs are lightly browned, about 20 minutes. (They will flatten out during baking.) Remove the baking sheet from the oven and decrease the oven temperature to 300°F (150°C). Let the logs cool on the baking sheet for 10 to 15 minutes.

Transfer the logs to a cutting board. With a serrated bread knife, cut each log diagonally into slices $^{1}/_{2}$ inch (1.5 cm) thick. Place the cookies, cut sides up, in a single layer on the baking sheet. (If necessary, use an additional baking sheet.) Bake until the biscotti are firm, about 20 minutes, flipping them midway through baking. Let cool completely; they'll continue to firm up as they cool.

STORAGE: The biscotti will keep in an airtight container for up to 1 week.

VARIATION: You can substitute 1$^{1}/_{2}$ cups (240 g) chocolate chips for the chopped chocolate, if you like, although I prefer the irregularity of chocolate chunks in these cookies.

Peppery Chocolate-Cherry Biscotti

MAKES 50 TO 60 COOKIES

I love chocolate. But sometimes I want something that's packed with intense chocolate flavor yet not outrageously rich. These biscotti certainly fit the bill. Italians often add a dash of black pepper to desserts and give them the designation *pepato*. I share their affection for a hit of peppery flavor in desserts, but feel free to omit the pepper if you'd like.

$^{3}/_{4}$ cup (90 g) dried sour cherries, coarsely chopped

2 tablespoons (30 ml) kirsch, grappa, or rum

2 cups (280 g) all-purpose flour

$^{3}/_{4}$ cups (75 g) unsweetened Dutch-process cocoa powder

1 teaspoon baking soda

$^{1}/_{4}$ teaspoon salt

1 teaspoon freshly ground black pepper

3 large eggs, plus 1 large egg for glazing

1 cup (200 g) granulated sugar

$^{1}/_{2}$ teaspoon almond extract

1 cup (125 g) almonds, toasted and coarsely chopped

$^{3}/_{4}$ cup (120 g) bittersweet or semisweet chocolate chips

2 tablespoons (30 g) coarse-crystal sugar, for sprinkling (see Tip)

Preheat the oven to 350°F (175°C). Line a baking sheet with parchment paper or a silicone baking mat.

In a small saucepan, combine the dried cherries and kirsch, grappa, or rum. Bring to a boil, then remove from the heat, cover, and let cool to room temperature.

Into a medium bowl, sift together the flour, cocoa powder, baking soda, salt, and pepper.

In a large bowl, whisk together the 3 eggs, granulated sugar, and almond extract. Gradually stir in the flour mixture, then add the cherries and their soaking liquid, the almonds, and the chocolate chips and mix just until the dough comes together.

On a lightly floured work surface, divide the dough in half. Using dampened hands, shape each half into a log 3 inches (8 cm) in diameter. Set the logs lengthwise on the prepared baking sheet, evenly spacing them apart. Dampen your hands and gently flatten the tops of the logs.

In a small bowl, whisk the remaining egg. Generously brush the logs with the egg wash, then give the logs a second coat. Sprinkle each log with 1 tablespoon coarse-crystal sugar.

Bake, rotating the baking sheet midway through baking, until the logs feel firm to the touch, about 25 minutes. Remove the baking sheet from the oven and decrease the oven temperature to 300°F (150°C). Let the logs cool on the baking sheet for 10 to 15 minutes.

Transfer the logs to a cutting board. With a serrated bread knife, cut each log diagonally into slices $^{1}/_{2}$ inch (1.5 cm) thick. Place the cookies, cut sides up, in a single layer on the baking sheet. (If necessary, use an additional baking sheet.) Bake until firm, 20 to 30 minutes, flipping them midway through baking. Let cool completely; they'll continue to firm up as they cool.

STORAGE: The biscotti will keep in an airtight container for up to 1 week.

VARIATION: Add $^{1}/_{3}$ cup (55 g) of cocoa nibs to the dough along with the almonds and chocolate chips.

TIP: Coarse-crystal sugar, such as turbinado, Demerara, or raw sugar, is available in well-stocked supermarkets, specialty stores, or online (see Resources, page 270). If you can't find it, use regular granulated sugar, or simply omit the egg wash and sugar coating.

Lemon Quaresimali Cookies

MAKES ABOUT 50 COOKIES

These cookies are like supersized biscotti, but, unlike biscotti, they've never gained wide acceptance outside their native Italy, probably because their name is a bit more of a challenge to pronounce. Thankfully, they're just as easy to make, and every bit as good.

1³/₄ cups (245 g) all-purpose flour

1¹/₂ teaspoons ground cinnamon

1 teaspoon baking soda

¹/₂ teaspoon salt

2 large eggs, plus 1 large egg for glazing

1¹/₃ cups (265 g) sugar

³/₄ teaspoon vanilla extract

Grated zest of 2 lemons, preferably organic

1¹/₂ tablespoons freshly squeezed lemon juice

2 cups (250 g) almonds, toasted

Position racks in the upper and lower thirds of the oven; preheat the oven to 350°F (175°C). Line 2 baking sheets with parchment paper or silicone baking mats.

In a small bowl, whisk together the flour, cinnamon, baking soda, and salt. In a medium bowl, whisk together the 2 eggs, sugar, vanilla, lemon zest, and lemon juice. Add the flour mixture and stir until well blended, then mix in the almonds.

Divide the dough in half and place each half on a prepared baking sheet. Using dampened hands, shape each half into a 13 by 2¹/₂-inch (33 by 6-cm) log.

In a small bowl, whisk the remaining egg. Generously brush the logs with the egg wash, then give the logs a second coat.

Bake, rotating the baking sheets midway during baking, until the logs are firm and golden brown, 25 to 30 minutes. (They will flatten out during baking.) Remove the baking sheets from the oven and decrease the oven temperature to 300°F (150°C). Let the logs cool on the baking sheets for 10 to 15 minutes.

Transfer the logs to a cutting board. With a serrated bread knife, slice each log crosswise into 1-inch (3-cm) bars. Place the cookies, cut sides up, in a single layer on the baking sheets and bake for 20 minutes. Let cool completely.

STORAGE: The cooled cookies will keep for up to 1 week stored in an airtight container.

VARIATION: Substitute toasted hazelnuts for the almonds.

Chocolate-Port Truffles

MAKES 25 TO 30 TRUFFLES

I thought I knew all about chocolate truffles until I enrolled in an advanced course in chocolate making at a school for professionals next to the Valrhona factory in France's Rhône Valley. I spent three very intense days there learning how to combine three simple ingredients—chocolate, cream, and butter—into silky smooth ganache. In the class were eight of the top chocolatiers in the world, plus a ninth person, who quickly realized that he had a lot more to learn about chocolate than he thought he did.

Ganache seems simple, but chef Philippe Givre taught us how to whip these three ingredients into a velvety paste that needed several days of rest before it was ready to be tasted. (It's worth the wait!) It would take a whole book to explain his technique and a professionally equipped kitchen attached to a chocolate factory to try it out, so for this recipe, I've shortened the process a bit.

Of course, to make these truffles, it's worth seeking out the best chocolate you can find, which, if you're lucky like I was, might be right next door.

$^1/_2$ cup (125 ml) heavy cream

8 ounces (225 g) plus 5 ounces (140 g) bittersweet or semisweet chocolate, chopped

3 tablespoons ($1^1/_2$ ounces/45 g) unsalted butter, at room temperature, cut into pieces

3 tablespoons (45 ml) ruby or tawny port

$^3/_4$ cup (75 g) unsweetened natural or Dutch-process cocoa powder

In a medium saucepan, bring the cream to a boil over medium-high heat. Remove from the heat and add the 8 ounces (225 g) chocolate. Let stand for 1 minute, then gently stir with a spatula until melted. Add the butter and port, then stir until combined.

Using an immersion blender (see page 17), blend the ganache until completely smooth and glossy, about 1 minute. (You can use a whisk or a stand mixer on very low speed, but avoid incorporating air into the ganache; you simply want to make an emulsion, not whip it.) Pour the ganache into a shallow container, cover, and refrigerate until firm, at least 3 hours.

Using a melon baller or two teaspoons, scoop out balls of the chilled ganache about 1 inch (3 cm) in diameter and place them on a large plate; you should have 25 to 30 balls. (If using a melon baller, to get the ganache to release, dip the tool in hot water between scoops and tap out excess water each time.) With your hands, roll each truffle into a not-quite perfect ball, return it to the plate, and refrigerate again until firm, about 30 minutes.

Sift the cocoa into a pie plate or a deep, wide dish with sides. Add the 5 ounces (140 g) chocolate to a small heatproof bowl. Set the bowl over a saucepan of simmering water and stir occasionally until the chocolate is just melted and smooth. Remove from the heat.

Gather up some of the melted chocolate with your dominant hand. Pick up a truffle with your other hand and drop it into the chocolate in your hand. Coat the truffle with chocolate, then drop the truffle into the cocoa powder. Repeat with the remaining truffles and melted chocolate. When done, jiggle the dish of cocoa around until the truffles are well coated. Place the truffles in a mesh strainer and gently shake to remove any excess cocoa.

SERVING: The truffles should be served at room temperature. If refrigerated, let them stand at room temperature for at least 1 hour before serving.

STORAGE: The truffles will keep in the refrigerator for up to 1 week. Leftover chocolate and cocoa powder can be reused for another project.

VARIATIONS: Replace the port with 3 tablespoons (45 ml) of your favorite liquor—whiskey, Grand Marnier, crème de cassis, or dark rum all work well.

You can skip the step of coating the truffles with chocolate and make traditional chocolate truffles that are simply ganache formed into lumpy rounds and rolled in cocoa powder.

Almond Ding

MAKES ³/₄ POUND (350 G), 20 TO 25 PIECES

It was the name of this candy that first won me over, but it's the taste of this easy-to-make treat that continues to make me smile. Both novice and intrepid candy makers will be happy because this simple confection doesn't require a candy thermometer or any fancy equipment and it can be made in minutes.

Serve pieces of almond ding as part of a cookie or candy plate, chop it into bits and fold them into just-churned ice cream, or offer some alongside a favorite sorbet. (It goes particularly well with Simple Cherry Sorbet, page 165.) Be sure to use flaky sea salt which will provide dramatic bits of salty sparks when you crunch into the buttery caramelized almonds. This recipe is from Cindy Pawlcyn, chef-owner of Mustard's Grill in the Napa Valley.

1 cup (125 g) blanched almonds (see Tips)

¹/₂ cup (100 g) sugar

2 tablespoons (1 ounce/30 g) unsalted or salted butter, cut into pieces

¹/₄ teaspoon flaky sea salt

TIPS: It's important to use blanched almonds for this recipe. Almond skins make it difficult for the syrup to permeate the nuts and your ding won't be as crunchy.

I recommend using a very delicate but flavorful sea salt, such as *fleur de sel* or Maldon Sea Salt (see Resources, page 270).

Lightly oil a baking sheet with nonstick spray or line it with a silicone baking mat.

In a medium saucepan or skillet, combine the almonds, sugar, and butter. Cook over medium heat, stirring ever so gently as the mixture begins to darken (vigorous stirring encourages crystallization). Continue to cook, stirring gently, until the mixture is deep amber in color (similar to a cup of coffee with a touch of cream). Gently stir in the salt, then pour the mixture out onto the prepared baking sheet. Avoiding spreading out the almonds except to ensure that they're in a single layer. Using a heatproof spatula, push any spreading caramel back toward the almonds. Let cool completely.

Once cooled, break into bite-size pieces.

STORAGE: The candy pieces will keep in an airtight container for up to 1 week.

Pistachio, Almond, and Dried Cherry Bark

MAKES ABOUT 1¼ POUNDS (565 G)

It was a happy day when an enterprising midwesterner decided that the surplus of sour cherries could be dried instead of left neglected on the trees. And thus, one of my favorite baking ingredients was born.

But this recipe is eminently adaptable and you can use any kind of dried fruit or toasted nuts that suits you. Diced apricot pieces and cranberries, walnuts and toasted pecans, and roasted cocoa nibs have all found their way into various batches of this bark. I even got really crazy once and crumbled candied bacon into a batch. That one met with a few raised eyebrows, but was gobbled up by all.

1¼ pounds (565 g) bittersweet or semisweet chocolate, coarsely chopped

¹/₂ cup (65 g) almonds, toasted

¹/₄ cup (35 g) shelled pistachios

¹/₄ cup (30 g) dried sour (or sweet) cherries

Flaky sea salt (optional)

Stretch taut a sheet of plastic wrap across a baking sheet.

Add the chocolate to a large heatproof bowl. Set the bowl over a saucepan of simmering water and stir frequently until the chocolate is almost melted.

Remove the bowl from the heat, wipe off the bottom of the bowl, then stir the chocolate until completely melted and smooth. Mix in the almonds, pistachios, and dried cherries.

Scrape the mixture onto the prepared baking sheet and use a spatula to spread it to the desired thickness. Flick bits of salt, if using, across the top. Refrigerate the baking sheet until the chocolate sets.

Once the bark is firm, break it into pieces.

STORAGE: The bark should be stored in the refrigerator until ready to serve or it may turn gray and streaky. Remove it about 30 minutes before you plan to enjoy it. It will keep for 1 to 2 weeks.

VARIATION: To make ALMOND AND CANDIED BACON BARK, chop the almonds and replace the pistachios and dried cherries with candied bacon. To make candied bacon, lay 5 strips of bacon on a baking sheet lined with aluminum foil (shiny side down) or parchment paper. Sprinkle each strip with about 2 teaspoons light brown sugar. Bake in a 400°F (200°C) oven for 12 to 15 minutes, flipping the strips over midway through baking, and dragging them through any melted sugar that's collected on the baking sheet. They're done when they're mahogany colored. Cool on a wire rack until crisp, then crumble and mix into the chocolate along with the almonds. It's best to make the candied bacon the same day you plan to use it. Candied bacon bark should be eaten within 3 days.

Spiced Candied Pecans

MAKES 4 CUPS (400 G)

If there's an easier candy out there, I haven't found it. When I worked as a pastry chef, I think I made a batch of these every day. And since they're so easy, why not? (Actually, I pretty much had to since I discovered all the other cooks in the kitchen couldn't resist dipping into the container when I wasn't looking.)

Great nibbled on their own, these nuts are also good used in place of the toasted nuts in Chocolate Chip Cookies (page 188) and Robert's Absolute Best Brownies (page 196), or in place of the almonds in Pistachio, Almond, and Cherry Bark (page 223). They can be chopped and folded into just-churned ice cream, or sprinkled on top of scoops of ice cream that are sauced with a ladleful of warm Rich Caramel Sauce (page 241).

1 large egg white

$^1/_2$ cup (120 g) packed light brown sugar

2 tablespoons ground cinnamon

1 teaspoon ground ginger

1 teaspoon ground cloves

1 teaspoon cayenne or pure chile powder

$^1/_2$ teaspoon salt

2 teaspoons vanilla extract

4 cups (14 ounces/400 g) pecan halves

Preheat the oven to 300°F (150° C). Spray a baking sheet with nonstick cooking spray or oil it lightly.

In a large bowl, whisk the egg white until frothy, about 10 seconds. Stir in the brown sugar, cinnamon, ginger, cloves, cayenne or chile powder, salt, vanilla, and pecans until the nuts are well coated.

Distribute the nuts in an even layer on the prepared baking sheet and bake until the pecans are well toasted and the glaze is dry, about 30 minutes, stirring every 10 minutes. Let cool completely, separating the pecans as they cool.

STORAGE: The nuts will keep in an airtight container at room temperature for up to 2 weeks.

VARIATION: You can substitute walnut halves for the pecans.

Quince Paste

MAKES SIXTY 1-INCH (3-CM) SQUARES

With all the recent interest in Spanish cuisine, it's no surprise that *membrillo*—Spanish quince paste—has become a global hit. Anyone who has tasted it paired with Manchego cheese and a glass of sherry understands why it's become so popular the world over.

But that popularity doesn't come easy: it takes at least 30 minutes of almost-constant stirring to make quince paste. I always wear an oven mitt while stirring with a wooden spatula because the hot mixture occasionally pops and sputters as it thickens.

4 medium quinces (1^1/$_2$ pounds/675 g)

^{1}/$_2$ lemon, preferably organic

4 cups (1 liter) water

3 cups (600 g) sugar

Wash and rub the quinces to remove any fuzz and leaves and cut them into quarters.

In a medium saucepan, combine the quince pieces, lemon half, and water and cook over medium heat, covered, until the quince is tender, about 1 hour. Remove from the heat and discard the lemon half.

With a melon baller or spoon, scoop out the quince seeds and discard them. Pass the quince pieces and the cooking liquid through a food mill or press them through a coarse-mesh strainer. You should have 3 to 4 cups of purée.

Put the quince purée and the sugar in a large heavy-duty saucepan or wide skillet and cook over low heat, stirring constantly, until the mixture forms a thick, shiny, solid mass, 30 to 40 minutes. (Be careful as you stir because the hot mixture will sputter and pop.)

Line a baking sheet with parchment paper or oil it very lightly. Spread the quince paste into a layer ^{1}/$_2$ inch (1.5 cm) thick on the prepared baking sheet and let cool slightly. Once cooled enough to touch, wet your hand and smooth the surface of paste, then let cool completely.

Using a sharp knife, cut the paste into 1-inch (3-cm) squares. If the paste is sticky, dip the knife in hot water and wipe it dry between each cut.

SERVING: Serve the quince paste by itself, or with slices of a dry, sharp cheese, such as Manchego or Cheddar.

STORAGE: Stored in a container in a cool, dry place, quince paste will keep for at least 3 months. Do not store it in a very tightly sealed container or it will become soggy. Some folks layer a bay leaf between squares of the quince paste, which gives it a unique flavor.

VARIATION: You can make APPLE PASTE by using 3 large baking apples (about 2 pounds/1 kg). Cook the quartered apples in 1 cup (250 ml) water until soft, purée them, then cook the purée down to a paste with 2 cups (400 g) sugar and ^{1}/$_4$ vanilla bean, split lengthwise.

Basics, Sauces, and Preserves

The recipes in this chapter are not only the foundations of many of the desserts in this book, but many can be used as springboards for creating your own inspired combinations. To start things off, there are a few pastry doughs, including a very simple galette dough (page 231) that takes just a few moments to make. It's a very forgiving mixture that's nothing to fear—and I'm not just saying that because I've made it at least 5,000 times in my lifetime.

When I first learned to make pie dough a few decades ago from my friend's Norwegian grandmother, she told me "If the dough doesn't fall apart when you make it, it's not going to be good." It's true: the enemy of any pastry dough is overworking the mixture in an effort to bring it together. For the tenderest, flakiest results, keep your movements and mixing swift and don't overdo it. Don't worry if the dough falls apart slightly or doesn't look like a professional rolled it out. Any dough made from scratch, no matter how questionable it looks, tastes infinitely better than store-bought refrigerator dough or one made from a boxed mix.

Pastry cream, sabayon, and crème anglaise often serve as the bases for desserts like soufflés and ice creams, but they are also accompaniments to cakes, pies, and tarts. A mound of Cider Sabayon (page 238) is a natural alongside a wedge of Apple-Frangipane Galette (page 89), and who wouldn't want a pool of cold crème anglaise (page 237) with a slab of Chocolate Pavé (page 25)?

In addition to two recipes for chocolate sauce, plus one for white chocolate sauce, this chapter contains a colorful variety of fruit sauces and caramel accompaniments. Caramel doesn't always want to share the stage with anything else, so I'm offering options—a couple thick, rich sauces and a few thin, lighter ones—depending on if you want a full-on, gooey experience or a neat, sophisticated drizzle of flavor.

Preserving also plays an important role in my kitchen, so I've included some favorite recipes for candied fruits and homemade jams. These get served inside, alongside, and sometimes on top of, many of my desserts. I hope you'll find some ways to use them creatively in your own baking as well.

And because man cannot live by dessert alone (although I know of one who is working on proving that dictum wrong), I sometimes like a little something to drink before and after dinner. *Vin d'orange* (page 262), a slightly bitter orange-flavored fortified wine, makes a wonderful aperitif that's meant to perk up your appetite before you sit down at the table.

After dinner, a digestif is equally inviting and balances the meal. I have many friends with walnut trees who provide me with green walnuts to make *nocino* (page 263), a syrupy, mildly spiced Italian liqueur. *Nocino* is wonderful digestif, but it's also superb poured over Vanilla Ice Cream (page 143) or made into smooth custards (page 263).

Prebaked Tart Shell

MAKES ONE 9-INCH (23-CM) TART SHELL

This dough is cookielike and sturdy, and it doesn't need to be weighed down with pie weights for prebaking. But best of all, it's pressed into the tart pan, so there's no need for rolling.

6 tablespoons (3 ounces/85 g) unsalted butter, at room temperature

$^{1}/_{4}$ cup (50 g) sugar

1 large egg yolk

1 cup (140 g) all-purpose flour

$^{1}/_{8}$ teaspoon salt

In a stand mixer fitted with the paddle attachment, beat together the butter and sugar on low speed until just smooth, about 1 minute. Add the egg yolk and mix for 30 seconds on low speed. Add the flour and salt and mix just until the dough comes together in a smooth, homogeneous mass. Don't overmix. Pinch off a jelly bean–size piece of dough, wrap it in plastic wrap, and set aside.

Place the remaining dough in the center of a 9-inch (23-cm) tart pan with a removable bottom. Use the heel of your hand to press the dough evenly across the bottom of the pan; try to get the dough as smooth as possible. Use your fingers to press the dough up the sides and to the rim of the pan; make sure that the dough is not too thick in the corners.

Freeze the dough-lined tart pan until the dough is firm, at least 1 hour.

Preheat the oven to 375°F (190°C).

Set the tart pan on a baking sheet and prick the frozen tart dough about 10 times with a fork. Bake the tart shell on the baking sheet for 7 minutes, then check if the bottom has puffed up; if it has, gently press it down with the back of a metal spatula. Continue baking until deep golden brown, 15 to 20 minutes more.

Remove from the oven. While the tart shell is hot, if there are any large fissures, pinch off small pieces of the reserved unbaked dough, and use your fingertip to gently smooth them into the cracks until the cracks are filled. (There's no need to bake longer as the heat from the still-warm tart shell will firm it up.)

STORAGE: Tart dough can be frozen for 1 month, either formed into a disk or pressed into the tart pan. The tart shell needs to be used the day that it's prebaked, so don't bake it until you need it.

Pie Dough

MAKES ENOUGH FOR ONE 9- OR 10-INCH (23- OR 25-CM) DOUBLE-CRUST PIE
OR TWO 9- OR 10-INCH (23- OR 25-CM) SINGLE-CRUST PIES

There's lots of controversy about which fat makes the best pie crust: butter, shortening, or lard. I'm not a fan of shortening or lard because I always feel like I'm being unfaithful to butter by not baking with it. And besides, I like its taste. As long as you keep the butter cold and the ice water to a minimum, this dough bakes up plenty flaky.

I prefer to use glass pie plates as they make it easy to check on the browning underneath, but metal pie pans work well, too.

2^1/$_2$ cups (350 g) all-purpose flour

1 tablespoon sugar

^{1}/$_2$ teaspoon salt

1 cup (8 ounces/225 g) unsalted butter, cut into
  1-inch (3-cm) cubes and chilled

6 to 8 tablespoons (90 to 120 ml) ice water

In a large bowl using a pastry blender, in a stand mixer fitted with the paddle attachment, or in a food processor fitted with the metal blade, mix together the flour, sugar, and salt. Add the chilled butter cubes and mix just until the butter is broken up into rough ^{1}/$_4$-inch (6-mm) pieces.

Add 6 tablespoons (90 ml) of the ice water all at once and continue mixing just until the dough begins to hold together. If necessary, mix in the additional 2 tablespoons (30 ml) ice water.

Turn the dough out onto a work surface. Divide the dough in half and form each half into a disk about 1 inch (3 cm) thick. Wrap the disks in plastic wrap and refrigerate until chilled and firm, at least 1 hour.

STORAGE: The disks of dough can be refrigerated for up to 2 days or frozen for up to 2 months.

TIP: If the dough is chilled for more than 1 hour, before you roll it out, let it stand at room temperature for about 5 minutes until it becomes slightly malleable again.

PREBAKING A PIE SHELL

- For a prebaked 9- or 10-inch (23- or 25-cm) pie shell, lightly flour the work surface and roll out one disk of dough into a 14-inch (36-cm) circle. To make it easier to move, fold it in half, and fit it into a 9- or 10-inch (23- or 25 cm) pie plate.

- Unfold the dough, centering it and gently pressing it into the dish with your fingers. Tuck the excess dough under itself, leaving a generous amount of pastry around the rim. Use your fingers or a fork to decoratively crimp the edges. Freeze for about 30 minutes.

- Preheat the oven to 375°F (190°C).

- Line the dough-lined pie plate with a sheet of aluminum foil, fill halfway with pie weights (or dried beans), and bake until the bottom of the crust is beginning to brown, about 20 minutes. Remove the foil and weights, and continue baking until deep golden brown, about 10 minutes more.

Galette Dough

MAKES ENOUGH FOR ONE 12-INCH (30-CM) GALETTE

Anyone intimidated by making dough will quickly get over it in the 3 minutes that it takes to make this one. It's very easy to put together, very forgiving, and almost impossible to botch. Any flaws, cracks, or imperfections are part of its rustic charm, although I'm confident that even the most inexperienced baker will master it with the very first try. It will likely become your favorite dough to use for any number of open-faced fruit tarts.

This recipe can be doubled—an extra disk is good to have on hand in the freezer for later use.

1¹/₂ cups (210 g) all-purpose flour

1 tablespoon sugar

¹/₂ teaspoon salt

¹/₂ cup (4 ounces/115 g) unsalted butter, cut into 1-inch (3-cm) cubes and chilled

6 tablespoons (90 ml) ice water

In a large bowl using a pastry blender, in a stand mixer fitted with the paddle attachment, or in a food processor fitted with the metal blade, mix together the flour, sugar, and salt. Add the chilled butter cubes and mix until the butter is broken into pieces about the size of large corn kernels. Don't worry if a few pieces are in larger, rough chunks; they will make the dough nice and flaky.

Add the ice water all at once and continue mixing just until the dough begins to hold together.

Shape the dough into a 5-inch (13-cm) disk, wrap it in plastic wrap, and refrigerate until chilled and firm, at least 30 minutes. Use as directed in the recipe.

STORAGE: The disk of dough can be refrigerated for up to 2 days or frozen for up to 1 month.

TIP: This dough can be used to create a rustic tart using almost any type of fruit. Cut 3 pounds (1.5 kg) of fruit such as nectarines, apricots, plums, or peeled pears or peaches into ¹/₂-inch (1.5-cm) slices. Roll out the galette dough according to the directions for Apple-Frangipane Galette (page 89), and transfer to a parchment paper–lined baking sheet. Top with the fruit, leaving a 2-inch (5-cm) border. Fold the edges over the fruit, sprinkle with ¹/₄ cup (60 g) sugar and bake in a 375°F (180°C) until the fruit is tender and the crust is deep golden brown, about 1 hour.

Pâte à Choux Puffs

MAKES 25 TO 30 PASTRIES

The batter for these French puffs is made on the stovetop, then shaped and baked until the eggy mounds balloon into airy, hollow spheres. The puffs take to all sorts of fillings, from simple whipped cream (page 239) to scoops of ice cream, as for Anise-Orange Ice Cream Profiteroles with Chocolate Sauce (page 172). No special equipment is required to make them, and they come together with ingredients you probably already have on hand.

A few things to keep in mind: Measure the ingredients carefully—too much liquid results in flat puffs. Dump in the flour just when the butter is melted; if you wait too long, too much of the water will cook off. The finished batter should be thick and shiny and should stick to the spatula when you lift it. Finally, be sure to bake the puffs until they're deep golden brown all the way around. If they're underbaked, they may collapse cooling; the darker color means the puffs will stay crisper, too.

PUFFS

1 cup (250 ml) water

$^1/_2$ cup (4 ounces/115 g) unsalted butter, cut into $^1/_2$-inch (1.5-cm) pieces

2 teaspoons sugar

$^1/_2$ teaspoon salt

1 cup (140 g) all-purpose flour

4 large eggs

GLAZE (OPTIONAL)

1 large egg yolk

1 teaspoon whole milk

Preheat the oven to 425°F (220°C). Line a baking sheet with parchment paper or a silicone baking mat.

In a medium saucepan, bring the water, butter, sugar, and salt to a boil over medium-high heat, stirring gently to encourage the butter to melt. As soon as the mixture begins to boil, add the flour all at once and stir rapidly with a spatula until the mixture forms a thick paste and pulls away from the sides of the pan.

Remove from the heat. Wait for 2 minutes, stirring the paste a couple of times to cool it slightly, then vigorously beat in the eggs one at a time, making sure each one is completely incorporated before adding the next. (I do this by hand, but some folks prefer to use a stand mixer fitted with the paddle attachment.)

Using a pastry bag fitted with a plain $^1/_2$-inch (1-cm) tip, pipe the choux paste into mounds $1^1/_2$ inches (4 cm) high on the prepared baking sheet, spacing them 3 inches (8 cm) apart. Or, use 2 teaspoons to drop the paste into mounds.

If you want puffs with a shiny glaze, in a small bowl, whisk together the egg yolk and milk and brush the tops of the puffs without letting the glaze drip down the sides, which will inhibit rising.

Bake until the puffs are golden brown on the tops and sides, 25 to 30 minutes. Turn off the oven and let them rest in the oven for 5 minutes. Remove from the oven and poke each puff in the side with a paring knife so that it releases its steam. Let cool completely.

STORAGE: Pâte à choux puffs can be stored at room temperature for several hours. I prefer not to freeze them because there is a noticeable difference in quality between fresh and frozen puffs, but if you have leftovers, you can freeze them for up to 1 month and recrisp them in a low oven before serving.

Sponge Cake

MAKES ONE 12 BY 18-INCH (30 BY 46-CM) SHEET CAKE OR ONE 9-INCH (23-CM) ROUND CAKE

This feather-light sponge cake recipe was given to me by the always-gracious food writer Shirley Sarvis. When I asked her the reason for adding water to sponge cake batter, she replied, "For moisture, of course!" It is indeed a wonderfully moist sponge cake, and I use it in many desserts, including Coconut Layer Cake (page 59), Lemon Semifreddo (page 65), and Coconut and Tropical Fruit Trifle (page 70). The cake can be baked in a baking sheet with sides, often referred to as a jelly-roll pan, or in a 9-inch (23-cm) round springform pan.

$1^1/_2$ cups (195 g) cake flour

$^1/_2$ teaspoon baking powder

$^1/_4$ teaspoon salt

5 large eggs, separated, at room temperature

$^1/_4$ cup (60 ml) cold water

1 cup (200 g) sugar

1 teaspoon vanilla extract

Preheat the oven to 350°F (175°C). Lightly butter just the bottom of a 12 by 18-inch (30 by 46-cm) rimmed baking sheet or 9-inch (23-cm) springform pan with sides at least 2 inches (5 cm) high. Line the bottom with a piece of parchment paper.

Into a small bowl, sift together the flour, baking powder, and salt.

In a stand mixer fitted with the whip attachment, whisk together the egg yolks and water on high speed for 1 minute. Decrease the speed to medium, add the sugar and vanilla, then increase the speed to high and continue to whisk until the mixture forms a ribbon when the whip is lifted, about 5 minutes. Set aside.

In a clean, dry bowl and with a clean whip attachment, whisk the egg whites on high speed in the stand mixer until they form stiff peaks.

Using one hand, gradually sift the flour mixture over the beaten yolks, and using a whisk with the other hand, fold it in. (Setting the bowl on a damp towel will help steady it while you sift and fold.) When the flour is completely incorporated, use a rubber spatula to fold in one-third of the whipped egg whites to lighten the batter, then fold in the remaining whites.

Pour the batter into the prepared baking sheet or springform pan and quickly spread it in an even layer. Bake until the cake is browned and the center springs back when gently pressed with a finger, 15 to 18 minutes in a baking sheet or 40 to 45 minutes in a cake pan. Let cool in the pan.

Run a knife around the sides of the cake to loosen it from the pan. Invert the cake onto a cutting board or large plate.

STORAGE: The cake will keep at room temperature for 3 days, or in the freezer for 1 month.

VARIATIONS: You can add the grated zest of 1 lemon or orange to the batter along with the egg whites. Instead of the vanilla extract, you can use $^1/_2$ teaspoon almond extract.

TIP: Sponge cake is easier to slice if made a day in advance.

Frangipane

MAKES ABOUT 1 CUP (250 ML), ENOUGH FOR ONE 12-INCH (30-CM) GALETTE

A thin layer of frangipane baked under a pinwheel of sliced fruit in a tart shell crust not only adds richness and the flavor of almonds to complement the sweet-tangy fruit, it also helps keep the tart shell crisp because it acts as a barrier between fruit juices and the pastry.

Almond paste is available in the baking aisle of supermarkets. It is not marzipan, which has more sugar and is usually used for modeling and shaping.

4 ounces (115 g) almond paste, crumbled

1¹/₂ teaspoons sugar

1¹/₂ teaspoons all-purpose flour

¹/₈ teaspoon almond extract

6 tablespoons (3 ounces/90 g) unsalted or salted butter, at room temperature

1 large egg, at room temperature

1 teaspoon rum, kirsch, or Calvados (optional)

In a food processor fitted with the metal blade or in a stand mixer fitted with the paddle attachment, mix together the almond paste, sugar, flour, and almond extract until the almond paste is in fine pieces. Add the butter and mix until completely incorporated, then add the egg and rum, kirsch, or Calvados, if using, and continue mixing until the frangipane is as smooth as possible. Don't worry if there are a few tiny bits of almond paste; they'll disappear with baking.

STORAGE: Frangipane will keep in the refrigerator for up to 1 week, or in the freezer for up to 1 month. For easier spreading, bring it to room temperature before using.

VARIATIONS: To make PISTACHIO FRANGIPANE, substitute pistachio paste (see Resources, page 270) for the almond paste.

To make BOSTOCK (a snack made by frugal French bakers with leftover frangipane), spread slices of day-old eggy bread, such as brioche or challah, or a firm-textured sandwich bread, with a thick layer of frangipane—about ¹/₃-inch (8-mm) thick. Sprinkle with sliced almonds, and bake in a 425°F (220°C) oven until the frangipane is crusty and deep golden brown, about 10 minutes. Serve warm or at room temperature, alone or with a fruit compote.

Pastry Cream

MAKES ABOUT 2½ CUPS (625 ML)

One of the basics in any baker's repertoire is *crème pâtissière*, or pastry cream. Though the word "cream" appears in its name, there is, in fact, no cream in pastry cream. Cooking egg yolks and milk with a bit of flour creates a smooth, rich custard that looks and tastes as if it were made with cream.

Pastry cream is used as the base for many soufflés. It can also be spread in a prebaked tart shell (page 229) and topped with fresh fruit to make a seasonal fruit tart, or piped as a filling into pâte à choux puffs (page 232) that are then smothered in warm Bittersweet Chocolate Sauce (page 243).

6 tablespoons (60 g) all-purpose flour

½ cup (100 g) sugar

Pinch of salt

2 cups (250 ml) whole milk

6 large egg yolks

½ teaspoon vanilla extract

2 tablespoons (1 ounce/30 g) unsalted or salted butter

In a small bowl, whisk together the flour, sugar, and salt.

In a medium saucepan, warm the milk until it begins to steam. Whisk in the flour mixture and cook over medium heat, whisking constantly to prevent lumps from forming, until the mixture is thick and beginning to bubble, 1 to 2 minutes.

In a small bowl, lightly whisk the egg yolks. Whisk in some of the hot milk mixture to warm them, then scrape the warmed yolks back into the thickened milk. Cook, stirring constantly, until the pastry cream just begins to boil.

Remove from the heat, whisk in the vanilla and the butter until melted, and pour the pastry cream through a mesh strainer into a shallow container. Cover and refrigerate until chilled.

STORAGE: Pastry cream will keep in the refrigerator for up to 3 days.

VARIATIONS: Add 1 vanilla bean, split lengthwise, to the milk before warming it. After straining, the pod can be rinsed, dried, and used for another purpose (see page 14).

To make CITRUS PASTRY CREAM, grate the zest of 2 lemons or limes into the warm milk and let steep for 15 minutes. Make the pastry cream as indicated (with our without the vanilla extract) and let cool. Stir 2 tablespoons freshly squeezed lemon or lime juice into the cooled pastry cream.

Crème Anglaise

MAKES 2½ CUPS (625 ML)

I've seen fights break out among pastry chefs over what constitutes crème anglaise, so I'll stick with the classic. This versatile custard sauce isn't so rich that it overwhelms, but it is smooth enough to provide a creamy, luxurious component to desserts such as cakes and cobblers. Although not traditional, try a pour of crème anglaise in a bowl of fruit sorbet—the silken richness is a spot-on counterpoint to the icy scoop.

2 cups (500 ml) whole milk

6 tablespoons (75 g) sugar

Pinch of salt

1 vanilla bean, split lengthwise

6 large egg yolks

½ teaspoon vanilla extract

Make an ice bath by nesting a medium metal bowl in a larger bowl filled with ice water. Set a mesh strainer across the top.

In a medium saucepan, combine the milk, sugar, and salt. Scrape the seeds from the vanilla bean and add them to the saucepan, then drop in the pod. Warm the mixture, stirring to dissolve the sugar.

In a small bowl, lightly whisk the egg yolks. Whisk in some of the warmed milk mixture, then scrape the warmed yolks back into the saucepan. Cook over medium-low heat, stirring constantly with a heatproof spatula and scraping the bottom of the pan, until the custard is thick enough to coat the spatula. Don't let the mixture boil.

Immediately strain the custard through the mesh strainer into the chilled bowl. (The vanilla pod can be rinsed, dried, and used for another purpose; see page 14.) Add the vanilla extract and stir the crème anglaise with a clean spatula to help cool it down. Once cool, cover and refrigerate.

SERVING: Crème anglaise should always be served cold. I like to chill it in a pitcher, bring the pitcher to the table, and allow guests to help themselves.

STORAGE: Crème anglaise will keep in the refrigerator for up to 3 days.

VARIATIONS: Instead of infusing the milk with a vanilla bean, in its place, use 4 to 6 crushed cinnamon sticks, 1¼ cups (100 g) coffee beans, or the grated zest of 3 oranges or 4 lemons; omit the vanilla extract.

If you like, you can spike the cooled custard with 2 to 3 tablespoons (30 to 45 ml) of spirits such as Cognac, rum, or Grand Marnier.

> **TIP:** You can rescue crème anglaise that you've accidentally overcooked. If it looks curdled after straining, pour it into a blender while it's still warm, filling the jar no more than halfway (or use an immersion blender directly in the bowl), and blend on low speed until smooth.

Champagne Sabayon

MAKES ABOUT 3½ CUPS (875 ML)

Sabayon is the French version of Italian zabaglione, an airy egg-and-wine custard. It requires a certain amount of energy—and strength—to whip up a batch. If you've ever heard a frenzy of whisking coming from the kitchen at an Italian restaurant, you've heard why many Italian cooks (especially the sturdy grandmas) have such well-developed arms. But one lick of the boozy, frothy dessert is enough to make you forget those few furious minutes of whipping. If you don't think you're up to the task, you can use an electric handheld mixer. But I always feel that if I've worked hard to make something, I've earned the right to eat it.

You can serve the sabayon hot from the stove, although here, it is cooled and whipped cream is added so it can be held before serving.

7 large egg yolks

⅓ cup (65 g) sugar

⅔ cup (160 ml) Champagne or other sparkling wine

½ cup (125 ml) heavy cream

Fill a large bowl with ice water.

In a large heatproof bowl, whisk together the egg yolks, sugar, and Champagne or other sparkling wine. Set the bowl over a saucepan of simmering water and whisk vigorously and constantly. The mixture will first become frothy, then as you continue to whisk, thick and creamy. When the mixture holds its shape when you lift the whisk, remove the bowl from the heat. Set the bowl in the ice water bath and whisk gently until cooled.

In a stand mixer fitted with the whip attachment (or in a bowl by hand), whisk the cream on medium-high speed until it holds soft peaks. Fold the whipped cream into the sabayon.

STORAGE: Sabayon can be refrigerated for up to 2 days, but it is best used the day it's made.

VARIATIONS: Don't limit yourself to sabayon flavored with Champagne. In Italy, the traditional flavoring is Marsala, but any dry or sweet white wine is also delicious.

To make CIDER SABAYON, use 6 large egg yolks and replace the Champagne with ½ cup (125 ml) sparkling apple cider and ¼ cup (60 ml) applejack or Calvados.

Whipped Cream

MAKES 2 CUPS (500 ML)

A wonderful revolution has taken place in America over the last decade: small local dairies have been sprouting up all across the land and many of them are producing heavy cream with rich, unmistakable, and honest-to-goodness flavor. Once you taste real cream, you'll never want to use the bland ultrapasteurized stuff that has taken over supermarket dairy cases.

For whipped cream, the freshest non-ultrapasteurized cream not only tastes the best, but it whips up much better. I highly recommend tracking some down. Make sure the cream is very cold before whipping, and if the weather is warm, chill the bowl and the whisk ahead of time.

1 cup (250 ml) heavy cream

1 tablespoon sugar

$^1/_2$ teaspoon vanilla extract

In a stand mixer fitted with the whip attachment (or in a bowl by hand), whisk the cream on medium-high speed until it just begins to hold its shape.

Add the sugar and vanilla and continue to whisk on medium-high speed just until the cream mounds gently. Don't whip it until it is superstiff, or it will become grainy.

STORAGE: Whipped cream is best used the same day you make it. If whipped in advance, it may be necessary to rewhisk it slightly just before serving, because it tends to separate as it sits.

VARIATIONS: If you like specks of vanilla seed in your whipped cream, split $^1/_2$ vanilla bean and scrape its seeds into the cream before whipping it.

To flavor whipped cream with a spirit such as Cognac, rum, whiskey, or Grand Marnier, fold in a few tablespoons to taste once the cream is sweetened and fully whipped.

> TIP: You can rescue whipped cream that you've accidentally overwhipped by stirring in a few tablespoons of unwhipped cream, gently folding until the whipped cream smoothes out.

Cognac Caramel Sauce

MAKES 1 1/2 CUPS (375 ML)

This thin sauce with a fiery personality adds a direct hit of liquor, tempered by caramel, to any dessert that it's drizzled over. I particularly like it made with Armagnac, Cognac's rowdy cousin, and paired with Creamy Rice Pudding (page 138). If you wish, you can use bourbon, rum, or any favorite liquor in place of the Cognac.

1 cup (200 g) sugar

1/3 cup (80 ml) plus 1/2 cup (125 ml) water

Pinch of cream of tartar or a few drops of lemon juice

3/4 cup (180 ml) Cognac

> Before preparing this recipe, see Caramelization Guidelines, page 265.

Spread the sugar in an even layer in a medium heavy-bottomed skillet or saucepan. Pour the 1/3 cup (80 ml) water over the sugar to dampen it, but don't stir. Cook over medium heat until the sugar dissolves and add the cream of tartar or lemon juice. Continue to cook without stirring, but swirling the pan if the sugar clumps or begins to brown unevenly. When the caramel turns dark amber in color and begins to foam a bit, remove from the heat and immediately add the remaining 1/2 cup (125 ml) water. The caramel will bubble up vigorously, then the bubbling will subside. Stir with a heatproof utensil until any hardened bits of caramel completely dissolve. Let cool completely, then stir in the Cognac. Serve at room temperature.

STORAGE: This sauce can be stored at room temperature or refrigerated for up to 2 weeks.

Rich Caramel Sauce

MAKES ABOUT 1$^1/_2$ CUPS (375 ML)

Burnt caramel is all the rage lately, and for good reason. The slightly bitter notes counter the sugar's sweetness so that the result is a complex and balanced flavor, not just direct sweetness. It's important to stop cooking the caramel at just the right moment, which is only a few seconds before it's scorched. Recipes often advise cooking the caramel until it just begins to smoke, but it isn't until it begins to foam a bit that its best flavor comes forward.

To one-up burnt caramel, you can make salted-butter burnt caramel sauce by using salted butter and stirring in additional salt (preferably flaky sea salt) to taste. It's delicious!

$^1/_2$ cup (4 ounces/115 g) unsalted or salted butter, cut into pieces

1 cup (200 g) sugar

1 cup (250 ml) heavy cream

$^1/_4$ teaspoon vanilla extract

$^1/_8$ teaspoon salt, or more to taste

TIP: The caramel will bubble up extra vigorously when the heavy cream is added, so it is important that you use a large saucepan or a Dutch oven for this recipe.

In a large heavy-bottomed saucepan or a Dutch oven, melt the butter over medium heat. Add the sugar and cook, stirring occasionally, until the sugar begins to caramelize, then turns dark amber in color and begins to foam a bit (it should smell and look like it's just on the verge of burning). Remove from the heat and immediately add the heavy cream. Stir until the sauce is smooth, then stir in the vanilla and salt. Let cool, then taste, and add more salt, if desired. Serve the sauce warm.

STORAGE: This sauce can be stored in the refrigerator for up to 2 weeks. Rewarm before serving.

Orange Caramel Sauce

MAKES 1 CUP (250 ML)

I make this sauce with blood oranges when they're available because I like the deep, vivid color their juice adds. One of my favorite and simplest of desserts is a platter of chilled navel and blood orange slices scribbled with this tangy-sweet sauce and sprinkled with chopped pistachios. But this sauce is also good drizzled over a neat slab of Gâteau Victoire (page 32) or a serving of Ricotta Cheesecake with Orange and Aniseed (page 55).

1 cup plus 2 tablespoons (230 g) sugar

$^1/_3$ cup (80 ml) water

A pinch of cream of tartar or a few drops of lemon juice

$^3/_4$ cup (180 ml) freshly squeezed orange juice

> Before preparing this recipe, see Caramelization Guidelines, page 265.

Spread the sugar in an even layer in a medium heavy-bottomed skillet or saucepan. Pour the water over the sugar to dampen it, but don't stir. Cook over medium heat until the sugar dissolves and add the cream of tartar or lemon juice. Continue to cook, without stirring, but swirling the pan if the sugar clumps or begins to brown unevenly. When the caramel turns dark amber in color and begins to foam a bit, remove from the heat and immediately add half of the orange juice. The caramel will bubble up vigorously, then the bubbling will subside. Stir with a heatproof utensil until any hardened bits of caramel completely dissolve. Let cool for 3 minutes, then stir in the remaining orange juice. Serve the sauce at room temperature.

STORAGE: This sauce can be stored at room temperature or refrigerated for up to 2 weeks.

Tangerine Butterscotch Sauce

MAKES ABOUT 1$^1/_2$ CUPS (375 ML)

With the addition of sprightly tangerine juice, this twist on traditional butterscotch sauce goes very well drizzled over Buckwheat Cake (page 44) paired with orange or tangerine sections instead of the cider-poached apples, or spooned over Pâte à Choux Puffs (page 232) filled with Caramel Ice Cream (page 144) and topped with toasted or candied nuts.

4 tablespoons (2 ounces/60 g) unsalted or salted butter, cut into pieces

1 cup (215 g) packed light brown sugar

$^1/_3$ cup (80 ml) heavy cream

$^1/_8$ teaspoon salt

$^1/_4$ cup (60 ml) freshly squeezed tangerine juice

2 tablespoons (30 ml) orange-flavored liqueur, such as Grand Marnier, Cointreau, or Triple Sec

In a large saucepan, combine the butter, brown sugar, cream, and salt. Bring to a boil over medium-high heat and boil for 3 minutes without stirring.

Remove from the heat, let cool for 2 minutes, then stir in the tangerine juice and orange-flavored liqueur. Serve the sauce warm.

STORAGE: This sauce can be stored in the refrigerator for up to 2 weeks. Rewarm before serving.

Bittersweet Chocolate Sauce

MAKES ABOUT 2 CUPS (500 ML)

This is my all-time favorite chocolate sauce and the one I've been making for almost three chocolate-filled decades. Don't let the fact that it doesn't contain any cream or butter make you think that this sauce is lacking in any way—it gets maximum intensity from ramped-up amounts of chocolate and cocoa powder. I do prefer to use Dutch-process cocoa powder here because of its stronger flavor and darker color, but you can use natural cocoa powder if that's what you prefer or have on hand.

Since it has no cream or butter, I don't feel any guilt liberally pouring this sauce over desserts like Anise-Orange Ice Cream Profiteroles (page 172) or a wedge of Pear Tart with Brown Butter, Rum, and Pecans (page 91).

$^3/_4$ cup (75 g) unsweetened cocoa powder, preferably Dutch-process

$^1/_2$ cup (100 g) sugar

$^1/_4$ cup (80 g) light corn syrup or agave nectar

1 cup (250 ml) water

2 ounces (60 g) bittersweet or semisweet chocolate, chopped

TIP: The sauce is even better made a few hours or a day ahead of serving to allow the cocoa to thicken it properly.

In a medium saucepan, whisk together the cocoa powder, sugar, corn syrup or agave nectar, and water. Bring to a boil over medium-high heat, whisking occasionally to break up any lumps of cocoa. Once it reaches a full boil, remove from the heat. Add the chocolate and whisk until the chocolate is melted and the sauce is smooth. Serve the sauce warm.

STORAGE: This sauce can be stored in the refrigerator for up to 2 weeks. Rewarm before serving.

Rich Chocolate Sauce

MAKES 2 CUPS (500 ML)

For those who like their chocolate sauce rich and thick, this sauce has more body than the Bittersweet Chocolate Sauce (page 243), courtesy of a modest amount of cream. It is particularly appealing when served side by side or gently swirled with White Chocolate Sauce (below) as an accompaniment to wedges of chocolate cake.

12 ounces (340 g) bittersweet or semisweet chocolate, chopped

3/4 cup (180 ml) water

3/4 cup (180 ml) heavy cream

2 teaspoons whiskey, rum, or Cognac

In a medium saucepan, combine the chocolate, water, and cream. Warm over low heat, stirring gently until the chocolate is melted and the sauce is smooth. Remove from the heat and stir in the whiskey, rum, or Cognac. Serve the sauce warm.

STORAGE: This sauce can be stored in the refrigerator for up to 2 weeks. Rewarm before serving.

VARIATION: For a slightly richer sauce, stir in 2 tablespoons unsalted or salted butter, at room temperature, along with the whiskey, rum, or Cognac.

White Chocolate Sauce

MAKES 1 CUP (250 ML)

I fall into the camp of white chocolate lovers because, unlike white chocolate critics, I don't compare it to dark chocolate. Instead, I appreciate it for its own lavishly rich merits. Because it's on the sweeter side, white chocolate sauce pairs especially well with desserts with the puckery punch of lemon, such as the Lemon Semifreddo (page 65), Super-Lemony Soufflés (page 130), or Freestyle Lemon Tartlets (page 94.) Be sure to use real white chocolate, one which lists only cocoa butter in the list of ingredients, and no other vegetable fats. Since white chocolate plays such an important part in this sauce, you want it to be as good as it possibly can be.

3/4 cup (180 ml) heavy cream or half-and-half

9 ounces (255 g) white chocolate, chopped

In a small saucepan, warm the cream or half-and-half over low heat. When it just begins to boil, remove from the heat and add the white chocolate. Let stand for 1 minute, then whisk until the chocolate is melted and the sauce is smooth. Serve the sauce warm.

STORAGE: This sauce can be stored in the refrigerator for up to 1 week. Rewarm before serving.

Blueberry Compote

MAKES 2 CUPS (500 ML)

One day while cooking some blueberries, it occurred to me that the sharp taste of a sizable shot of gin would nicely complement the berries, so I reached for the bottle and poured some in. Gin's herbaceous flavor does indeed marry nicely with blueberries—it can hardly be tasted once cooked, but somehow it just rounds out the blueberry notes. Now, whenever I cook with blueberries, a bit of gin finds its way into the mix.

$2^1/_2$ cups (12 ounces/340 g) fresh or frozen blueberries

$^1/_4$ cup (50 g) sugar, plus more to taste

2 tablespoons (30 ml) gin

In a medium saucepan, combine the blueberries, sugar, and gin. Cook over medium heat, stirring occasionally, until the berries soften and release their juices.

Remove from the heat and let stand, uncovered, and let cool to room temperature. Taste for sweetness and add more sugar, if desired.

STORAGE: This compote can be stored in the refrigerator for up to 3 days. It's actually better when prepared a day in advance, which gives it time to thicken nicely.

VARIATION: If you don't wish to use gin, you can substitute water and a good squeeze of fresh lemon juice.

Raspberry Sauce

MAKES ABOUT 1 CUP (250 ML)

Although fresh raspberries are terrific in this sauce, frozen raspberries also work very well—especially good news when the berries aren't in season. I can't think of a lemony dessert that this sauce doesn't complement.

2¹/₂ cups (12 ounces/340 g) fresh raspberries, or 12 ounces (340 g) frozen raspberries, thawed

1¹/₂ tablespoons sugar, or more to taste

¹/₄ cup (60 ml) water

¹/₂ teaspoon freshly squeezed lemon juice

1 teaspoon kirsch (optional)

Purée the berries and remove the seeds by passing them through a food mill fitted with a fine disk into a medium bowl. Or, process the berries in a food processor fitted with the metal blade, then, using a rubber spatula, press the purée through a fine-mesh strainer set over a medium bowl.

Whisk in the sugar, water, lemon juice, and kirsch or framboise until the sugar dissolves. Taste for sweetness and add more sugar, if desired.

STORAGE: This sauce can be stored in the refrigerator for up to 3 days.

Mango Sauce

MAKES ABOUT 1¹/₄ CUPS (310 ML)

Mangoes, like most tropical fruits, will tip you off to their ripeness with their aroma. A good, ripe mango has a heady, syrupy scent, and when you hold it in your hand, it should feel slightly soft and a bit too heavy for its size. Although the plump, sweeter varieties, such as Hayden and Tommy Atkins, are the most tempting, slender and wrinkly Champagne or Manila mangoes that you might come across will surprise you with their gentle nuances. Depending on which variety you choose to use in this sauce, start with the smaller amount of sugar and add more if necessary.

A spoonful of mango sauce is a nice complement to Coconut and Tropical Fruit Trifle (page 70) or scoops of Toasted Coconut Sherbet (page 152) nestled in cookie cups made with Sesame-Orange Almond Tuiles (page 212).

1 large or 2 small mangoes (about 8 ounces/240 g total weight), peeled, pitted, and cut into pieces

1 tablespoon water

2 to 4 tablespoons (30 to 60 g) sugar

2 teaspoons rum

2 teaspoons freshly squeezed lime juice

In a food processor fitted with the metal blade or in a blender, purée the mango pieces with the water, 2 table-spoons of the sugar, the rum, and lime juice. Taste for sweetness and add more sugar, if desired.

STORAGE: This sauce can be stored in the refrigerator for up to 3 days.

Strawberry Sauce

MAKES 1 CUP (250 ML)

The best strawberry sauce is made from the ripest strawberries. Look for ones that are red from top to bottom and all the way through to the core. If you take a sniff, they should smell like, well, ripe, sweet, strawberries. I don't always strain out all the seeds since I sometimes like their texture and appearance in the sauce.

2¹/₂ cups (1 pound/450 g) strawberries

2 tablespoons (30 g) sugar, or more to taste

1 teaspoon freshly squeezed lemon juice or kirsch

In a food processor fitted with the metal blade, pureé the berries along with the sugar and lemon juice or kirsch. If you wish to remove the seeds, using a rubber spatula, press the purée through a fine-mesh strainer set over a medium bowl.

Taste for sweetness and add more sugar, if desired.

STORAGE: This sauce can be stored in the refrigerator for up to 3 days.

TIP: If the strawberries are less than perfect, add 1 to 2 teaspoons crème de cassis, which works wonders to heighten their flavor.

Blackberry Sauce

MAKES 1 CUP (250 ML)

This very glossy, deeply colored sauce is especially good with Vanilla Ice Cream (page 143), but it also shines brightly alongside a fruit tart or a summer fruit galette.

2¹/₂ cups (12 ounces/340 g) blackberries

3 tablespoons (45 g) sugar, or more to taste

¹/₄ teaspoon freshly squeezed lemon juice

Purée the berries and remove the seeds by passing them through a food mill fitted with a fine disk into a medium bowl. Or, process the berries in a food processor fitted with the metal blade, then, using a rubber spatula, press the purée through a fine-mesh strainer set over a medium bowl.

Whisk in the sugar and lemon juice until the sugar dissolves. Taste for sweetness and add more sugar, if desired.

STORAGE: This sauce can be stored in the refrigerator for up to 3 days.

Apricot Sauce

MAKES 2½ CUPS (625 ML)

Even when they're in season, fresh apricots aren't always easy to find, so I turn dried apricots that are available everywhere and at any time of the year into this delightfully tangy apricot sauce. I always use California dried apricots, which have a much deeper flavor than imported ones, and I highly recommend you do the same.

2¼ cups (560 ml) orange juice (freshly squeezed or store-bought), plus more as needed

2 tablespoons (30 g) sugar

3 ounces (85 g) dried California apricots, cut into quarters

¼ teaspoon vanilla extract

In a medium saucepan, combine the orange juice, sugar, and apricot pieces. Bring to a boil, remove from the heat, cover, and let stand 15 minutes.

In a food processor fitted with the metal blade or in a blender, purée the softened apricots and their liquid, along with the vanilla, until smooth. If necessary, thin with a bit more orange juice.

STORAGE: This sauce can be stored in the refrigerator for up to 3 days.

Orange-Rhubarb Sauce

MAKES 2 CUPS (500 ML)

This sauce bridges two seasons—it marries the citrus fruit of winter and spring's rhubarb. Its delicate color and bright flavor makes it the ideal accompaniment to Ricotta Cheesecake with Orange and Aniseed (page 55).

1 cup (250 ml) orange juice (freshly squeezed or store-bought)

½ cup (100 g) sugar, or more to taste

¾ pound (340 g) rhubarb, leaves trimmed, and stems cut into ¼-inch (6-mm) slices (about 3 cups)

In a medium saucepan, combine the orange juice, sugar, and rhubarb pieces. Bring to a boil over medium-high heat, stirring occasionally, then remove from the heat, cover, and let stand until the rhubarb is tender, about 10 minutes.

In a food processor fitted with the metal blade, or in a blender, purée the rhubarb and its cooking liquid until smooth. Taste for sweetness and add more sugar, if desired.

STORAGE: This sauce can be stored in the refrigerator for up to 5 days.

Candied Cherries

MAKES ABOUT 2 CUPS (250 ML)

During the brief cherry season when fresh cherries are abundant (and inexpensive), I make as many batches of candied cherries as I can, as they keep beautifully in their syrup for months in the refrigerator. I'll add a handful of candied cherries to a fruit crisp before baking, or drain them well and fold them into a batch of just-churned ice cream. They are particularly good spooned over lemon desserts, such as Tangy Lemon Frozen Yogurt (page 174) and Lemon Semifreddo (page 65), and are delicious used in place of the chocolate-covered peanuts in White Chocolate-Ginger Ice Cream (page 149). Or, if no one's looking, I just pluck one from the jar and pop it into my mouth.

2 cups (12 ounces/340 g) sweet cherries, pitted

1 cup (250 ml) water or apple juice

1 cup (200 g) sugar

1 tablespoon freshly squeezed lemon juice

In a large saucepan, combine the cherries, water or apple juice, sugar, and lemon juice. Cook over medium-high heat, stirring occasionally, until the juices are quite syrupy and thickened to the consistency of warm honey, 15 to 20 minutes. If you like, you can use a candy thermometer to gauge doneness; the mixture should register about 220°F (105°C).

Transfer the cherries to a jar. Let cool, then cover and refrigerate.

STORAGE: The cherries in their syrup will keep for at least 6 months in the refrigerator.

VARIATION: To boost the cherry flavor, stir $1/8$ teaspoon almond extract or 1 teaspoon amaretto liqueur into the cherries just before placing them in the jar.

> **TIP:** You can double or even triple this recipe, to take advantage of the cherry season. If you do make a big batch, simmer a lemon half or a lemon slice or two with the cherries, then remove it before transferring to the jars.

Candied Ginger

MAKES ABOUT $1/2$ POUND (225 G)

If I have a jar of candied ginger within arm's reach, there's an excellent chance that you'll find my hand reaching into it. Yes, you can buy candied ginger, but it's not at all difficult to make your own. From one good-size knob of fresh ginger, you can make enough so that even if you are caught with your hand in the ginger jar as much as I am, you'll have some left to toss with fruit dessert, such as the Nectarine-Berry Cobbler with Fluffy Biscuits (page 104) or to add to a batch of Nonfat Gingersnaps (page 200).

Take time to cut the ginger across the grain into thin slices no thicker than a coin because you want to make sure that any fibers in the ginger are minimized. If you can find young giner in the spring, you should definitely use it.

$1/2$ pound (225 g) fresh ginger

3 cups (750 ml) water

3 cups (600 g) sugar, plus 1 cup (200 g) for coating the ginger slices

Pinch of salt

1 tablespoon light corn syrup (optional; see Tip)

Peel the fresh ginger and slice it as thinly as possible, cutting crosswise against the fibers. Put the ginger slices in a large saucepan, add water to cover, and bring to a boil over medium-high heat. Decrease the heat to medium-low and simmer for 3 minutes. Drain the ginger and repeat this step twice more. You will have blanched the ginger slices a total of 3 times.

After the third draining, return the ginger to the saucepan and attach a candy thermometer to the side. Add the 3 cups (750 ml) water, 3 cups (600 g) sugar, salt, and corn syrup, if using, and cook until the liquid reaches 225°F (110°C). Remove from the heat and let the ginger rest in the syrup for 1 hour.

Place the ginger slices in a strainer and stir a few times to make sure as much syrup drips off as possible. (If you wish, save the syrup for another use, such as for sweetening lemonade or mixing with sparkling water and fresh lime juice.) Spread the ginger slices out on a wire rack set over a baking sheet and allow to dry for 2 to 3 hours.

Spread the remaining 1 cup (200 g) sugar on a baking sheet. Place the ginger slices in the sugar and toss with your fingers to separate the pieces and coat them well with sugar. Lift out the slices and shake off the excess sugar with your hands or place them in a colander and shake well. Set the sugar-coated ginger slices on the wire rack and let dry overnight at room temperature.

STORAGE: The candied ginger will keep in an airtight container for up to 6 months. The ginger can also be left in its syrup, without draining and tossing in sugar, and kept for a similar length of time in the refrigerator.

TIP: In the candying process, ginger slices or citrus peels are cooked in a thick sugar syrup to preserve them. But, over time, the sugar has a tendency to recrystallize, causing the ginger or citrus peel to dry out a bit. Adding a bit of corn syrup inhibits this recrystallization. (Most other liquid sweeteners, like honey and maple syrup, don't behave the same way, so they're not interchangeable for corn syrup.) I've made the corn syrup optional, so you can decide whether to use it.

Soft-Candied Citrus Peel

MAKES ABOUT 1 CUP (240 G)

Thin strips of soft-candied citrus peel enliven the flavor of desserts and look beautiful as garnishes for cakes, fruit compotes, sherbets, custards, and, especially, Champagne Gelée (page 114). Although it's convenient to have a jar on hand to use on a whim, they're quick and easy to make.

5 lemons, oranges, or limes (preferably organic), washed

2 cups (500 ml) water

1 cup (200 g) sugar

1 tablespoon light corn syrup (optional; see Tip, page 252)

Using a sharp vegetable peeler and working from pole to pole, remove the zest from the citrus fruits in strips about 1 inch (3 cm) wide. Try to remove only the colored portion of the rind and leave the bitter white pith on the fruit. (If you've peeled too deeply, you can lay the strips flat on a counter, pith side up, and carefully trim away the pith with a knife.) Using a sharp knife, cut the strips of zest length-wise into pieces about as narrow as a wooden match.

Put the peel in a medium saucepan and add water to generously cover. Bring to a boil and cook until the peel is soft and translucent, 5 to 6 minutes.

Drain the peel and discard the water. In the same saucepan, bring the 2 cups water, sugar, and corn syrup, if using, to a boil, stirring to dissolve the sugar. Add the drained peel, decrease the heat to maintain a gentle boil, and cook until the peel is translucent and the syrup is thick, about 20 minutes.

If you like, you can use a candy thermometer to gauge doneness; the mixture should register about 210°F (100°C).

Let cool, then transfer the peel and syrup to a clean jar, cover tightly, and refrigerate until ready to use.

STORAGE: The peel will keep in the refrigerator for at least 2 months. If you don't use the corn syrup, it might recrystallize. If it does, warm it slowly, adding a little water if necessary, to untangle the pieces.

Candied Orange Peel

MAKES ABOUT 1 POUND (450 G)

There's no reason to ever buy candied orange peel since it's so much better when you make it at home. I can't bear throwing away anything remotely edible, so when I have rinds left over from juicing oranges or tangerines for sorbet, I always make a batch of candied peels and serve them alongside.

Finely chopped bits of candied orange peel enliven a batch of cookies like Gingersnaps (page 199) and add an unexpected, but delicious, twist when tossed into a fruit dessert such as Apple-Blackberry Crisp (page 101). This candied orange peel is thicker and more substantial than Soft-Candied Citrus Peel (page 253). In addition to being used an an ingredient or garnish, it can be enjoyed on its own as a confection.

10 oranges, preferably organic, washed

3 cups (750 ml) water

$4^1/_2$ cups (900 g) sugar, plus $1^1/_2$ cups (300 g) for coating the strips of peel

2 tablespoons (30 ml) light corn syrup (optional; see Tip, page 252)

Halve and juice the oranges. Reserve the juice for another use and put the orange rinds in a large saucepan or Dutch oven. Add water to cover and bring to a boil over medium-high heat. Decrease the heat to medium-low and simmer until the rinds are tender, 30 minutes to 1 hour. How long this will take depends on the thickness of the rinds, so start checking them after 30 minutes to make sure they're not overcooking and turning mushy. To check for doneness, pluck one out and let it cool a minute; the rinds are cooked when you can easily scrape away most of the inner white pith with a spoon or a knife.

Drain the rinds, and when cool enough to handle, cut each piece in half. Using a spoon or paring knife, scrape or cut away the inner white pith. Cut the rinds into strips $1/_4$ inch (6 mm) wide.

In a large saucepan fitted with a candy thermometer, combine the 3 cups (750 ml) water, $4^1/_2$ cups (900 g) sugar, and the corn syrup, if using. Bring to a boil, then add the strips of orange peel and cook over medium heat until the temperature reaches 225°F (110°C) and the peel turns translucent.

Place the candied peel in a strainer and stir a few times to make sure as much syrup drips off as possible. Spread the strips out on a wire rack set over a baking sheet and allow to dry for 2 to 3 hours.

Spread the remaining $1^1/_2$ cups (300 g) sugar on a baking sheet. Place the orange peel strips in the sugar and toss with your fingers to separate the pieces and coat them well with sugar. Lift out the strips and shake off the excess sugar with your hands or place them in a colander and shake well. Set the sugar-coated strips on the wire rack and let dry overnight at room temperature.

STORAGE: The candied peel will keep in an airtight container in the refrigerator for up to 6 months.

VARIATIONS: You can substitute tangerines for the oranges. Note that the initial cooking time might be shorter because tangerine peels tend to be thinner. Lemon rinds can be candied this way, too.

TIP: Letting the peel dry thoroughly overnight is important because excess moisture can shorten the lifespan of the candied peel. If for some reason the peel gets too dry during storage, you can rehydrate it and make it more flavorful by soaking it in an orange-flavored liqueur such as Grand Marnier, Cointreau, or Triple Sec before chopping and adding to a batter.

Pineapple-Ginger Marmalade

MAKES ABOUT 5 CUPS (1.6 KG)

I make this marmalade in the dead of winter whenever my collection of confitures is running low, since, happily, good pineapple is always available. One pineapple yields a lot of jam—another thing to be happy about.

The best way to judge if a pineapple is truly ripe is to take a whiff. If the fruit is ripe, it will smell strong and sweet and the flesh will be sweet, too. Using the old wives' tale method of plucking a leaf from the top just means you're going to get strange looks from the people in the produce department. And if you do it in France, where I live, you might even be reprimanded.

1 large pineapple, peeled, eyes removed, cored, and quartered

1 navel orange, preferably organic

10 cups (2.5 liters) water

5 cups (1 kg) sugar

6 tablespoons (3 ounces/85 g) chopped Candied Ginger (page 252)

1 tablespoon dark rum

Cut the pineapple into $1/4$- to $1/2$-inch (6-mm to 1.5-cm) cubes. Cut the orange, unpeeled, into quarters. Slice each quarter as thinly as possible, then chop the slices into $1/4$-inch (6-mm) bits.

Put the chopped pineapple and orange in a large pot or a Dutch oven. Add the water, bring to a boil over high heat, then decrease the heat to medium-low and simmer for 30 minutes. Remove from the heat, cover, and let stand at room temperature for at least 2 hours, or up to overnight.

To finish the marmalade, add the sugar to the pineapple mixture, bring to a boil over medium-high heat, and cook until the mixture reaches the jelling point (use the wrinkle test, right, to judge when it's done).

Stir in the candied ginger and rum, then ladle the marmalade into clean jars. Cover tightly, let cool, and refrigerate.

STORAGE: The marmalade will keep for at least 6 months in the refrigerator.

THE WRINKLE TEST: The sugar, moisture, and pectin content of fresh fruits is so variable that it's difficult to know exactly how long jam or marmalade must cook in order to gel. In my recipes, I shy away from giving cooking times because I don't want anyone setting the kitchen timer and walking away from a pot of simmering fruit only to come back to an unfortunate surprise. Rather than rely on cooking times and candy thermometers, I use the "wrinkle test" to test jams and marmalades. You'll need a cold plate for testing the preserves with the wrinkle test, so be sure to put one in the freezer before you start cooking.

In most cases, it'll appear that not much is happening until 15 or 20 minutes into cooking. Then, the bubbles will get larger; this is when you should be more vigilant and stir the mixture, scraping the bottom of the pot to make sure nothing is sticking. When the juices become a thick, heavy syrup and the fruit mounds a bit is the point at which you should start checking for doneness using the wrinkle test: Turn off the heat and put a little spoonful of the preserves on the chilled plate. Return the plate to the freezer and, after a few minutes, nudge the jam with your finger. If it wrinkles, it's ready.

If you'd prefer to use a candy thermometer, jam and marmalades set at about 220°F (105°C). Always clip the thermometer to the pot before cooking begins to avoid breakage that can result from temperature shock.

Seville Orange Marmalade

MAKES 8 CUPS (2 KG)

After making many, many pots of Seville orange marmalade and spending countless hours plucking out the over-abundance of seeds (the seeds provide the pectin so that the marmalade will set), I figured out a great trick for preparing the oranges quickly: Place a mesh strainer over a small bowl. Halve the oranges and firmly squeeze out their juice and seeds into the strainer. Add the juice to the marmalade pot and wrap the seeds in cheesecloth so that they can be easily retrieved after cooking. A sharp serrated knife works very well for slicing the oranges very thinly.

6 Seville oranges or other sour oranges (2 pounds/1 kg total weight), preferably organic

1 navel orange, preferably organic

10 cups (2.5 liters) water

Pinch of salt

8 cups (1.6 kg) sugar

2 tablespoons (30 ml) Cognac or whiskey

Halve the Seville and navel oranges and squeeze out the juice and seeds from each half into a mesh strainer set over a small bowl. After all the oranges have been squeezed, place the seeds on a piece of cheesecloth, gather up the sides, and tie securely. Cut each rind in half and then slice as thinly as possible.

Put the orange slices in a large pot or a Dutch oven. Add the orange juice, water, the bag of seeds, and salt. Bring to a boil over medium-high heat, then decrease the heat to medium-low and simmer for 20 minutes. Remove from the heat, cover, and let stand overnight at room temperature.

The next day, stir in the sugar and set the pot over high heat. Bring the mixture to a boil, then decrease the heat to medium-low to maintain a gentle simmer. Cook, stirring occasionally to make sure the mixture is not burning on the bottom, until the marmalade reaches the jelling point (use the wrinkle test, page 256, to judge when it's done). If white scum occasionally rises to the top, skim it off with a large spoon.

Stir in the Cognac or whiskey and remove the bag of seeds, squeezing it with a pair of tongs to extract as much marmalade from it as possible. Ladle the marmalade into clean jars. Cover tightly, let cool, and refrigerate.

STORAGE: The marmalade will keep for at least 6 months in the refrigerator.

TIP: The salt is said to help soften the fruit. I've not made two batches side by side to test this theory (16 cups of Seville orange marmalade is a bit too much to have on hand), but it certainly doesn't hurt to add it, so I always throw in a pinch.

Plum-Strawberry Jam

MAKES ABOUT 4 CUPS (1.25 KG)

In my humble opinion, red plums make the best preserves, and certainly one of the easiest. Their skins give the jam a pleasant tartness and contain so much pectin that even inexperienced jam makers will be blushing like rosy plums with the pride of success. Tossing the fruit with sugar and letting it stand for a few hours intensifies the color of the strawberries so that the jam cooks up with a vivid crimson color.

2^1/$_2$ cups (1 pound/450 g) strawberries, hulled and diced into ^{1}/$_4$-inch (6-mm) pieces

1 pound (450 g) red plums (about 10), halved, pitted, and cut in ^{1}/$_2$-inch (1.5-cm) slices

2^1/$_4$ cups (450 g) sugar

In a large pot or a Dutch oven, toss the strawberries and plums with the sugar. Let stand for at least 1 hour, tossing occasionally to encourage the fruits to release their juices.

Bring the mixture to a boil over medium-high heat, then decrease the heat to medium-low to maintain a gentle simmer. Cook, stirring occasionally to make sure the mixture is not burning on the bottom, until the jam reaches the jelling point (use the wrinkle test, page 256, to judge when it's done).

Ladle the jam into clean jars. Cover tightly, let cool, and refrigerate.

STORAGE: The jam will keep for at least 6 months in the refrigerator.

Fig Jam

MAKES 4 CUPS (1.25 KG)

Figs have two seasons—the first figs appear in late summer and the second batch shows up around mid-autumn. If you miss the first one, not to worry—the second is usually more prolific and the figs are even tastier. Don't be put off by fresh figs with skins that are split and syrupy; those are the ones that taste the best. For jam making, I like black Mission figs, which are the most common variety, but this recipe will work with others as well. Figs are high in natural sugar, which means that the jam cooks relatively quickly.

3 pounds (1.35 kg) fresh figs, hard stems removed, and quartered

$^1/_2$ cup (125 ml) water

3 cups (600 g) sugar

$^1/_4$ cup (60 ml) freshly squeezed lemon juice

Place the figs in a large pot or a Dutch oven and add the water. Cover and bring to a boil over medium-high heat, then decrease the heat to medium-low to maintin a gentle simmer. Cook until the figs are completely soft and tender, about 15 minutes.

In a food processor fitted with the metal blade or in a blender, purée the figs and their cooking liquid (if using a blender, don't fill the jar more than halfway, as the hot liquid might burst through the top when the blender is turned on). Or, pass the figs through a food mill.

Return the purée to the pot. Stir in the sugar and lemon juice. Cook over medium heat until thickened, stirring constantly to prevent the mixture from burning on the bottom, until the jam is thick appears slightly jelled. (Because figs are low in pectin, the wrinkle test, page 256, won't work with this jam.)

Ladle the jam into clean jars. Cover tightly, let cool, and refrigerate.

STORAGE: The jam will keep for at least 6 months in the refrigerator.

VARIATION: Before ladling into jars, stir in $^1/_2$ cup (80 g) coarsely chopped Soft-Candied Citrus Peel (page 253) made with lemons.

Quince Marmalade

MAKES ABOUT 3 CUPS (900 G)

This is one of the most beautiful marmalades I know of. As the delicate shreds of quince cook, they turn brilliant red and intensify in color as the fruit reduces to a fragrant, shimmering jelly.

This preserve is terrific at breakfast or as a filling for Easy Marmalade Tart (page 93). It's also great paired with slices of Manchego or Cheddar cheese, served with a glass of sherry. This marmalade was inspired by a recipe from Helen Witty's book *Fancy Pantry*.

4 cups (1 liter) water

3 cups (600 g) sugar

3 large quinces (about 1 pound/450 g), peeled, quartered, cored, and seeded

1/2 lemon, preferably organic

In a Dutch oven or large saucepan, bring the water and sugar to a boil over high heat. Meanwhile, in a food processor fitted with a coarse grating disk or on the largest holes of a box grater, shred the quince.

Add the grated quince and the lemon half to the boiling sugar mixture. Decrease the heat to medium and cook at a simmer, stirring occasionally, until the mixture is thick. Use the wrinkle test (page 256) to judge when the marmalade is done.

Remove and discard the lemon half. Ladle the marmalade into clean jars. Cover tightly, let cool, and refrigerate.

STORAGE: The marmalade will keep for at least 6 months in the refrigerator.

TIP: Quince tend to turn brown as soon as they're cut. With cooking, any minor discoloration will fade away. But do try to get them into the hot syrup as soon as possible after they're grated.

Tomato Jam

MAKES 2 CUPS (600 G)

This jam is the filling for the Rosemary Cookies with Tomato Jam (page 205). I often serve a small pot of it to accompany a sumptuous platter of perfectly ripened cheeses, one of my favorite desserts of all.

2¼ pounds (1 kg) ripe tomatoes (about 5 large)

2¼ cups (450 g) sugar

2 or 3 grinds of black pepper

Big pinch of salt

1 teaspoon freshly squeezed lemon juice

Bring a large saucepan of water to a boil. Using a paring knife, cut out the stem end of each tomato, then slice a shallow X in the bottom.

Plunge the tomatoes into the boiling water until their skins loosen, about 30 seconds. Remove them with a slotted spoon and let cool. When cool enough to handle, slip off their skins. Discard the water, but save the saucepan for cooking the jam.

Halve the tomatoes at their equator and gently squeeze out the seeds and juice. Cut the tomatoes into ½-inch (1.5-cm) pieces.

Return the tomatoes to the saucepan and stir in the sugar, pepper, and salt. Cook over medium heat, stirring frequently to ensure that the mixture is cooking evenly, until most of the liquid has cooked off. If foam occasionally rises to the top, skim it off with a large spoon. Remove from the heat and stir in the lemon juice.

Ladle the jam into clean jars. Cover tightly, let cool, and refrigerate.

STORAGE: The jam will keep for at least 6 months in the refrigerator.

TIP: I don't use the wrinkle test (page 256) for this jam. If you wish to use a candy thermometer to gauge doneness, when ready, the temperature of the jam should register 220°F (105°C) degrees.

Vin d'Orange

MAKES ABOUT 6 CUPS (1.5 LITERS)

I often serve small glasses of *vin d'orange* as a warm-weather aperitif. Anyone who enjoys Lillet is likely to enjoy this fruity and slightly bitter fortified wine. But be careful—it's quite potent.

To stay true to its humble Provencal roots, I use very inexpensive vodka and dry white wine. I've even made it with wine from a box—with excellent results!

$^2/_3$ cup (130 g) sugar

5 cups (1.25 liters) white wine

1 cup (250 ml) vodka

3 Seville or sour oranges (1 pound/450 g), preferably organic, quartered

1 lemon, preferably organic, quartered

$^1/_2$ vanilla bean, split lengthwise

In a large glass jar, mix together the sugar, white wine, and vodka until the sugar dissolves. Add the orange and lemon quarters. Scrape the seeds from the vanilla bean and add them to the jar, then drop in the pod. Cover, and let stand undisturbed for 1 month in a cool, dark place.

After 1 month, remove and discard the fruit; remove the vanilla pod (it can rinsed, dried, and used for another purpose; see page 14). Pour the mixture through a mesh strainer lined with a double thickness of cheesecloth or a coffee filter, then funnel the *vin d'orange* into clean bottles. Cork tightly and refrigerate.

SERVING: Serve over ice in small glasses with a twist of orange or lemon zest.

STORAGE: *Vin d'orange* will keep for at least 6 months in the refrigerator.

VARIATION: Although *vin d'orange* is usually made with sour oranges, if you can find only regular oranges, try this version, which is also quicker: In a large glass jar, mix together $^1/_2$ cup (100 g) sugar; $^1/_2$ cup (125 ml) vodka; one bottle (750 ml) rosé wine; $^1/_2$ vanilla bean, split lengthwise; and 1 cinnamon stick. Add 2 navel oranges and 1 lemon, each quartered. Cover and let stand in a cool, dark place for up to 2 weeks, shaking every few days. Strain through cheesecloth and funnel into clean bottles.

Nocino

MAKES 4 CUPS (1 LITER)

My friends who live in the countryside were surprised one morning to wake up and see me climbing their walnut tree in my pajamas, swiping the rock-hard, unripe green orbs off the branches. Once I'd picked enough, I climbed down and confessed that I could barely sleep the night before in anticipation of collecting enough of them to make a batch of *nocino*, an Italian liqueur made from unripe walnuts. It took a while for them to figure out what I was talking about. When I returned a few months later with a tub of Vanilla Ice Cream (page 143) and drizzled inky-brown *nocino* over each scoop, no one questioned my early-morning motives.

If you know someone with a walnut tree, give this liqueur a try. And be sure to give them a bottle as a thank you, so you'll get invited back to gather more green walnuts the following year.

30 green walnuts, rinsed and dried

2 cinnamon sticks

5 whole cloves

4 strips lemon zest, each about 1 inch (3 cm) wide

$2^{1}/_{2}$ cups (500 g) sugar

$^{1}/_{2}$ vanilla bean, split lengthwise

1 quart (1 liter) vodka

Using a chef's knife or cleaver, quarter each walnut. (Use caution, as the husks are tough to cut through. I press a cleaver gently into the skin, then, holding my hands far away from the blade, crack the nut in half on a cutting board.)

Put the quartered walnuts in a large glass container along with the cinnamon, cloves, lemon zest, and sugar. Scrape the seeds from the vanilla bean and add them to the container, then drop in the pod. Add the vodka. Cover and let stand 6 to 8 weeks at room temperature, agitating the container daily.

When ready to bottle, using a slotted spoon, remove and discard the walnuts and remove the vanilla pod (it can be rinsed, dried, and used for another purpose; see page 14). Pour the mixture through a mesh strainer lined with a double thickness of cheesecloth or a coffee filter, then funnel the *nocino* into clean bottles and cork tightly.

STORAGE: *Nocino* will keep for several years stored in a cool, dry place or in the refrigerator.

VARIATION: To make *NOCINO* CUSTARDS, in a medium saucepan, warm 2 cups (500 ml) heavy cream, 1 cup (250 ml) half-and-half, and 9 tablespoons (135 g) sugar, stirring to dissolve the sugar; remove from the heat. In a medium bowl, whisk 6 large egg yolks, then gradually whisk in the warmed cream mixture along with $^{1}/_{8}$ teaspoon vanilla extract. Pour the mixture through a mesh strainer into a large measuring cup, then stir in $^{1}/_{2}$ cup (125 ml) *nocino*. Divide the mixture among eight 4- to 6-ounce (125- to 180-ml) ramekins or custard cups set in a roasting pan. Add enough hot water to come halfway up the sides of the ramekins, cover tightly with aluminum foil, and bake in a 350°F (175°C) oven until the custards are just barely set, about 30 minutes.

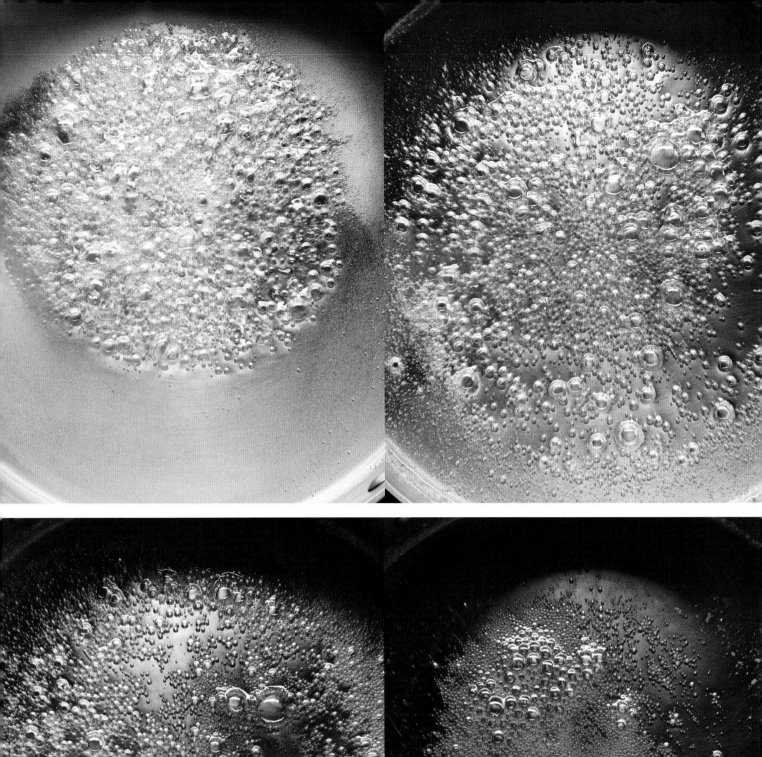
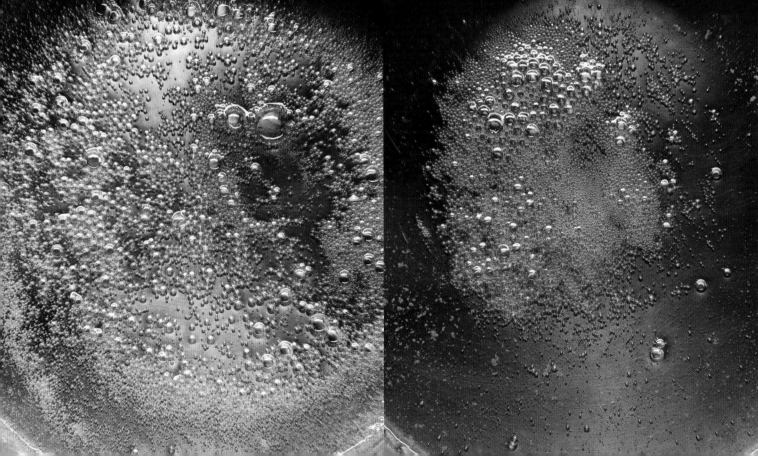

Appendix:
Caramelization Guidelines

Caramel frequently shows up in my recipes because it's one of my favorite flavors. Although it's not difficult to caramelize sugar, if you haven't done it before, the process can be intimidating, and it might take a couple of tries before you're comfortable taking it to the right degree of darkness: a deep amber liquid, on the edge of burnt, but still sweet in flavor.

When sugar is heated, it melts into liquid. As the sugar continues to cook, it begins to take on a bit of color, or caramelize. Because cookware and heat sources don't always distribute heat evenly, you need to stand guard during the entire process, encouraging the sugar to cook at an even rate.

The two things to watch out for when making caramel are **recrystallization**—what happens when sugar crystals join together in a lumpy mass—and **burning** the sugar. You can avoid recrystallization by making sure that the sugar is free of impurities and that the pan used to cook the caramel is clean. If you're making a wet caramel—one that begins with sugar and water (more on that in a bit)—limiting the amount that the mixture is stirred during cooking helps guard against recrystallization.

To avoid burning the caramel, it's just a matter of being vigilant. The melted sugar should be cooked until it's a deep amber color—it's done when it starts to smoke and begins to foam just a little bit. At this point, it should be removed from the heat immediately to stop the sugar from darkening any further. Usually, a liquid is then quickly added, which also helps halt the cooking.

After making caramel, to clean the pan and dissolve any stuck-on bits, either soak it in warm water or fill the pan with water, bring it to a boil, and continue boiling until the caramel dissolves.

WET AND DRY CARAMEL

There are two kinds of caramel made in this book: wet and dry. A wet caramel is made by heating sugar and water together in the pan. Since wet caramel doesn't get too hard when cooled, I use it for sauces and to line ramekins for flan. A dry caramel is simply sugar heated without any liquid and can handle being stirred gently.

Wet Caramel

When making caramel, especially wet caramel, your main nemesis will be the sugar's natural tendency to recrystallize. The sugar crystals have jagged edges and, even after liquefying, want to regroup into a solid mass. Stirring a wet caramel encourages these crystals to hook up—and cause clumping.

One common technique for preventing recrystallization is to cook the sugar in a covered pot until the sugar is completely melted; the trapped condensation washes away crystals clinging to the side of the pot. Another is to use a clean brush dipped in water to wash down the sides, dissolving any crystals that may have formed. I don't recommend the latter technique as I've lost a few bristles in the caramel—and found them later, when dessert was served. You can also add an interfering agent—a tiny amount of cream of tartar or lemon juice—near the beginning of cooking to help inhibit recrystallization.

To make a wet caramel, begin by sprinkling the sugar in an even layer in a heavy-bottomed skillet or saucepan. Pour water over the sugar until is it completely and evenly moistened—you don't want any dry spots. Cook the sugar and water over medium heat until the sugar dissolves. At this point, add a pinch of cream of tartar or a few drops of lemon juice, if indicated or desired. Continue cooking, watching carefully as the sugar begins to brown. If it starts to recrystallize, swirl the pan and continue to cook. Usually, the lumps will melt as the caramel continues to cook.

When the caramel has darkened to the point of being almost burnt—when it's dark amber in color, smoking, and beginning to gently foam—take it off the heat and stop the cooking by pouring in the liquid called for in the recipe. Then stir or whisk the caramel over low heat until it's smooth. If the lumps persist, you can always strain them out.

Dry Caramel

In some ways, making dry caramel is easier than making wet caramel, but it can be difficult to control the rate of caramelization because it happens much more quickly.

To make dry caramel, sprinkle an even layer of sugar in a heavy-bottomed skillet or saucepan. As you heat the sugar, the edges and bottom will melt first and start browning. With a heatproof utensil, gently push the liquefied sugar toward the center, which encourages the still-solid sugar to begin melting. Once the sugar begins to color, watch very closely because dry caramel cooks rapidly, so don't take your eyes off it until it's the proper color. If the recipe calls for a liquid, add it now. Then stir or whisk the caramel over low heat until smooth. If there are any small bits of sugar remaining, you can strain the caramel to remove them.

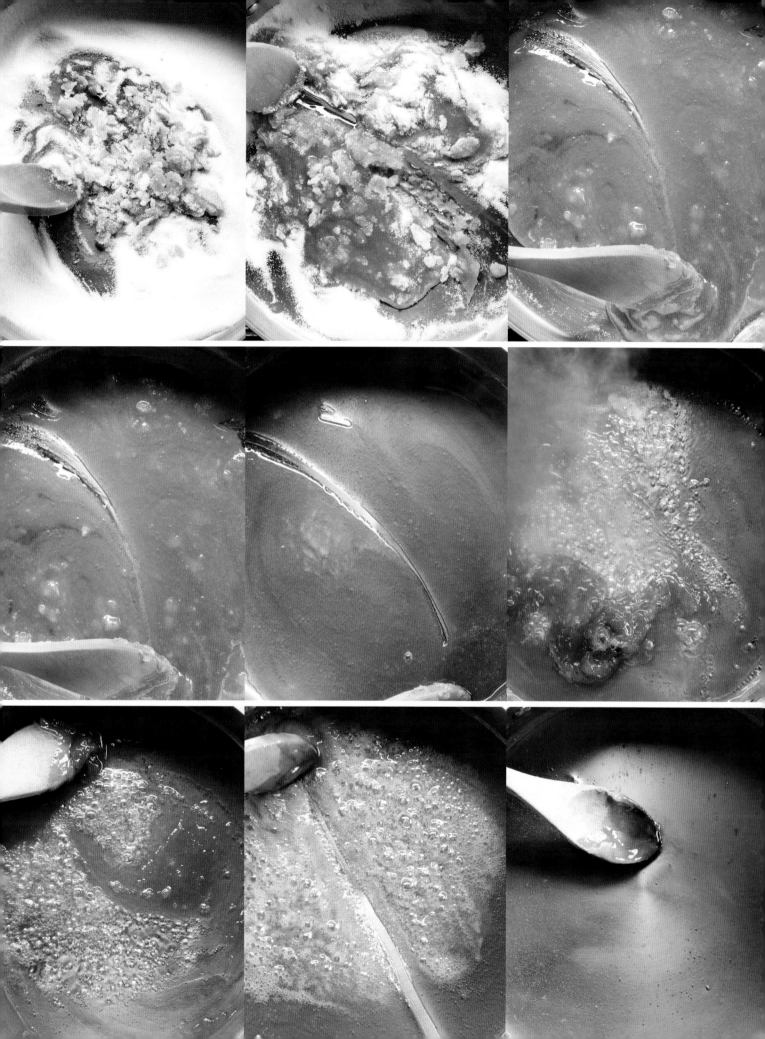

*This book is dedicated to Robert Steinberg,
who changed how we think about chocolate
in America. You are missed.*

Acknowledgments

When people ask, "How long did it take you to write this book?" the answer for this particular one is "Thirty years!"

That may seem like a long time, but this book really was that long in the making, as it's the culmination of years and years of baking professionally, and, subsequently, at home. Thankfully, I've had some great help along the way.

Fritz Streiff provided his truly invaluable help on my first two books. I learned much of what I know about recipe writing from him, sitting side by side and taking breaks to run down to the kitchen to taste something just out of the oven.

Thanks to my agent Fred Hill and his associate Bonnie Nadell who've taken good care of me—and brought me back home.

I loved working with Clancy Drake on a previous book and I couldn't have been happier to be paired up with her again. And Dawn Yanagihara came in at the eleventh hour and took on the enormous task of wrapping it all up, adding her very sharp eye and making sure I crossed the finish line.

When I was told that Maren Caruso was going to be taking the photographs, the word "Great!" couldn't come out of my mouth fast enough. I loved her work in other books and was thrilled when she signed on to shoot my desserts.

Thanks to Nancy Austin, for coming up with such a striking book design, and being such a pleasure to work with, once again. And to Susan Friedland, who did such a great job editing and guiding me through my first two books, which are generously borrowed from here.

I'm incredibly fortunate to be part of a large and generous baking community. I've been lucky to be able to count on Flo Braker, Marion Cunningham, Fran Gage, Emily Luchetti, Nick Malgieri, Alice Medrich, John Scharffenberger, Nancy Silverton, Kathleen Stewart, and Dede Wilson, for advice, encouragement, and a few recipes here and there along the way.

Virtual hugs to my online pals Matt Armendariz, Elise Bauer, Jesse Gardner, and Deb Perelman for keeping me sane.

Without the many, many people I worked with at Chez Panisse, I don't know where I'd be. Mary Jo Thoresen, Mary Canales, Lisa Saltzman, Diane Wegner, Linda Zagula, and Shari Saunders were the best pastry buddies a guy could hope for. It was owner Alice Waters who told me to write my own book when I left the nest. Thanks most of all to Lindsey Shere who deserves a medal for putting up with me.

And to Romain Pellas, for going through yet another round.

Resources

All-Clad Metalcrafters
800-255-2523
www.allclad.com
Sturdy, professional-grade cookware and bakeware.

Askinosie Chocolate
417-862-9900
www.askinosie.com
Handcrafted chocolates, including bean-to-bar white chocolate, plus natural cocoa powder and cocoa nibs.

Bridge Kitchenware
973-287-6163
www.bridgekitchenware.com
Comprehensive selection of cake pans, baking equipment, and kitchen appliances.

C&H Sugar Company
www.chsugar.com
Makers of various types of sugars, including Hawaiian washed sugar, a coarse-crystal sugar.

The Chef's Warehouse
718-842-8700
www.chefswarehouse.com
Frozen passion fruit purée, French sea salt, and fine chocolates.

Chocosphere
877-992-4626
www.chocosphere.com
Enormous selection of chocolates and cocoa powders from around the world.

Cowgirl Creamery
866-433-7834
www.cowgirlcreamery.com
Crème fraîche, plus handcrafted artisan cheeses.

Cuisinart
800-726-0190
www.cuisinart.com
Manufacturer of ice cream machines and other baking appliances and equipment.

Gourmet Country
800-665-9123
www.gourmetcountry.com
Rain's Choice vanilla beans and pure vanilla extracts, including pure—and extraordinary—Mexican vanilla extract.

Guittard Chocolate Company
800-468-2462
www.guittard.com
American-made chocolate and cocoa powder, including the E. Guittard line of premium chocolates.

India Tree
800-369-4848
www.indiatree.com
Purveyors of spices and sugars, including coarse-crystal sugars such as turbinado and muscovado.

Kendall Farms Crème Fraîche
805-466-7252
www.kendallfarmscremefraiche.com
Crème fraîche made from milk from Holstein cows.

King Arthur Flour Company
800-827-6836
www.kingarthurflour.com
Specialty baking flours (including tapioca flour), citric acid, cocoa powder, chocolate, unsweetened coconut, plus almond and pistachio pastes.

KitchenAid
800-541-6390
www.kitchenaid.com
Electric stand mixers (including an ice cream attachment) and other kitchen appliances.

Love 'n Bake
www.lovenbake.com
Excellent almond and pistachio pastes.

Patric Chocolate
www.patric-chocolate.com
Handmade microbatch chocolate.

Penzeys Spices
800-741-7787
www.penzeys.com
Extensive selection of spices and vanilla beans and extract.

The Perfect Purée of Napa Valley
866-787-5233
www.perfectpuree.com
Fruit purées, including frozen passion fruit purée.

St. George Spirits
510-769-1601
www.stgeorgespirits.com
Wonderful distillations made in California, such as kirsch and pear eau-de-vie.

Sur La Table
800-243-0852
www.surlatable.com
Equipment for home bakers, including ice cream makers and electric mixers.

Taza Chocolate
www.tazachocolate.com
617-623-0804
Stone-ground chocolate and cocoa nibs.

Theo Chocolate
206-632-5100
www.theochocolate.com
Seattle-based maker of organic and fair-trade chocolates.

Trader Joe's
www.traderjoes.com
Bulk chocolate, cocoa powder, apricot kernels, and top-quality nuts and dried fruit.

Valrhona Chocolate
www.valrhona.com
Fine-quality French chocolate—I'm especially fond of their very dark cocoa powder.

Vermont Butter & Cheese Company
800-884-6287
www.butterandcheese.net
Crème fraîche, mascarpone, and cultured butter.

Williams-Sonoma
877-812-6235
www.williams-sonoma.com
Specialty kitchen equipment, such as ice cream makers, electric mixers, and baking tools.

Index

Also by David Lebovitz

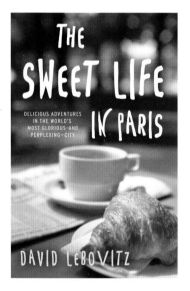

PERFECT SCOOP
Ice Creams, Sorbets, Granitas, and Sweet Accompaniments
$18.99 paper (Canada: $21.99)
ISBN 978-1-58008-219-8
Ten Speed Press

THE GREAT BOOK OF CHOCOLATE
The Chocolate Lover's Guide with Recipes
$16.99 paper (Canada: $21.99)
ISBN 978-1-58008-495-6
Ten Speed Press

THE SWEET LIFE IN PARIS
Delicious Adventures in the World's Most Glorious—and Perplexing—City
$24.95 hardcover (Canada: $28.95)
ISBN 978-0-7679-2888-5
Broadway

AVAILABLE FROM THE CROWN PUBLISHING GROUP WHEREVER BOOKS ARE SOLD

WWW.CROWNPUBLISHING.COM